OHIO YESTERDAY & TODAY

By Robert T. Howe

Roblen Publishing Company
Cincinnati, Ohio

Ohio: Yesterday and Today

Author: Robert T. Howe
Professor Emeritus, University of Cincinnati • Cincinnati, Ohio

Editor: Helen Cooper Howe
Retired teacher of history, Walnut Hills High School • Cincinnati, Ohio

Design and Artwork: Slaughter & Slaughter, Inc. • Cincinnati, Ohio

Printing and Binding: The C. J. Krehbiel Company • Cincinnati, Ohio

Library of Congress 94-068683

ISBN: 0-9631313-7-0

10 9 8 7 6 5 4 3 2 1

Roblen Publishing Company
1516 Northview Avenue
Cincinnati, Ohio 45223-1629

Supplementary materials:
Teacher's Handbook
Student Workbook

 Roblen Publishing Company

Acknowlegements and Credits

The following people made helpful comments on the first draft of the manuscript:

Ricki Blair, 4th-grade teacher,
Westbrook School, Brookville, Ohio

Jill W. Carothers, 4th-grade teacher
Plain School, Plain City, Ohio

Patricia A. Cooke, 4th-grade teacher
Plain School, Plain City, Ohio

Margaret Coughlin, 4th-grade teacher
Lakeview School, Summit County, Ohio

Margaret Haney, Curriculum Coordinator
Madison County Schools

Dana L. Kessinger, Supervisor
Fred Kesssinger, 4th-grade teacher
Meigs County Schools

Eric Bender, 4th-grade student
Princeton Schools, Glendale, Ohio

Abbey Meistrich, 4th-grade student
Cincinnati City Schools

The following people made helpful comments on the second draft of this manuscript:

Linda Allendorf, 4th-grade teacher
Monfort Heights School, Hamilton County

Sally Auble, 4th-grade teacher
Weigel School, Hamilton County

B.J. Beason, 4th-grade teacher
Welch School, Hamilton County

Sally Dumford, 4th-grade teacher
Huston School, Hamilton County

Susan Waksmundski, Coordinator of Elementary Studies
Northwest Local Schools, Hamilton County

Table of Contents

Title Page i
Front Piece ii
Acknowledgements iii
Table of Contents iv

Chapter 1   Where and what is Ohio? 1
Where is Ohio in the world? 3
What are the symbols of Ohio? 5
Why is Ohio an interesting place to live? 7
What will you learn? 9

Chapter 2   How has nature shaped Ohio? 11
Part 1 — How did the forces of nature create rocks and soil? 12
Part 2 — How did glaciers change the land? 20
Part 3 — What are the natural resources of Ohio? 26

Chapter 3 Who lived in Ohio before 1600? 33
Part 1 — How can we learn about prehistoric people? 34
Part 2 — Who lived in the Ohio Country 2,000 years ago? 38
Part 3 — How did prehistoric people live? 44

Chapter 4 What happened to the natives when Europeans came? 51
Part 1 — How did traders and settlers from Europe affect the natives? 53
Part 2 — Why did natives move into the Ohio Country? 58
Part 3 — How did wars affect the Ohio Country? 63
          The American Revolution 66

Chapter 5 How did the Americans displace the natives? 73
Part 1 — How was the Northwest Territory established? 74
Part 2 — How was Ohio divided for settlement? 82
Part 3 — How did the natives defend themselves? 89

Chapter 6 What happened during the earliest years of Ohio? 97
Part 1 — What problems did the United States face? 98
Part 2 — How did Ohio become a state? 101
Part 3 — How did the War of 1812 affect Ohio? 105

Chapter 7 How did travel change during the 19th century?...................117
Part 1 — How does movement affect our lives? 118
Part 2 — How were highways developed? 121
Part 3 — How were waterways improved? 131
Part 4 — How did railroads become important? 139

Chapter 8 How did people live during the 19th century? 145
Part 1 — How did events in Europe affect Ohio? 146
Part 2 — How did slavery affect Ohio? 155
Part 3 — How did people live in rural areas? 160
Part 4 — Why did religious groups come to Ohio? 166

Chapter 9 How did the cities of Ohio develop? 173
Part 1 — Why did some settlements grow into big cities? 174
Part 2 — How did people live in cities? 185

Chapter 10 How did industry develop during the 19th century? 195
Part 1 — How are knowledge, energy, and tools related? 196
Part 2 — How did industries develop? 207

Chapter 11 What was the role of government during the 19th century? 219
Part 1 — What does it mean to be ruled by laws? 220
Part 2 — How were schools established? 226
Part 3 — What were the social problems in 1900? 230
Part 4 — Which presidents came from Ohio? 234

Chapter 12 How did life change in the 20th century? 247
Part 1 — How did turmoil in the world affect Ohio? 248
Part 2 — How did working conditions change? 255
Part 3 — What happened during the Great Depression? 261
Part 4 — How can we enjoy our free time? 266

Chapter 13 How did patterns of living change? 275
Part 1 — How did forms of energy change? 276
Part 2 — How did forms of transportation change? 281
Part 3 — How did energy and transportation change cities? 288

Chapter 14 How did the economy of Ohio change? 303
Part 1 — What is a business? 304
Part 2 — What are the industries of Ohio today? 307
Part 3 — What role has Ohio played in the Space Age? 325

Chapter 15 How is Ohio governed today? 335
Part 1 — How is the government of Ohio organized? 336
Part 2 — How do we pay for government? 341
Part 3 — How are people elected to political office? 345
Part 4 — How are laws created? 355
Part 5 — How are local areas governed? 359

Chapter 16 What are the challenges of the 21st century? 367
How can we preserve freedom? 368
How can natural resources be used wisely? 370
How can we live in peace? 377
What have we learned in this book? 379

Appendix A: The Counties of Ohio 381

Appendix B: Population Information for Ohio Counties 383

Glossary 385

Illustration Credits 391

Bibliography of Books to Read 393

Bibliography of References 398

Index 401

Map List

Satellite map of the world 2
The United States in 1958 3
Ohio counties in 1802 8
Location of Ohio caves 14
Geological map of Ohio 17
Glacial map of Ohio 23
Drainage pattern of Ohio 24
Ohio counties with coal and/or petroleum 29
Land bridge from Asia to North America 34
Locations of prehistoric mounds 40
Time line and map of settlement of East Coast 54
Native tribal locations about 1600 55
Northeastern United States about 1760 60
Northeastern United States about 1780 64
The United States in 1783 77
Public land surveys of Ohio 81
Subdivision plat of Nassau 83
The Northwest Territory 91
Greenville Treaty line 93
Ohio counties in 1802 102
1815 reservations for natives in Ohio 114
Zane's Trace and Natchez Trace 122
The National Road 124
Ohio canals 134
Ohio railroads in 1861 141
Europe in 1939 148
Underground Railroad in Ohio 157
Population of Ohio counties in 1900 180
Selected countries of Asia 252
Pipelines in Ohio 278
Ohio House of Representatives districts 352
Ohio Senate districts 353
Congressional districts 354

Chapter 1

Where and what is Ohio?

Let's learn...

- where Ohio is in the world.

- about the symbols of Ohio.

- why Ohio is an interesting place to live.

If someone asks you where you live, do you tell them the address of the building you call home? Perhaps you live on a street called *Main, Market, Elm, Maple, High,* or another popular name. If so, there are people all over the United States who live on streets with the same name. Each of us also lives in a city, a village, or a township, and in a county. The name of this place is also a part of our address. In this book, you will learn how the neighborhood where you live is related to the State of Ohio. You will also learn why our state is an important part of the United States of America.

Where is Ohio in the world?

The picture below was made by an artist from satellite photographs of our planet *earth*. As you know, earth has the shape of a ball, so many photos had to be laid side-by-side to make this picture. When you travel across Ohio, it seems to be very big, but on this picture it is such a small speck that you cannot put a label on it.

The map on the next page shows the United States as it looked until almost 1960. Today Alaska and Hawaii are also states, but they are not shown. Ohio looks

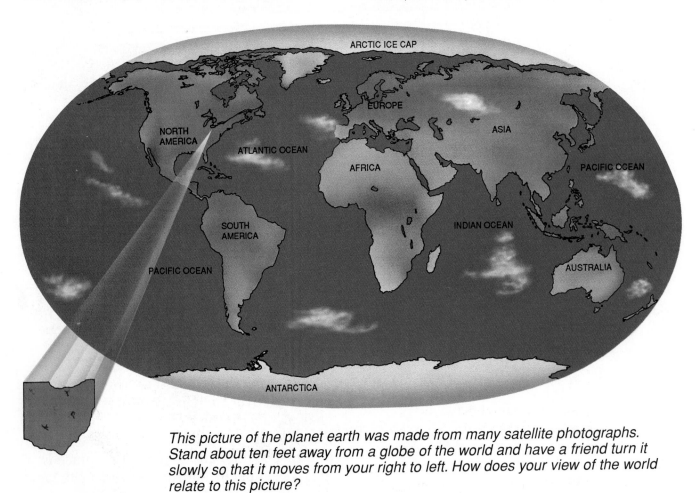

This picture of the planet earth was made from many satellite photographs. Stand about ten feet away from a globe of the world and have a friend turn it slowly so that it moves from your right to left. How does your view of the world relate to this picture?

This map shows the United States as it was from 1912 until 1959. Look at the globe of the world from a place where you can see this same image plus Alaska and Hawaii. How big would Ohio seem to be if the entire United States was shown on this map?

much bigger on this map. If we tried to show Alaska and Hawaii in their true positions in the same space, Ohio would appear much smaller.

How would you describe where Ohio is in the United States? People living in the other 49 states look at Ohio in different ways. People living in Massachusetts (marked MASS on the map) think we are

"out west." People living in California think we are "back east." People living in Louisiana think we are "Northerners." People living in Minnesota think we are "Southerners." People living in Kentucky, Indiana, Michigan, and Pennsylvania think we are "neighbors." We Ohioans usually say that we live in the "Middle West," but the people of Iowa, Nebraska, Kansas, and Missouri are closer to the

State Symbols of Ohio

State symbol used on all official documents

State flag of Ohio

"With God, all things are possible" is the state motto.

The state beverage is tomato juice.

The state fossil is the trilobite.

The state bird is the cardinal.

The state animal is the deer (proposed but not yet officially adopted).

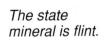

The state mineral is flint.

The state insect is the ladybug.

The state flower is the scarlet carnation.

The most important symbols of Ohio are the seal and the flag. Go to your public library and ask to see a legal paper that has the seal on it. Have you ever seen the Ohio flag on a flag pole?

"Beautiful Ohio"

The following words to the state song were written by Ballard MacDonald. The music was composed by Mary Earl.

Long, long ago, someone I know
Had a little red canoe
In it room for only two
Love found its start,
Then in my heart
And like a flower grew.

Chorus:

Drifting with the current down a
 moonlit stream
While above the Heavens in their
 glory gleam
And the stars on high
Twinkle in the sky
Seeming in a Paradise of love divine
Dreaming of a pair of eyes that looked
 in mine
Beautiful Ohio, in dreams again I see
Visions of what used to be.

This song tells about a love story that took place on the Ohio River and was adopted as the state song in 1969. It really says nothing about our state. From time to time, people have suggested alternative words to the beautiful music.

"middle" of the United States than we are. Geography books often say that Ohio is one of the "Great Lakes States" because it touches Lake Erie. In 1990 the lawmakers of Ohio decided to advertise that Ohio is *The heart of it all*. For several years, this slogan has been on our automobile license plates.

What are the symbols of Ohio?

How do you recognize a person, place, or thing? Do you carry an identification card that tells your name and address? Long ago, people who could not read or write made marks on their bodies or wore certain objects, so that other people could identify them. Today many people wear symbols, in the form of pins, caps, or T-shirts, to show that they belong to certain groups. Our state has adopted the symbols shown on the opposite page to represent *Ohio*. Only the flag and the seal are widely used. In later chapters, you will learn why some of these symbols were adopted.

Why is our state called Ohio?

Do you know what is "round on the ends, and high in the middle?" The answer to this old riddle is *O-hi-o*. Our state was named after the river that forms all of its southern boundary and part of its eastern boundary. Before any people from Europe came to North America, a tribe of Native Americans,

5

Events in the Early History of the United States

1770's
1770 — 13 British Colonies
1774 — Continental Congress
        organized
1776 — Declaration of Independence
1777 — Articles of Confederation

1780's
1780 — American Revolution
1783 — War ends with American
        victory
1787 — Constitution written
    States agree to Constitution
    in order:
    Delaware, Pennsylvania,
    New Jersey, Georgia,
    Connecticut, Massachusetts,
    Maryland, South Carolina,
    New Hampshire, Virginia,
    New York, North
    Carolina, Rhode Island

1790's
1791 — Vermont becomes 14th state
1792 — Kentucky becomes 15th state
1796 — Tennessee becomes 16th state

1800's
1803 — Ohio becomes 17th state

called the *Iroquois*, lived in what is now New York State. They knew how to travel great distances on rivers and lakes, including the river that forms a boundary of our state. When explorers from Europe asked the Iroquois the name of this river, the natives spoke a word that sounded like *Ohio*, but no one knows what they really meant by this.

Later, the Europeans began to call the area to the north and west of the Ohio River the *Ohio Country*. When the United States of America was formed, this area was called the *Territory Northwest of the Ohio River*. In 1803, when the first state was formed in the Northwest Territory, it was named *Ohio*. The time line on this page shows how Ohio fits into the early history of the United States. You will learn more about this time line in Chapters 5 and 6.

Why is Ohio called the "Buckeye State"?

Early explorers traveling in the Ohio Country found many trees whose nuts reminded them of the eyes of deer. For this reason, they called them **buckeye** trees (a *buck* is a male deer). Buckeye trees are closely related to horse chestnut trees, but buckeye trees have five leaflets — which look something like spread-out fingers of your hand — while chestnut trees have seven leaflets. The picture on the next page shows the leaf and flower of a buckeye tree, but these trees are hard to find today.

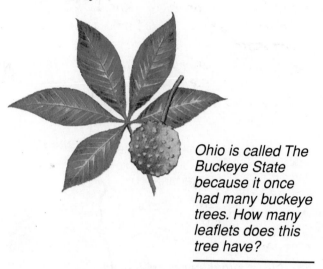

Ohio is called The Buckeye State because it once had many buckeye trees. How many leaflets does this tree have?

A man named William Henry Harrison lived most of his life in Ohio. When he ran for President of the United States in 1840, he used a buckeye tree as a symbol of his campaign. People everywhere began to refer to Ohio as *The Buckeye State*. The Ohio General Assembly made the buckeye the official state tree in 1953.

How did Ohio get its shape?

As you can see on the map of the United States, the shape of Ohio is different from that of any other state. You will learn how it got this shape in a later chapter. On the next page, you can see the largest map of Ohio in this book. When you travel across our state from east to west, you go about 200 miles (320 kilometers). When you travel across it from north to south, you

also go about 200 miles (320 km). Of the fifty states in the United States of America, thirty-four have more land than Ohio, but only six have more people.

This map also shows the 88 counties of Ohio. In **Appendix** (addition to a book) A, beginning on page 381, you will find information about each county, including the year in which it was organized, its area, its **county seat** (place of government), and the meaning of its name.

Why is Ohio an interesting place to live?

Although our state is rather small in area, it has many outstanding features that you will be learning about in the following chapters. One interesting feature is represented by the yellow band on the map on the following page. This band from the southwest corner of Ohio to the northeast corner is shown as 50 miles (80 kilometers) wide. If you live to the northwest of this band, you may think that Ohio is very flat. If you live to the southeast, you may think that it is very hilly. If you live within the yellow band, you may think that Ohio is just one city after another. If you live outside the band — except in Lucas County — you may think that Ohio is mostly farm land or woods. In Chapter 2, you will learn how nature divided Ohio into these parts that are so different.

The yellow band on this map shows how Ohio is divided into roughly three parts.
Where is the county you live in?
How does it fit the pattern of flat and hilly, urban and rural?

Why should you learn about Ohio?

How long have you lived in Ohio? Will you live in this state for all of your life? Why learn about a state that you may live in for only a short time? No matter where you may live in the future, the history of Ohio will help you understand the history of each of the other states. For this reason, what you learn about Ohio will help you understand places where you may someday live or visit.

In Chapters 2 through 4, you will learn how nature shaped the lands of our state, and how the earliest humans lived on the land. In Chapters 5 and 6, you will learn how white settlers moved into the Ohio Country and pushed out the natives. In Chapters 7 through 11, you will learn how millions of people from Europe moved to America during the **19th century** (1801 - 1900). Many of these people came to Ohio and used the resources of nature to create the foundations of the cities, industries, and transportation systems we have today.

In Chapters 12 through 15, you will learn how the population of our state grew and how the lives of people changed during the **20th century** (1901 - today). Since 1950 things have changed so fast that it is hard to remember what some people call "the good old days." Yes, Ohio is a great place to live, as you will soon discover!

What will you learn?

For over 200 years, Ohio has been an exciting place to live. As you study our state, you can expect to learn:
1. Why events happened in the past.
2. How these events affect you today.
3. How laws are made to deal with new events.
4. How to understand the world around you.

No matter where you may live in the future, you can use these ideas to understand your new community.

Let's Review

New Words

appendix
buckeye
county seat
19th century
20th century

Note: The United States Government began using the International System of units in 1994; therefore, all present measurements will be given in both English and metric form. Old measurements will be given only in English form.

New Things to Do

1. Find your county on the map of Ohio. Is the land where you live hilly or flat? Do you live in a town or country area? How do these answers compare to the diagonal band on page 8?

2. Practice until you can draw a map of Ohio from memory. Write on this map the name of each state and body of water around Ohio.

3. Practice until you can draw a map of your county from memory. Write on this map the name of each county, state, or body of water that touches your county.

4. Begin to make a scrapbook about Ohio. Ask an adult in your home to help you find information about people, places, and events of your local community, county, and the state as a whole. Keep the information in the order of the chapters of this book.

Books to Read

America The Beautiful Ohio, by Deborah Kent, uses many beautiful pictures to tell the story of our state. It includes lists of important dates, people, and events.

Enchantment of America Ohio, by Allan Carpenter, is a short summary of your textbook, including several of the same illustrations.

Ohio, by Mary Virginia Fox, is a brief history of our state with black and white pictures.

Portrait of America Ohio, by Kathleen Thompson, is a very short summary of Ohio history.

Who Put the Cannon in the Courthouse Square?, by Kay Cooper, is a guide to discovering the history of your neighborhood and to writing stories about it.

Chapter 2

How has nature shaped Ohio?

Let's learn...

- **how forces of nature created rocks and soil.**

- **how glaciers changed the land.**

- **about the natural resources of our state.**

How old is the earth? How large is the universe? **Scholars** (people who study things carefully) have been seeking answers to these questions for thousands of years. Today we know that earth is a very small planet moving in a space so large we cannot understand the size. You now know almost as much about outer space as the wisest people who lived just 100 years ago.

Geologists (scholars who study the formation of the earth) now believe that our planet is from 4 to 5 billion years old. The oldest rocks we can see in Ohio are only about 500 million years old. In this chapter, we will explore how the history of earth affects our lives today.

Part 1

How did the forces of nature create rocks and soil?

The forces of nature that created the place we call *Ohio* operate in the same way everywhere on our planet. Some forces,

Running water can erode sandy soils very quickly. Have you ever cleaned a sidewalk or driveway with a garden hose?

including weathering, erosion, and chemical action, break down the surface of the earth. Other forces, including chemical action, heat, and pressure, cause new rocks to form from small pieces of old rocks. Over millions of years, this combination of breaking down and cementing together created the rocks that you can find everywhere under Ohio today.

Igneous Rocks

Do you know that most of planet earth is so hot that it is a thick liquid? When geologists drill holes into the surface of earth, the deeper they go, the hotter the drill becomes. When you see pictures of a volcano, you see some of this hot material from the center of the earth breaking through the surface. When it reaches the surface, it cools and hardens to produce **igneous** rocks. We live on the hard crust of earth, which is called **bedrock**. All of the igneous rock under our state is covered by thick layers of *sedimentary* rocks that nature made from igneous rocks. You can travel north into Canada and see igneous rocks at the surface of earth.

We will now look at the forces of weathering, erosion, and chemical action that break down igneous rocks. Then we will look at the forces of nature that created the three kinds of sedimentary rocks that you can see in Ohio.

Effects of Weathering

How does the weather affect our lives? When the temperature and humidity go up, we become uncomfortable. When the weather turns cold, we must protect ourselves by wearing warm clothing or by staying in warm buildings. We need rain to grow food, but it can interfere with our work or play. These ordinary events of weather also affect the surface of the earth. When the natural events of **weathering** (heating and cooling, wetting and drying, freezing and thawing) go on for thousands of years, whole mountains of igneous rock are broken down.

Effects of Erosion

Have you ever turned a stream of water from a garden hose against a pile of dirt or sand? If so, you have seen **erosion** at work. Flooded streams can remove large rocks, and high waves can change shore lines. The picture on the previous page shows how running water can erode sand.

Wind can also cause erosion. Have you ever seen a "whirlwind" behind a tractor as a farmer plows a field? A strong wind blowing across a bare field picks up fine pieces of dirt and rock. When these tiny pieces hit a hard object, they act like sandpaper and erode away the surface.

LAKE ERIE
CAVES

CRYSTAL ROCK CAVE

SENECA CAVERNS

INDIAN TRAIL CAVERNS

ZANE CAVERNS

OHIO · OLENTANGY CAVERNS
CAVERNS

SEVEN CAVES

Each of these caves is owned by the State of Ohio. Have you visited any of them?

Effects of Chemicals

Have you ever been in a *cave* or *cavern*? Caves are formed when water containing weak acids **dissolve** (melt) certain kinds of rocks. The map above shows the names and locations of the most important caves that you can visit in Ohio. In some caves, the water and rock combine to form strange and beautiful formations like those shown on the next page. If you live near Hocking County in central Ohio, you may wonder why the map does not show Ash Cave and Old Man's Cave. These "caves"

were formed by the erosion of water rather than by chemical action.

Sedimentary Rocks

What happens to igneous rocks under the forces of nature? Over millions of years, the actions of weathering caused the surfaces of some forms of igneous rocks to break into smaller and smaller pieces that we call *sand* and *gravel*. The actions of chemicals caused other forms of igneous rock to break into even smaller pieces that we call *clay*. In most places, rain water carried the small materials away and the igneous rock was again exposed to nature.

Have you ever looked at a flooded stream? What color was it? Flooded streams carry large amounts of clay and sand so the water usually looks brown. Over thousands of years, moving water played an important part in creating the rocks of Ohio. It broke large pieces of rock into smaller and smaller pieces. When it reached an ocean, all the clay and sand dropped to the bottom.

As bits of clay and sand laid on the ocean floor for millions of years, the forces of nature changed them into **sedimentary** rocks. The sandy sediments became **sandstone**. The picture on page 16 shows the layers of sandstone under Lorain County, in north-central Ohio. The clay sediments became **shale**. The picture on page 16 shows the layers of shale and

14

limestone you can see in southwestern Ohio and in places along Interstate Highway 71.

As more millions of years passed, small living creatures appeared on the earth and in the waters. Some of these creatures had **calcium** in their bodies. In fact, the hard parts of all animals, such as bones, shells, and teeth, contain calcium. When these creatures died, the calcium from their bodies was washed into the still waters. Some of it mixed with other chemicals to form *calcium carbonate*, which we often call **limestone**.

The Age of Rocks

You have learned that the earth is perhaps 4 or 5 billion years old and that the oldest

In Ohio Cavern you can see beautiful scenes like this. What must be done to a cave so that visitors can see such sights?

rocks in our state are about 500 million years old. These numbers are so big that no one can really understand them, so you may be thinking, "How can they possibly say that rocks are so old?" Geologists and other scholars have been studying rocks all over the world for about 150 years. From these studies, they have been able to explain the forces of nature and rock formation in useful ways.

In some parts of Ohio you can see alternate beds of limestone and shale. How is this bedrock different from sandstone in Lorain County?

For more than 100 years sandstone was taken from this quarry in Lorain County. Judging by the size of the people, how large are these blocks of stone?

The geological map on the next page shows the ages of rocks found in our state. Sandstone, shale, and limestone are found in many places around the world. Because these rocks were formed under water, geologists know that most of the earth's surface was at the bottom of a saltwater sea at sometime in the past. Because Ohio has many layers of sedimentary rocks, we know that our state was at the bottom of an ocean many times. We also know something about forms of life that existed millions of years ago, because the rocks contain **fossils**. These are stone objects that look like pieces of plants and/or animals.

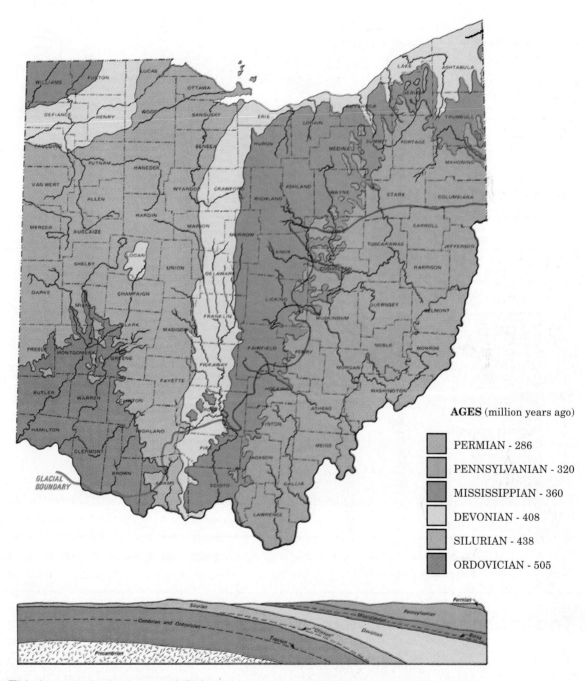

AGES (million years ago)

- PERMIAN - 286
- PENNSYLVANIAN - 320
- MISSISSIPPIAN - 360
- DEVONIAN - 408
- SILURIAN - 438
- ORDOVICIAN - 505

This is a geological map of Ohio. It shows the ages of the rocks of our state. What age rocks are under your home?

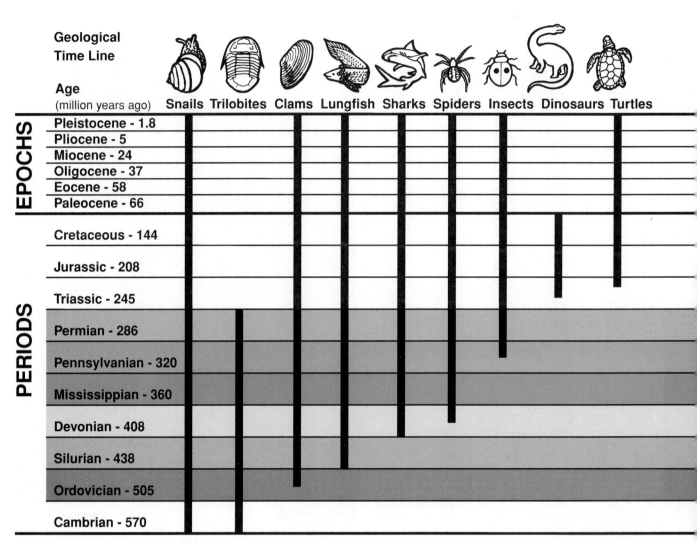

	Geological Time Line Age (million years ago)	Snails	Trilobites	Clams	Lungfish	Sharks	Spiders	Insects	Dinosaurs	Turtles
EPOCHS	Pleistocene - 1.8									
	Pliocene - 5									
	Miocene - 24									
	Oligocene - 37									
	Eocene - 58									
	Paleocene - 66									
PERIODS	Cretaceous - 144									
	Jurassic - 208									
	Triassic - 245									
	Permian - 286									
	Pennsylvanian - 320									
	Mississippian - 360									
	Devonian - 408									
	Silurian - 438									
	Ordovician - 505									
	Cambrian - 570									

The rocks of Ohio contain fossils of creatures that lived millions of years ago. Why are no dinosaur bones found in the rocks of Ohio?

The Importance of Fossils

Above, you can see a geological time line of earth. The colored bands on this time line match the colored areas of the map on the previous page. As you can see from these two illustrations, all of the rocks of Ohio are more than 250 million years old. On page 4, you learned that the **trilobite** is our state fossil. Near the left end of the

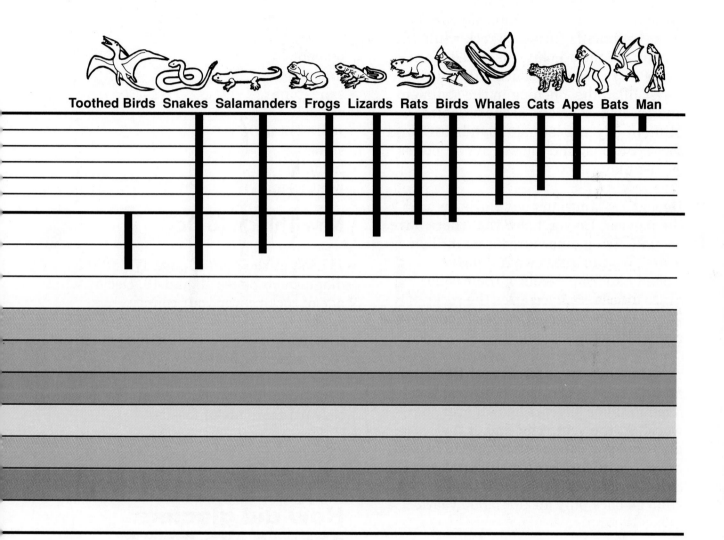

Toothed Birds   Snakes   Salamanders   Frogs   Lizards   Rats   Birds   Whales   Cats   Apes   Bats   Man

time line, you can see that trilobites existed for almost 300 million years. Almost all the rocks of Ohio contain some fossils, but those in the southwestern part of the state contain many fossils.

Nature used special combinations of chemicals, time, and pressure to create these fossils. Suppose a trilobite died and was washed into a body of salt water. Over a period of years, nature packed sediments around its shell. Thousands of years later, these sediments turned to rock while the remains of the trilobite dissolved. Over many more years, chemicals from the water filled the opening in the sediment and created a "model" of the trilobite. Millions of years later, human beings find these "models" and know what trilobites looked like.

Do you see dinosaurs on television or in the movies? Do you know that there have been no living dinosaurs for 65 million years? We can guess what dinosaurs looked like from fossils of their bones. Since dinosaurs lived after the rocks of Ohio had been formed, none of their fossils can be found in Ohio.

The time line on pages 18 and 19 includes an artist's idea of other creatures that lived millions of years ago all over the world. At the very right end of the diagram, you can see that human beings have existed for about 2 million years. The oldest records of human activity found in Ohio go back only about 15,000 years.

Let's Review Part 1

New Words

bedrock
calcium
dissolve
erosion

fossil
geologist
igneous
limestone
sandstone
scholar
sedimentary
shale
trilobite
weathering

New Things to Do

1. Look at the map of page 17 and the diagram on pages 18 and 19. Decide what age of rocks cover your county.

2. What kinds of fossils should you be able to find in your county?

3. Go to a library and read an encyclopedia to learn more about fossils.

Part 2

How did glaciers change the land?

What is the biggest piece of ice you have ever seen? Maybe it was a large piece of ice floating on a pond. Maybe it was a river or lake frozen so hard that you could walk on it. The picture on the next page shows a moving sheet of ice called a **glacier** that may be large enough to cover your county.

Today you can walk through a model of a glacier at the Cincinnati Museum of Natural History.

This is a glacier in Alaska. What kind of clothes would you wear to take a hike on a glacier?

Events During The Ice Age

The period of time from 1,000,000 to 15,000 years ago is often called the *Ice Age*. No one knows why it happened, but during the Ice Age, four huge sheets of ice moved over parts of North America, including Ohio, Indiana, and Michigan. About 15,000 years ago, the ice melted back to about where you can see the Arctic Ice Cap across the top of the map on page 2.

Beginning far to the north in Canada, these masses of ice acted like huge "bulldozers" as they pushed soil and broken rock over the areas to the south.

On Kelleys Island in Lake Erie, the moving rocks created grooves in the bedrock of the island, which you can see on the next page. The map on page 23 shows the parts of Ohio covered by the last three glaciers. The soil and rocks carried by the first glacier covered the bedrock of a large part of our state. Each later glacier covered the materials left by the earlier ones. The picture on the next page shows large igneous rocks from Canada that have been found in southern Ohio.

If you look at the maps on pages 8 and 23, you can see that the diagonal line on page 8 almost matches the edge of the glaciers. If you live to the northwest of this line, you may have to travel some distance to see bedrock, because the glaciers leveled off the old hills and filled all of the old valleys. If you live to the southeast of the line, you must travel to see large areas of level land because the glaciers did not affect your area.

How Glaciers Affected Hills

As the weather grew colder or warmed during the four glacial periods, the southern edges of the glaciers moved forward and back. As they moved to the south, they scraped the tops off of the hills of northern Ohio. As they melted back, they dropped the soil and rocks picked up while moving southward. Some of this material filled in old valleys and some created long mounds called **moraines**.

These glacial grooves on Kelleys Island were made by ice pushing hard rocks across limestone. How is this limestone different from that shown on page 16?

The dark green areas on the map on the next page are moraines. If you live in the northwestern half of our state, you can see that these moraines are your *hills*. Can you guess how the city of *Moraine* in Montgomery County got its name?

How Glaciers Affected Waterways

As the glaciers pushed southward, they changed the drainage pattern of the entire area they covered. Geologists know from drilling deep holes into the earth that most of the rivers of Ohio once flowed to the north. As the glaciers blocked these streams, the waters had to create new channels to the south.

The glaciers moved these granite boulders to Warren County from Canada. Have you seen boulders like these decorating someone's yard?

22

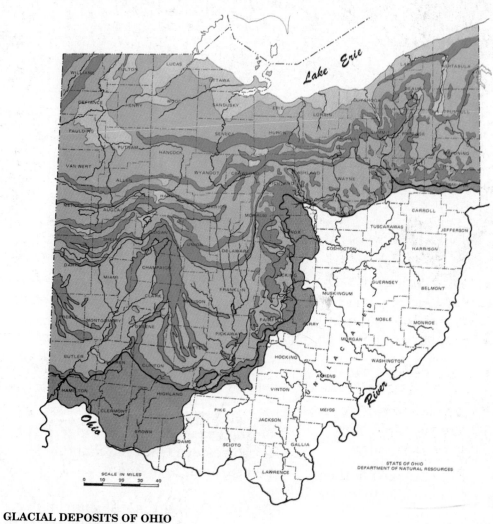

GLACIAL DEPOSITS OF OHIO

WISCONSINAN

- KAMES AND ESKERS
- LAKE DEPOSITS
- GROUND MORAINE
- END MORAINE

ILLINOIAN

- UNDIFFERENTIATED

KANSAN

- GROUND MORAINE

This map shows how the glaciers affected our state.
What does the map tell you about your county?

23

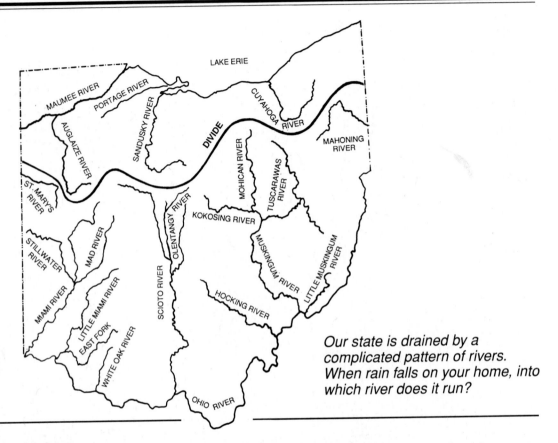

Our state is drained by a complicated pattern of rivers. When rain falls on your home, into which river does it run?

The map above shows the most important streams of Ohio since the last glacier disappeared. As you can see, most of those that flow into Lake Erie are shorter than those that flow into the Ohio River. The **divide** shown on this map is the line of highest land across the state. Rain falling to the north of this divide flows to the Atlantic Ocean by way of Lake Erie, Lake Ontario, and the St. Lawrence River (see map on page 3). Rain falling to the south of this divide flows to the Gulf of Mexico by way of the Ohio and Mississippi Rivers. In northeastern Ohio, you can see this divide

on the ground as a clear ridge, but in northwestern Ohio you must make exact measurements to find it.

As you can see from the map on page 23, the glaciers stopped to the north of the present Ohio River. Large volumes of water were created as the southern ends melted, and this water had to cut through bedrock to create a new pattern of drainage. As a result, the Ohio River now flows between steep hills where it eroded the bedrock. The picture on the next page shows an artist's idea of these steep hills that begin close to the river.

In other places, where the last glacier found soft ground, it pushed the soil out to make huge pits. When the ice melted, the pits were filled with water. We now call the five largest pits the *Great Lakes*. You can turn back to page 3 to see these lakes.

When the last glacier melted back into Canada, the water we call *Lake Erie* covered a much larger area than it does today. In fact, all of the areas shown in blue on the map on page 23 were once part of it. The first explorers from Europe came into this area about 1700. They found a large wet area at the west end of Lake Erie that they called the *Black Swamp*. Later settlers found smaller wet areas in the northwestern half of Ohio and filled them in to create farm land. You can still see one of these glacial wetlands at Cedar Bog in Champaign County.

The Ohio River flows between steep hills in many places. What makes the boat move?

Let's Review Part 2

New Words

divide (drainage)
glacier
moraine

New Things to Do

1. Look at the map on page 23. How much of your county was covered by the glaciers? If any of it was covered, describe what the ground looks like in that area.

2. Find a valley in your neighborhood, and write a report on what has happened to a 600-foot (200-meter) length of it. If you live in a city, the stream that created the valley may be in a large sewer pipe that you cannot see. If you live in a very flat area, use a drainage ditch as a valley.

3. Find a divide in your neighborhood, and write a report on what has happened to a 600-foot (200-meter) length of it. (Hint: There may be a road on the divide.)

Part 3

What are the natural resources of Ohio?

Natural resources are materials found in nature that help humans live. Two hundred years ago, the most important natural resources of our state were soil, rocks, trees, coal, petroleum, salt, and iron. While the iron ore is gone, the other resources are still very important.

Soils

Earlier in this chapter, you learned how the forces of nature break hard rocks into small pieces. The very smallest pieces are called **soils**. Our lives depend on soils because most of what we eat comes from them. Farmers raise grains, vegetables, fruits, and other useful products from soils. They feed grains to animals to produce the meat that we eat.

Look back to the geological map on page 17. The reddish, pinkish, and yellow areas on this map are mostly limestone or mixed limestone and shale. When limestone breaks down by the processes of nature, it produces **fertile** soil (good for growing foods). The green, blue, and orange areas on the map are mostly sandstone, or sandstone and shale, which break down into poor soils. The picture on the next page might have been taken in many places in southeastern Ohio. The entire region is beautiful in the spring of each year, as the trees sprout new leaves, and in the autumn as the leaves turn to bright colors. But the hilly land and poor soils are used mostly for raising grass to feed cows and sheep.

Rocks

Human beings have used rocks for a variety of purposes throughout history. Each portion of the earth has a period of history called the *Stone Age* when people made tools and weapons from rocks. Many settlers in the Ohio Country built their houses on stacks of rocks to keep the wood away from the ground.

During the 19th century, sandstone from the **quarry** (source of bedrock) shown on page 16 was used to build county court houses and other important buildings throughout Ohio. It was also used to build foundation walls, sidewalks, curbs, and grave markers. Special kinds of sandstone were used to create *mill stones* for grinding grain. Sandstone is seldom used today.

During the 19th century, limestone was used to build the foundations of many houses. It was used to create sidewalks and curbs along streets. It was also used to make *whitewash*, which was the most important form of white paint for many years. The most important use of limestone today is in making **concrete**, which is an

You can see scenes like this in many places in southeast Ohio.
How would you describe the land in this picture?

important material for buildings and highways. Where the glaciers did not leave sand and gravel, limestone is crushed to create sand and gravel for concrete. Limestone and shale are used to make *Portland cement* which is the "glue" that makes concrete strong.

Trees

What is the largest tree you have seen? Have you ever "hugged" a tree? When the early settlers came into the Ohio country, many of the trees were so large that it would take four friends to help you "hug" one. These trees were "mixed blessings" to the settlers. On the one hand, they provided **lumber** (wood cut into usable pieces) for building houses, barns, fences, and furniture, and for fuel. On the other hand, the settlers had to cut down thousands of trees to clear the land for farming. It was not too hard to cut down the trees. But it was very difficult to remove the **stumps** (bases of the trees) so that farmers could plant seeds. In most cases, the stumps were left to rot over a period of years.

After most of the good timber in Ohio had been cut, some people worried about the loss of woodlands, the erosion of hillsides, and the damage to streams. These people, who are called **conservationists**, began to work to create areas where forests could grow again under protection of the law. Now there are state-owned forests and parks in all parts of Ohio. Wayne National Forest covers many square miles of southeastern Ohio. Today you seldom see trees larger than two feet (60 centimeters) in diameter, except in parks, because trees of this size are cut for lumber.

Coal

Coal is a black material that looks like rock. It will break easily if you hit it with a hammer. It is one of the most useful materials found in Ohio. Layers of coal were created millions of years ago as trees and plants fell into swamps. Later the surface of the earth dropped below sea level. The dead material — called **organic matter** — was then buried under sand and clay that settled to the bottom of the sea. Over a very long period of time, the great weight of the water, sand, and clay pressed the organic matter into what we call *coal*. The map on the next page shows where coal was mined in Ohio during 1987.

Petroleum

What makes your family automobile or your school bus run? What kind of fuel is used to heat your home? What is the salve made from that you use on a sore muscle? What kind of material was used to build the streets you use? The answers to all these questions may be one word, **petroleum**! We get gasoline, diesel fuel, home-heating oil, petroleum jelly, asphalt, and many other useful things from a dark-brown fluid that comes out of the ground. *Natural gas* is often found with petroleum. Today almost one-half of the petroleum used in the United States comes from other parts of the world. In the year 1890, about one-half of the petroleum used in the United States came from Ohio!

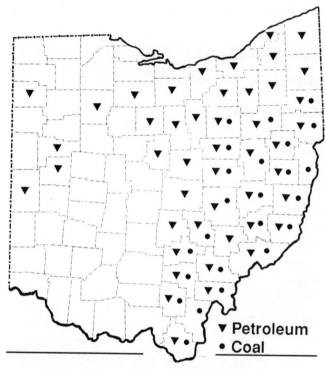

▼ Petroleum
• Coal

Coal and petroleum are important natural resources in some Ohio counties. How does your family use petroleum products?

The map above also shows the places in Ohio where natural gas and petroleum are found today. The picture on page 27 also shows the kind of petroleum pump you can see in many places in eastern Ohio.

Salt

Humans and all animals need salt to live. Early explorers of the Ohio country found many animal trails that led to **salt licks** (places were salt appears on the ground). Licking County was given its name because of the salt deposits used by animals, Native Americans, and settlers. In the days before ice was used, there were only three ways to preserve meat: it could be dried, treated with smoke, or packed into barrels with salt. Even today, Ashtabula, Cuyahoga, Lake, and Medina counties produce large amounts of salt.

Iron

Iron is a chemical found in soils and rocks in many parts of the world. Iron is useful only when it is removed from the rocks and purified by a process called **smelting**. People in some parts of the world learned to work with iron almost 4,000 years ago, and they created what is known as the *Iron Age*. When European explorers reached America, the native people knew nothing about iron.

During the last half of the 19th century (1851-1900), Ohio was one of the most important sources of iron in the United States. The message shown in the box on the next page is from a roadside marker in Jackson County, a short distance southeast of Wellston. It gives a very brief introduction to the iron industry you will learn about in Chapter 10. Of the 69 furnaces mentioned in the box, 23 were in Lawrence County. Can you guess why the county seat of Lawrence County was named *Ironton?*

Buckeye Furnace (1851-1874)

Buckeye Furnace is one of 69 charcoal iron furnaces in the famous Hanging Rock Iron Region. Extending more than 100 miles from Logan, Ohio, to Mt. Savage, Kentucky, this area contained all materials necessary to produce high grade iron. The industry flourished for over 50 years in the mid 19th century during which time the area was one of the leading iron producing centers in the world. The charcoal iron industry was responsible for the rapid development of southern Ohio, and the romance of the Hanging Rock Region forms a brilliant chapter in the industrial chapter of the Buckeye State.

You can see this sign near Wellston in Jackson County. What does the word "flourished" mean?

The Ohio Historical Society gained control of the Buckeye Iron Furnace almost one hundred years after it was closed. The Society repaired the buildings, as you can see on the next page, and you can visit this important place. You can also visit small communities in Scioto County named *Scioto Furnace, Franklin Furnace,* and *Ohio Furnace. Hanging Rock,* the name of the iron district, is a small community on U.S. Route 52 in Lawrence County.

Let's Review Part 3

New Words

concrete
conservation
fertile
lumber
natural resource
organic matter
petroleum
quarry
salt lick
smelt
soil
stump

New Things to Do

1. Which of the raw materials of Ohio is used to heat the house in which you live?

2. Make a list of all the things you eat in one day that contain salt. Look on the labels of food containers to see whether the food contains salt.

The Buckeye Furnace was used to make iron in Jackson County. What would happen to this building if no one took care of it?

3. Make a list of all the things you use in one day that are made of wood. (Some things that look like wood are really plastic!)

What have we learned?

Earth has a very long history. We can "read" parts of that history in the rocks we find in Ohio. By studying the fossils in these rocks, we can learn about plants and animals that lived on earth millions of years ago.

By studying the soils on top of the rocks, we can learn about glaciers that covered a large part of our state from about 1,000,000 to 15,000 years ago. These glaciers created the good farm land in northwestern Ohio. The fact that they did not cover southeastern Ohio left that area with poor land for farming. The rivers, streams, and lakes of Ohio were also shaped by the glaciers.

The forces of nature gave Ohio many natural resources including rocks, coal, petroleum, salt, iron, and trees. There are so many rocks that we can never "use" them all. Coal and petroleum are burned to create energy for many purposes. There is still enough coal to last for many years. Petroleum is being used so rapidly that it may all be gone by the year 2020. There are still large amounts of salt under the counties of northeastern Ohio. The iron was used up by 1900. The trees are renewable resources, and lumbering continues to be an important industry. In all of the remaining chapters of this book, you will learn how these natural resources influence our lives today.

Map Projects

Find the following places on your map of Ohio

Place	County
Franklin Furnace	Scioto
Hanging Rock	Lawrence
Moraine	Montgomery
Morrow	Warren
Ohio Furnace	Scioto
Scioto Furnace	Scioto
Wellston	Jackson

The Black Swamp around the west end of Lake Erie.

Books to Read

The following books will help you understand our planet earth and how our lives are related to the forces of nature. Your library may have other books on these subjects.

The Book of Dinosaurs, by Tim Gardom, tells why dinosaurs existed for so many millions of years.

How The Earth Works, by John Farndon, answers questions that you may have about our planet and suggests ways to explore the area where you live.

Icebergs and Glaciers, by Keith Branigan, describes how icebergs are created as glaciers reach the ocean.

The Illustrated Encyclopedia of Prehistoric Life, by Dougal Dixon, is a beautifully illustrated book about life on earth up to 1500 BC.

The Story of The Earth — Cave, by Lionel Bender, explains how and why caves form and includes many beautiful pictures.

The World Before Man, by David Lambert, explains how we learn about life on earth up through the glacial period.

Chapter 3

Who lived in Ohio before 1600?

Let's learn...

- about how we study prehistoric people.

- about the Woodland people.

- how prehistoric people lived.

The people who lived in the area we call *Ohio*, from about 13,000 **BCE**(before the common era) until Europeans found them, were **prehistoric**. This means that they did not have a written language. No one really knows where the first people of Ohio, and all of North and South America, came from. Some scholars believe that all of them were related to Asian people from the lands we call China, Japan, and Korea.

In recent years, scholars have found that the lives of people living in northeastern Asia are similar to those living in Alaska.

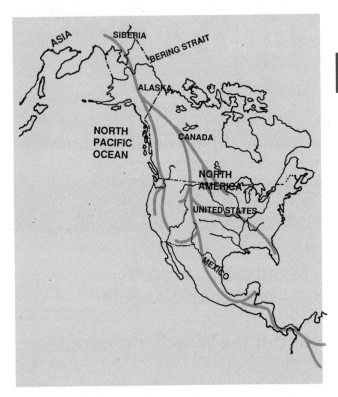

Some scholars believe that people were able to walk from Asia to North America during the times of the glaciers. Can you find the location of Ohio on this map?

If you look at the map above, you can see that the northeastern tip of Asia is very close to the northwestern tip of North America. Some geologists believe that Asia may have been connected to North America by a "land bridge." If people did move across such a "bridge" in ancient

times, the map also shows how they might have moved across North America in later times. In this chapter, we will look at the people who lived in the Ohio Country during these thousands of years.

Part 1

How can we learn about prehistoric people?

If prehistoric people could not write, how can we learn about them? During the past 200 years, **archaeologists** (scholars who study the remains of ancient peoples) have discovered the remains of ancient peoples in Ohio and many other parts of the world. They have learned to look for three kinds of prehistoric places: camp sites, trash piles, and burial places. In this part, you will learn why such places are important.

Camp Sites

Wherever prehistoric people lived, whether for a day or several years, they made fires to cook food and/or warm themselves. Perhaps you have roasted "hot dogs" or marshmallows over an open fire. If you used wood as the fuel, you created some **charcoal** because charcoal is made by heating wood but not burning it. Under the right conditions, charcoal can last for thousands of years. Scholars have learned to measure the age of a piece of charcoal

Trash Piles

Stop reading for a few minutes and think about the trash that your family throws out each week. Now think about the things you see your neighbors put out for the waste collectors. Almost all of this trash goes to what was once called a *dump* but is now a *sanitary land fill*. In the year 3000 **CE** (of the common era), archaeologists may learn about our civilization from this trash we leave behind. In the same way, we learn from the waste pits of prehistoric times.

One important form of waste is the bones of animals. Such bones have also been found in places where animals were trapped, as in a swamp. For example, we know that the largest animals that lived in the Ohio Country after the Ice Age were **mastodons**. These creatures were similar to elephants, as you can see on the next page. In 1926 a complete skeleton of a mastodon was uncovered at Johnstown in

The time line on this page shows the names that scholars have given to the groups of people who lived many years ago where we now live. How many "centuries" are shown on this diagram?

within a few hundred years. This means that they can relate prehistoric events to our calendar, as shown on the time line in the next column.

Prehistoric People in Ohio

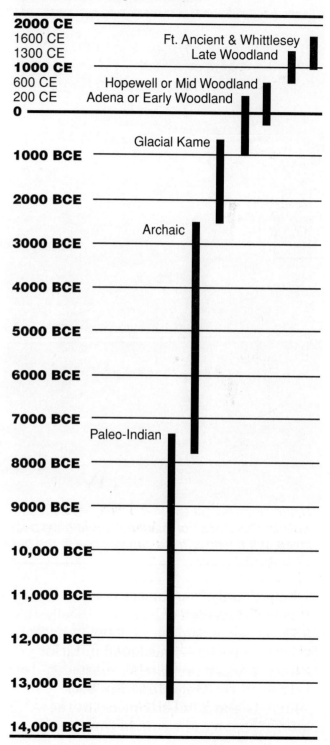

- 2000 CE
- 1600 CE
- 1300 CE — Ft. Ancient & Whittlesey / Late Woodland
- **1000 CE**
- 600 CE — Hopewell or Mid Woodland
- 200 CE — Adena or Early Woodland
- 0
- 1000 BCE — Glacial Kame
- 2000 BCE
- 3000 BCE — Archaic
- 4000 BCE
- 5000 BCE
- 6000 BCE
- 7000 BCE
- 8000 BCE — Paleo-Indian
- 9000 BCE
- 10,000 BCE
- 11,000 BCE
- 12,000 BCE
- 13,000 BCE
- 14,000 BCE

Based on the bones of mastodons that have been found in Ohio, scholars think they looked like this picture. What kind of trees can you see in the background?

Licking County. You can see it today in the Cleveland Museum of Natural History. In 1989 a whole mastodon skeleton — except for two leg bones — was found in Licking County. You can see another mastodon skeleton at the Ohio Historical Society in Columbus and a full-size model at the Natural History Museum in Cincinnati.

Another thing archaeologists look for in camp sites and dumps is **flint**. Flint is a very hard form of rock that has very sharp edges when broken. Flint from *Flint Ridge*, in Licking County, was the most important tool of prehistoric people in the eastern half of the United States. They used flint weapons to kill animals and flint knives to remove the skin and cut up the meat. The picture below was taken at Flint Ridge State Memorial where people worked for thousands of years. Can you guess why flint is our *state mineral*?

Burial Places

Now spend a few minutes thinking about a cemetery you have seen. In an effort to honor a mother, father, sister, or brother who dies, other members of the family often bury them with pieces of jewelry and/or other things they liked. The family often puts a bronze or stone marker over the grave. You can learn something about the history of your community by reading the messages on these markers. Archaeologists learn about prehistoric people by exploring their burial places.

Archaeologists have found very few remains of the people who lived in the Ohio Country before 1000 BCE as shown on the time line on page 35. They have found many remains of people who lived in this area from about 1000 BCE to about 1600 CE as you will soon learn.

The statues of people in this picture show how people worked with flint in Licking County thousands of years ago. What tools would we use today to dig in hard rock?

Let's Review Part 1

New Words

archaeologist
BCE
CE
charcoal
flint
mastodon
prehistoric

New Things to Do

Pretend that you and your classmates are archaeologists in the year 2,500:

(a) you visit the area where you now live. Discuss what parts of the buildings you now use might still remain.

(b) you dig into the area where your trash is dumped. Discuss what kinds of things you use today might last 500 years.

Part 2

Who lived in the Ohio country 2,000 years ago?

The time line on page 35 shows *Woodland* people living in the Ohio Country from 1000 BCE to 1300 CE. We know much more about them, and the Fort Ancient people, than we do about earlier Native Americans.

The earliest explorers from Europe found strange mounds of earth all across the Ohio Country. Later, scholars dug into these mounds and found remains of people who lived here for almost 2,300 years. For 200 years, farmers and construction workers have also found arrowheads and other **artifacts** (objects) made by these people. Perhaps someone you know has found such an object.

The Early Woodland people are also called the *Adenas*, and the Middle Woodland people are called the *Hopewells*. These two groups are also called the *Mound Builders*. We know very little about the Late Woodland people.

Adena and Hopewell Mounds

Most of the mounds found by explorers and settlers were rather small, but some were very high, very long, or built in strange patterns. Many of the smaller mounds were destroyed as settlers farmed and built homes, but some of the largest mounds are still visible today.

Why Adena? Why Hopewell?

During the late 1830s, archaeologists studied almost 300 prehistoric mounds east of the Mississippi River. Some of the mounds were on the farm of Thomas Worthington in Ross County. Mr. Worthington called his home *Adena*, which is a Hebrew word meaning "beautiful place." The archaeologists who explored these mounds called the people who once lived there the *Adena* people. Later, they explored mounds on the farm of M.C. Hopewell in Ross County. The artifacts found in these mounds were different from those at the Adena site, so archaeologists called them the *Hopewell* people.

Forty-one Adena and Hopewell mounds have been studied in the area of southern Ohio and nearby Indiana, Kentucky, and West Virginia. You can visit the places shown on the map on the next page and see these mounds. Several of the sites have small museums that display objects found in the mounds. A few small Hopewell mounds in northwestern Ohio are not shown on this map.

The two highest mounds are at Miamisburg in Montgomery County and just across the Ohio River from Belmont County in Moundsville, West Virginia. The first buildings at Circleville, the county seat of Pickaway County, were built inside two large rings of mounds. Some of the streets were laid out as circles to fit the mounds.

Serpent Mound: The most unusual Ohio mound is the *Serpent Mound* in the northeast corner of Adams County. As you can see in the picture on the next page and the map on page 41, this mound looks like a snake swallowing an egg. You must climb to the top of a tower to get the best view of this mound.

Ross County Mounds: If you visit the Mound City Group National Monument in Ross County, you can imagine that you are seeing the large Hopewell burial ground that early explorers found. What you are really seeing are rebuilt mounds. During World War I, the United States Army built a huge camp in this area and leveled the ancient mounds. You can see many of the relics found there in the museum on the site, and you can see the painting of a Hopewell ceremony shown on page 41.

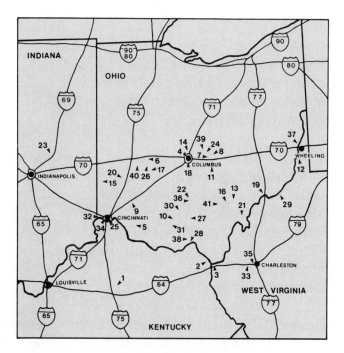

20. Miamisburg Mound
21. Mound Cemetery
22. Mound City Group National Monument
24. Newark Earthworks
25. Norwood Mound
26. Orator's Mound
27. Piketon Mound Cemetery
28. Portsmounth Mound Park
30. Seip Mound State Memorial
31. Serpent Mound State Memorial
32. Shawnee Lookout Park
34. Shorts Woods Park Mound
36. Story Mound
37. Titonsville Cemetery Mound
38. Tremper Mound
39. Williams Mound
40. Wright Brothers Memorial Mound Group
41. Zaleski State Forest Mound

Important remains of Adena and Hopewell people have been found at the places listed. Some of the mounds have been removed. You can visit prehistoric mounds at these places in Ohio and neighboring states. Which mound is closest to your home?

4. Campbell Mound
5. Elk Lick Road Mound
6. Enon Mound
7. Fairmount Mound
8. Flint Ridge State Memorial
9. Fort Ancient State Memorial
10. Fort Hill State Memorial
11. Glenford Fort
13. Hartman Mound and Wolfe's Plains Group
14. Highbanks Park Mound and Earthworks
15. Hueston Woods Campground Mound
16. Indian Mound Campground
17. Indian Mound Park
18. Indian Mounds Park
19. Marietta Earthworks

The best way to see Serpent Mound is from a helicopter. Why is a helicopter better than an airplane for viewing the mounds?

This map of Serpent Mound was made about 1846. Do you think the natives drew a plan of this before they built it? Explain your answer.

You can see this picture of a Hopewell death ceremony at the museum in Ross County. Why are death ceremonies important to human beings?

Newark Mounds: The most complicated system of mounds is in the city of Newark in Licking County. Again, many of the mounds were destroyed as the city grew, but two important ones are now owned by the Ohio Historical Society. The map on the next page shows how they looked in 1847. The large round mound is now a park. The large eight-sided mound is now part of a golf course. This may be the only golf course in the world where flag poles on prehistoric mounds show golfers the way to the next hole.

Fort Ancient: The map on the next page shows the mound called *Fort Ancient*. The Hopewell people built this on a hill above the Little Miami River. Today it is part of a state park with a museum of Hopewell artifacts in east-central Warren County. The mound is 3½ miles (5½ km) long, making it the longest prehistoric mound in the United States. Although we call it a *fort*, no one really knows why the Hopewells built it. Today some people think the Hopewells used it to study what they thought was the movement of the sun.

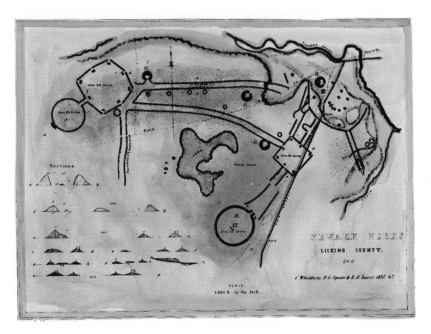

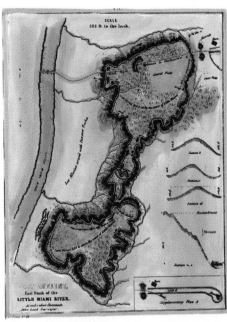

The map of mounds in Licking County was made in 1846. What do you think happened to many of these mounds as the City of Newark was built?

This map of Fort Ancient, in Warren County, was made in 1846. Can you think of reasons why the outline is so irregular?

Fort Ancient People

Between 1000 CE and 1600 CE, another group lived in the southern part of the Ohio Country near the Hopewell mound we call *Fort Ancient*. For this reason, they are called *Fort Ancient people*, but they did not have the skills of the Hopewells. People who lived in the northern part of our state at the same time were called *Whittlesey people*.

Today you can see the remains of a town called *Sun Watch* that Fort Ancient people

built about the year 1200 CE. It is in the southwestern corner of Dayton in Montgomery County. Many **volunteers** (people who work without pay) have helped a few archaeologists uncover this prehistoric town. In the Sun Watch Museum, you can see artifacts that were found nearby. Archaeologists believe that the people who lived there had a form of calendar based on the position of the sun at different times of the year. The picture on the next page shows how buildings have been reconstructed.

Archaeologists have found nothing relating to people who may have lived in the Ohio Country between about 1600 and 1750 CE. When Europeans came to North America, they called the people they found living here *Indians*.

Why The Natives Were Called Indians

Indians — that is what older books called the people who lived in North America before the Europeans arrived. But we use the same word for people who live in the country of *India*. Why is the same word used for two different people?

When Christopher Columbus sailed across the Atlantic Ocean in 1492, the rich people of Europe knew about the gold, spices, and other wonderful things of the *East Indies*. This was their name for the lands we know as India, Indonesia, Thailand, Vietnam, and China.

Sun Watch is a recreated village of the Fort Ancient people in Dayton, Ohio. Have you seen pictures of houses in other parts of the world today that look like these?

Because Columbus believed that the earth was round, he decided to go to the East Indies by sailing *west*. He had no idea that the continents of North America and South America would block his way. When he reached an island in the Caribbean Sea, he thought he was in the East Indies. In a letter he wrote in February of 1493, he referred to the dark-skinned, native people as *Indios*.

The explorers who followed Columbus called all the native peoples of North and South America *Indians*. Today these people prefer to be called *Native Americans*.

Let's Review Part 2

New Words

artifact
volunteer

New Things to Do

Visit the oldest cemetery that is convenient to where you live.

1. Write down the information on the oldest grave marker you can find. How old was the person when he/she died?

2. Find the grave of someone who was important in your community. What can you learn about this person from the grave stone?

3. Form a committee with several of your classmates to plan what to put into a *time capsule* for your school. Make a list of not more than twenty things you use or do in your school that can be fitted in a box that is 12 inches long on each side. Choose things that will help people living in the year 2100 CE to understand your life. If other committees in your class do the same project, compare your list with theirs.

Part 3

How did prehistoric people live?

Today we constantly try to *improve* the way we live and the world around us. Prehistoric people lived in harmony with nature. They did not try to change their surroundings. If conditions in one location became too difficult, they moved to a better place and changed their lives as necessary. Life in the Ohio Country changed less during the thousands of years between 13,000 BCE and 1600 CE than it did during the two hundred years between 1800 and 2000 CE. Since we know most about the Adena and Hopewell people, we will talk about the life-styles of only these two groups.

This is a wigwam made of tree bark. It is in a summer camp for young people. It was made entirely with simple hand tools. Why are there two "rings" around the wigwam?

Houses

These early people lived together in small villages. Several Adena families lived together in a large house, while each Hopewell family had its own **wigwam**, or **wigewa**. The picture to the right shows the support system for both kinds of houses. Small holes were dug, about two feet apart, around the outline of the building. Poles were made from tall, straight, young trees, and a pole was set into each hole. Archaeologists can find these holes today because the rotted wood of the poles is a different color than the

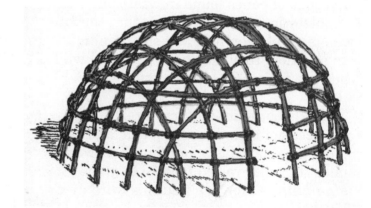

The frames of wigwams were made from poles set into the ground and tied together. Why were the poles set into holes in the ground?

45

surrounding soil. The tops of these poles were bent inward and tied together to form simple arches.

The Adenas made walls by weaving vines or small branches through the posts and filling the spaces with mud and straw. They made roofs by tying bundles of grass to the top of the arches. The Hopewells covered the pole frames with large pieces of tree bark, skins of animals, or woven mats. The picture on the previous page shows a wigwam that was built about 1990 to show children how the Native Americans once lived. There are people living in houses like this in some parts of the world today.

Food

The Adena and Hopewell people were primarily hunters and food-gatherers. Because of bones found in waste pits near prehistoric villages, we know that they ate the meat of deer, fish, and small animals. In addition, they may have gathered wild berries, fruits, nuts, and roots.

They also practiced agriculture, because the seeds of corn, beans, squash, and pumpkins have been found in their waste pits. They also raised tobacco to make *kinnikinnick*. You can find this word in a big dictionary, and you can find a town of this name in Ross County. The ability to plant and harvest crops encouraged the Adena and Hopewell people to build permanent villages. It also gave them leisure time in which to create arts and crafts.

Handicrafts

Pottery is one of the most important items for studying prehistoric people for several reasons. First, pottery lasts for thousands of years. Of course, most of it is found broken, but the pieces can often be put together again. Second, each group of people developed its own styles of making and decorating pottery. This fact helps archaeologists identify how people from various places traded with one another.

Perhaps the most interesting handicraft of the Adena and Hopewell people was a form of pottery. They made a wide variety of pipes for smoking tobacco like those shown below and on the next page. These are known as **effigy** pipes because they look

Adena and Hopewell effigy pipe bowls are true works of art. What creatures do these pipe bowls represent?

like real creatures. They were made from what is called *Ohio pipe stone*, a clay found in the Scioto River valley that can be easily carved and then baked to have permanent form. These pipes have been found in many places in the eastern half of the United States. Each pipe bowl has a small hole in one end. A short piece of hollow reed was slipped into this hole to make a stem to suck smoke from the burning tobacco in the bowl.

Tools

The most important tools were made from flint and bones. Large pieces of flint could be used to cut down small trees and strip bark from large ones. Sharp pieces of flint were tied to short sticks to make arrows for hunting birds and small animals. Larger pieces of flint were tied to long sticks to make spears for hunting larger animals. Sharp pieces of deer antler were used to scrape flesh and hair from the skins of animals for making clothing. Pointed pieces of bone were used to drill holes in skins or bark. Bone needles, threaded with fibers from plants, were used to sew together pieces of skin. Small **boulders** (hard round rocks brought into Ohio by the glaciers) were used to grind grain and to do jobs for which we might use a *hammer*.

Transportation

Walking was the most important form of transportation before Europeans brought horses to America. The natives also traveled along rivers and lakes in canoes. Frames for canoes were made by tying together straight young trees or small branches. These frames were covered with skins of animals or bark from trees. They were made waterproof with resin from pine trees.

Canoes were very useful because they could be used to carry heavy loads over water. At the same time, they were light enough in weight that they could be carried from one stream or lake to another over a **portage** path connecting two bodies of water.

Trade

We know that the Hopewells traded with people who lived far away. Archaeologists have found a variety of trade objects in their graves that are not found in Ohio. The closest place you can find **obsidian** (a black glass created by volcanos) is in the Rocky Mountains. The edges of broken obsidian are as sharp as broken glass. The closest place you can find copper is in northern Michigan. Pure copper is a very soft metal that can be shaped with simple tools. The closest place you can find **mica** (a very thin, flaky material) is in North and South Carolina. Large pieces of mica can be used as mirrors. The closest place you can find sea shells is on the shores of the Atlantic Ocean and the Gulf of Mexico. The closest place you can find alligator teeth is in Florida. On the other hand, Adena and Hopewell pipes have been found in all these far-off places.

Wampum

Because the natives of North America could not read or write, they made **wampum** belts to record important

events. Wampum was made by stringing together shell beads of different colors, sizes, and patterns. A simple wampum was a single string, perhaps 10 inches (25 cm) long, that told the owner's name and tribe. A very important wampum — perhaps recording an agreement between two

This picture was made by a 20th century Iroquois artist, John Kahionhes Fadden. Are the stars like those in the American flag?

tribes — might have fifty or more strings. Each string represented an idea. The picture on the previous page is an example of a wampum belt.

The Stone Age people of North America could not read or write, but they used their skills to create interesting lives in harmony with nature.

Let's Review Part 3

New Words

boulder
effigy
mica
obsidian
portage
wampum
wigwam-wigewa

New Things to Do

Pretend that you are a member of a Hopewell family, and the family wants to visit one of the places where the Hopewells traded. Write a plan for how you will travel, including methods of moving, how you will live along the way, and the equipment you must take with you.

What have we learned?

Scholars know that people moved into the Ohio country shortly after the last glacier melted back. Most of them now believe that the ancestors of these people were able to walk from Asia to North America over land now covered by water.

From 1000 BCE to 600 CE, the Adena and the Hopewell people lived in the Ohio Country and built mounds. From their burial places and from their waste areas, we know that these people were very skillful, and that they traded with others who lived far away from the Ohio Country. We know very little about people who may have lived here from 600 CE to 1000 CE.

From 1000 to 1600 CE, the less-skillful Fort Ancient and Whittlesey people lived in the Ohio Country. For some unknown reason, very few people lived here after these tribes disappeared about 1600. While prehistoric peoples lived in Ohio for over 14,000 years, each generation left the land as they found it.

Map Projects

Find the following places on your map of Ohio:

Place	County
Circleville	Pickaway
Dayton & Miamisburg	Montgomery
Flint Ridge, Johnstown & Newark	Licking
Fort Ancient	Warren
Mound City Group National Monument	Ross
Nettle Lake	Williams County
Serpent Mound	Adams County

Find the following places on your map of the United States:

Florida
Northern Michigan
North and South Carolina
Rocky Mountains

Find the following places on your map of the world:

In Asia:
China, India, Indonesia, Japan, Korea, Thailand, & Vietnam

Books to Read

The following books will help you understand the people who lived in the Ohio Country many years ago. Your library may have other books on these subjects.

Ancient America, by Marion Wood, is a beautifully illustrated explanation of how the earliest people moved across North and South America.

The Archaeology of North America, by Dean R. Snow, describes how archaeologists study the ancient people of North America. The book has many photographs and maps.

The Earliest Americans, by Helen Roney Sattler, uses line drawings and maps to explain prehistoric life in North America from the earliest times until the Europeans came.

Going on a Dig, by Velma Ford Morrison, explains how the digging done by archaeologists is different from digging "for fun" by children.

Indians of the Ohio Country, by Richard C. Knopf, shows how the objects that prehistoric people buried with the dead help us understand their way of life.

The Mound Builders, by William E. Schulte, has many pictures of the lives of the Adena and Hopewell people based on objects found in their mounds.

Prehistory, by Keith Branigan, describes how prehistoric people lived in Europe based on objects they left behind.

Chapter 4

What happened to the natives when Europeans came?

Let's learn...

- **how traders and settlers from Europe affected the natives.**

- **why several tribes moved into the Ohio Country**

- **about wars in the Ohio Country.**

During 1992, the citizens of the United States celebrated the 500th anniversary of Christopher Columbus discovering the western hemisphere. The City of Columbus, our state capital, is the largest city named for the explorer. As part of the celebration, the City of Columbus bought a copy of Christopher's largest ship, the *Santa Maria*, shown on the next page. You

This copy of the Santa Maria was moved to Columbus, Ohio in 1992.
How would you like to sail across the Atlantic Ocean in a ship like this?

can visit it today. In this chapter, you will learn how Christopher's discovery encouraged the nations of Europe to explore North America. You will also learn how the Europeans changed the lives of the Native Americans. The time line and map on the next page will help you understand the early history of the United States.

Part 1

How did traders and settlers from Europe affect the natives?

In the year 1492 CE, no one in Europe knew that the continent of North America existed! In October of that year, Columbus found an island that he named *San Salvador*. This island is shown in the southeastern corner of the map on the next page. Within a few years, **explorers** (people who look for new things) from Europe traveled along the east coast of North and South America. All of them were hoping to find riches for themselves in the *New World*. This map also shows the dates of the English **settlements** (new towns) along the East Coast of North America.

The Natives Meet The Europeans

Scholars think that there may have been from 200,000 to 500,000 natives living in the entire area we call the United States in 1700. The map on page 55 shows where the tribes important to the history of Ohio lived in that year.

The five tribes shown in the area we call New York State were very warlike. For many years, they fought with each other, but then united to fight the Europeans. When they worked together, they became so powerful that the whites called them the *Iroquois League*, or the *Five Nations*. After the Tuscaroras moved north, the league was known as the *Six Nations*.

The *Delaware* people lived in the states we call Delaware, New Jersey, and Pennsylvania. They called themselves the *Lenape*, which meant "original people." The *Shawnees* (meaning "people of the south") lived in present Maryland, Pennsylvania, and Virginia. As you can see, the map does not show any natives living in present Ohio or Kentucky in 1700.

The natives lived in harmony with the forces of nature. They thought that the *Great Spirit* had created the earth and its resources for them to enjoy and share with each other. Time after time during the **17th century** (1601-1700), the

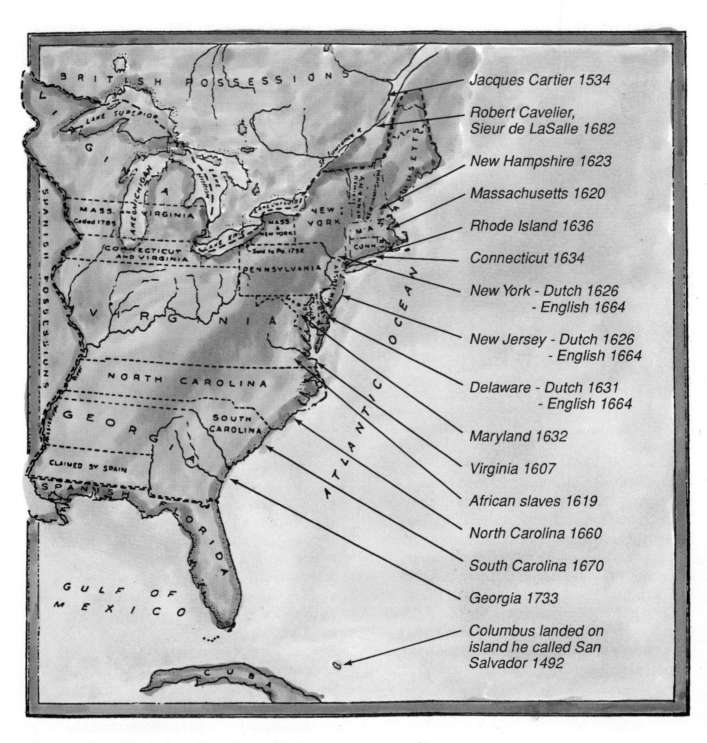

Jacques Cartier 1534

Robert Cavelier,
Sieur de LaSalle 1682

New Hampshire 1623

Massachusetts 1620

Rhode Island 1636

Connecticut 1634

New York - Dutch 1626
          - English 1664

New Jersey - Dutch 1626
            - English 1664

Delaware - Dutch 1631
          - English 1664

Maryland 1632

Virginia 1607

African slaves 1619

North Carolina 1660

South Carolina 1670

Georgia 1733

Columbus landed on
island he called San
Salvador 1492

This combination map and time line will help you understand Chapter 4.
What parts of Ohio can you see on this map?

54

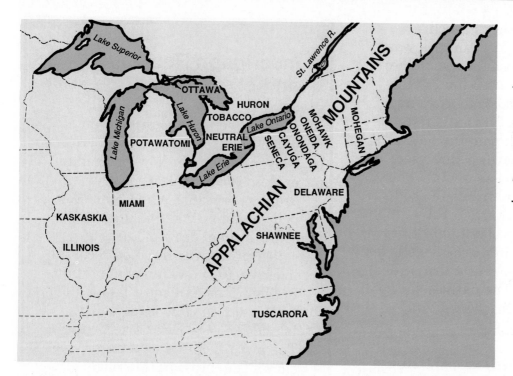

This map shows where native tribes important to Ohio lived about 1600 CE. Why are there no names on the states?

natives offered to *share* their lands with the Europeans.

The Europeans wanted to *own* the land and the natural resources. They tried to use their *knowledge* and *energy* to overcome the forces of nature. In the end, the Iron-Age weapons of the Europeans defeated the Stone-Age weapons of the natives.

Early French Explorers and Traders

Two French explorers were most important to our study of Ohio. In 1534, Jacques Cartier was looking for a northern route to the East Indies when he discovered the St. Lawrence River. As he sailed up this river, he claimed all the land for the King of France. There are still French-speaking people living along this river!

In 1682 Robert Cavelier, Sieur de la Salle — whom we will call *LaSalle* — traveled along the St. Lawrence River, through the Great Lakes, and down the Illinois and Mississippi Rivers. He claimed all of the land to the east of the Mississippi River and north of the Ohio River for the King of France. Can you find the areas marked *North America, Atlantic Ocean, Europe,* and *Asia* on the map of the world on page 2?

Cartier, LaSalle, and other French explorers found that North America was filled with animals whose furs would be valuable in Europe. By 1603 the French were building *trading posts* to exchange European goods for the furs gathered by the natives. The French paid the natives with things they had never before used: guns and gunpowder to use in place of bows and arrows; iron hatchets to use in place of stone tomahawks; colorful blankets to use in place of animal skins; and glass beads to use in place of shells for making wampum. The French also traded *alcohol* to the natives. The natives did not know how to use this "fire water," and many died from alcoholism.

When the Iroquois tribes learned that the Europeans would pay for furs, they set out to control the fur trade of nearby tribes shown on the map on page 55. Using their new guns, the Iroquois drove the Huron tribe further to the north and destroyed the Neutral, the Tobacco, and the Erie tribes. Some scholars once thought that the story in the box on this page was related to this defeat of the Erie people.

The British in The Ohio Country

By 1700 England controlled a large part of the East Coast of North America. About that time, the people of England joined with the people of North Ireland, Scotland, and Wales to form *Great Britain*. The people of this combined nation are usually

Inscription Rock on Kelleys Island

How did you put your ideas on paper before you learned to write? Do you remember how you had to explain to an adult what your drawings meant? While Stone Age people had no written language, some of them drew pictures — called **pictographs** — on rocks, or in caves, to show things important to their lives. The most famous pictograph in Ohio is on Kelleys Island, in Lake Erie (Erie County). The picture on the next page shows **Inscription** (Message) Rock as it looked about 100 years ago. The markings are no longer as clear as you see them.

In the 19th century, some scholars thought that the pictures were carved to tell the story of the Erie tribe when the Iroquois attacked them. Scholars no longer believe this, but they do not know who made the marks or what they mean.

called *British*. About this time, British traders began to compete with the French for the furs of the Ohio Country.

In 1749 the French sent Pierre Joseph Celeron de Blainville down the Allegheny and Ohio Rivers to mark the boundary of their lands. You might say that Celeron and his men put up *No Trespassing* signs around the area France claimed. The "signs" were actually lead plates set at the mouth of every important stream from what is now New York State to the southwest corner of Ohio. The picture on the right shows one of these plates. The stage was now set for almost seventy years of conflict.

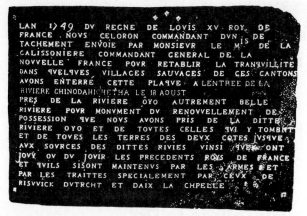

In 1749 the French put these lead "No Trespassing" signs along the Ohio River. How useful would such signs be?

A century ago the markings on Inscription Rock on Kelleys Island were clearly visible. Can you identify any of the symbols?

Let's Review Part 1

New Words

17th century
explorer
inscription
pictograph
settlement

New Things to Do

1. Use Appendix A, beginning on page 381, and make a list of the counties of Ohio that are named for native tribes shown on the map on page 55. Also write down the name of the county seat of each county listed.

2. Use Appendix A, and make a list of the county seats of Ohio that are named for the tribes shown on page 55. Also write down the name of that county.

Part 2

Why did natives move into the Ohio Country?

You have learned that the Fort Ancient and Whittlesey people left the Ohio Country about 1600 CE. The earliest French and British explorers found very few natives living in the lands we call Ohio and Kentucky.

Almost 250,000 Europeans lived in the American colonies in 1700. Fifty years later, there were over 1 million. As more and more Europeans arrived, the natives along the East Coast began to move westward. In this part, you will learn how several tribes moved into the Ohio Country by 1750.

Delawares

The Europeans who settled in eastern Pennsylvania were members of the *Society of Friends*, who are often call *Quakers*. One of the most important teachings of this group was to live in peace. They treated the Lenape with respect, but the growing number of Friends crowded the natives out of their home land. By 1751 some of the Lenape moved westward and became known as the *Delawares*, as explain in the box on the next page.

Shawnees

As more and more settlers moved into their lands, the Shawnees became restless. In 1748 they met with white settlers to sign a **treaty** (agreement). The whites promised not to move across the Appalachian Mountains, if the Shawnees would move into the Ohio Country.

How Did the Lenape Become the Delawares?

Sir Thomas West, who was called *Lord de la Warr*, was the first governor of the British colony of Virginia. When the British gained control of settlements made by Dutch people (see the map on page 54, they named the southern part of the area *Delaware* in honor of Lord de la Warr. Later the river and bay which separate New Jersey from Pennsylvania and Delaware were named *Delaware*. Finally, the Lenape people who lived along this river were given the same name.

Natives living in the West believed that the area south of the Ohio River was holy ground. All tribes could hunt in the area we call Kentucky, but none could live there. This made Kentucky very attractive to white settlers, and they soon began to move across the mountains. The Shawnees did not want settlers in their new hunting area, so they often attacked the white towns. They also attacked all white people who traveled north of the *Spay-lay-wi-theepi* — the Shawnee name for the Ohio River.

The Shawnee people were divided into five major groups, called septs. The **septs** cooperated with each other in many ways, but not as closely as the members of the Iroquois Nation. The central meeting place of the septs was on the bank of the Little Miami River in present Greene County. The natives called this — and all their meeting places — *chillicothe*.

Tecumseh: In 1768 the leaders of the Shawnee septs met to decide how to deal with the white settlers crossing the mountains. Some leaders wanted to fight, but others were afraid that their weapons could not compete with the guns of the settlers. During this meeting, Methotasa, the wife of Chief Pucksinwah, gave birth to a baby boy. When a comet, or "shooting star", crossed the sky that night, it helped the parents choose a name for their son. They named him Tecumseh — *panther passing across* — which was their word for a comet. Tecumseh became one of the greatest leaders of Native Americans at the time Ohio was becoming a state.

Blue Jacket: When Tecumseh was four years old, Shawnee hunters captured a seventeen-year-old white boy. The boy actually knew some Shawnee words and wanted to be adopted by the tribe. In order to prove that he was worthy of adoption, he had to run a **gauntlet**. This means that he had to run between two long lines of natives while they beat upon him with sticks. Tecumseh was in the gauntlet line

59

and saw the white boy beaten. Although he was badly hurt, the boy proved his courage and was adopted by the tribe. Because he was wearing a blue jacket when he was captured, the natives called him *Wey-yah-pih-ehr-sehn-wah*, which meant *Blue Jacket*. You will learn more about him later.

Other Tribes

The maps on pages 55 and this page will help you understand this section. Some of the Hurons you learned about earlier escaped from the Iroquois by fleeing to the north. Later they moved to the area around present Sandusky Bay in Ohio, where they were known as *Wyandots*. As white settlers moved into the area we call Western New York, some of the weaker Iroquois tribes, including Senecas, Cayugas, and Tuscaroras, moved into the Ohio Country. Here they became known as *Mingos*. The *Miami* and *Potawatomi* tribes traded peacefully with the French in the Ohio Country for many years. But their lives were disturbed as the Delawares, Shawnees, Mingos, and other tribes moved into the Ohio Country.

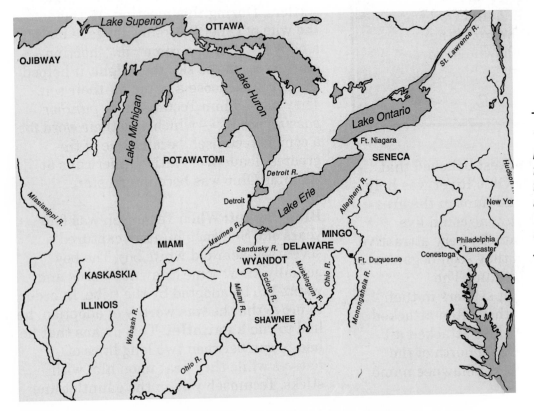

This map shows the locations of native tribes and European towns and forts about 1760. Where do you live on this map?

The Role of Indian Agents

The British government and some of the colonies appointed *Indian Agents* to work with the natives and encourage trade. We will look at only two agents who were important in the Ohio Country.

Conrad Weiser: Early in the **18th century** (1701-1800), the parents of Conrad Weiser moved from Germany to what is now New York State. When he was seventeen years old, he went to live with a Mohawk tribe for several years. He learned the languages and ways of life of all the Iroquois people. The diary he kept of his experiences is an important source of information about these natives.

Beginning in 1743, Weiser served as a guide for people exploring the Ohio Country. In 1748 he began to work with George Croghan. These two men met with leaders of many tribes at *Logstown* on the Ohio River near present East Liverpool, Ohio. At this meeting, they tried to discourage the natives from siding with the French against the British in the growing arguments about furs.

George Croghan: George Croghan, an Irishman, was an outstanding trader on the western frontier of Pennsylvania. By 1744 he had established a trading post at Logstown. From there, he sent white traders as far west as the Mississippi River. In 1748 he built a small fort and trading post at the Miami village of *Pickawillany*, in present Miami County. George Croghan traveled throughout the Ohio Country and encouraged the Miami tribes to attend annual meetings at Logstown. Much of what we know about the natives in the Ohio Country during the middle of the 18th century is based on Croghan's official reports and diaries.

Let's Review Part 2

New Words

18th century
gauntlet
sept
treaty

New Things to Do

1. Go to your public library and look at a history of your county that was written before 1900. Write a short report on what this book says about the natives who once lived in your area.

2. Which events in this chapter took place in or near your county?

An Outline of Events in American History That Affected Ohio

Years	Events	Location
1754	French and Indian War begins	St. Lawrence River Valley, New York, Michigan, Pennsylvania
1763	Pontiac's Rebellion	Ohio, Michigan, Pennsylvania
1763	French and Indian War ends	Treaty signed in Europe
Important People		
1755	Simon Kenton born	Western part of Virginia
1756	Simon Girty captured	Central Pennsylvania
1772	Moravians move to Gnadenhutten	Along Tuscarawas River in Ohio Country
1774	George Rogers Clark put in charge of defense of Kentucky	Moved from Virginia to Kentucky
American Revolution		
1774	First Continental Congress	Philadelphia
1774	First settlement in Kentucky	Harrodsburg
1775	Battle of Concord and Lexington	Massachusetts
1776	Declaration of Independence	Philadelphia
1778	Kaskaskia and Cahokia fall to George Rogers Clark	Illinois
1779	Vincennes falls to Clark	Indiana
1781	Battle of Yorktown	British defeated in Virginia
1782	Massacre at Gnadenhutten	Tuscarawas County
1783	End of American Revolutionary War	Treaty of Ghent, Belgium

Part 3

How did wars affect the Ohio Country?

The kings of England and France fought each other in Europe for hundreds of years. Both kings wanted to control the fur trade of North America. These problems led to wars in North America during the last half of the 18th century. The time line on the opposite page, and the maps on pages 60 and the next page, will help you understand what happened.

The French and Indian War 1754-1763

What Americans call the *French and Indian War* began in 1754 in North America. The French controlled the fur trade in the St. Lawrence River Valley and around the Great Lakes. The British controlled present New York State. All the traders needed the help of natives to get the furs they wanted, but the French and British treated them differently. The French traded more fairly and did not take land for farming. The British wanted to clear large areas of Iroquois land for farming. As a result, when the war began, most of the natives helped the French. Much of the fighting in the West was around Fort Detroit in present Michigan and Fort Duquesne in Pennsylvania. When

the British won the war, they changed the name of Fort Duquesne to Fort Pitt.

The war ended in North America in 1760, when the British took the great French city of Quebec. When the peace treaty was signed in Europe, the French gave up all their lands in North America. But French-speaking people continued to live in the St. Lawrence Valley and around the old French trading posts throughout the Ohio Country. In addition, they continued to give the natives guns and ammunition to fight the British. The picture on page 65 shows the reconstruction of Peter Loramie's French trading post of 1769. You can visit this today in Shelby County.

Pontiac's Rebellion - 1763

Pontiac, an Ottawa war chief, lived near Lake Huron. About 1761, he began to unite the tribes of the Great Lakes Region to drive out the British (see the map on the next page). For almost two years, Pontiac worked on a plan to capture Fort Detroit. The warriors were to set up camps around the fort for a council meeting. Some of the chiefs, with guns hidden under their blankets, were to enter the fort to talk with the commander. When Pontiac gave a signal, all the warriors were to attack and capture the fort. The commander learned of the plot so it did not work. The natives then surrounded the fort and almost starved the British into surrender.

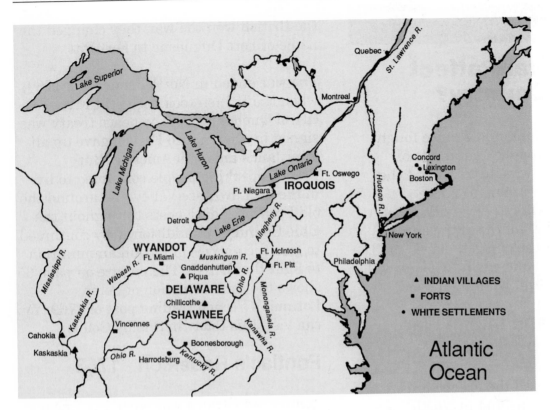

This map shows the location of native tribes and American towns and forts about 1780. What towns and forts were created between 1760 and 1780?

While Pontiac was urging the natives to continue fighting, he received word that France had turned over all of its land in North America to the British. Without French help, Pontiac's warriors could not continue the war. In August 1763, the British invited the natives to settle near Detroit, but Pontiac decided that they should stay in villages along the Maumee River (see the map above). From that time on, Pontiac chose to live at peace with the Europeans. But in 1769, he was murdered in Illinois by a native of another tribe.

The Mission at Gnadenhutten

In 1734 a large group of religious people moved from Moravia in eastern Germany to the colony of Pennsylvania. They built the town of Bethlehem and tried to live in peace with the natives and other Europeans in that area. David Zeisberger was a religious leader of these *Moravians*, as they were called.

By 1751 the Quakers had encouraged some of the Delawares to move westward. In 1772 some of them decided to move into the Ohio Country. David Zeisberger and his friend John Heckewelder, with their wives and children, led these Delawares to land along the Tuscarawas River in what is now Ohio.

The Moravians helped the Delawares build a village, which they named *Schoenbrunn* (meaning "beautiful springs"). They built a church and established the first school in the Ohio Country. Zeisberger wrote books for the natives in their language. Schoenbrunn was so successful that the Moravians created two more towns along the Tuscarawas River. The first was at *Gnadenhutten* (meaning "tents of grace") and the second at *Salem* (meaning "peace").

The Two Simons

Two outstanding men named *Simon* were good friends, and both played important roles in the Ohio Country during these years. In 1756 Simon Girty was fifteen years old when natives attacked his home in Pennsylvania. They took him and his brothers to their village. At the end of the French and Indian War, Girty was freed by the natives and served as a **translator** (person who changes words from one language to another) for the British at Fort Pitt.

Simon Kenton was born in the western part of Virginia in 1755. When he was

You can see this re-creation of Peter Loramie's trading post in Shelby County.

What is on this picture that would surprise Peter Loramie?

fifteen years old, he almost killed a man in a fight. He was so afraid of being punished that he fled and changed his name to Simon Butler. He then moved to the wilds of Kentucky to begin a lifetime of exploring. In 1774 he helped settlers from Virginia establish the first town in Kentucky.

You learned in Part 2 that the Shawnees agreed to move westward in 1748 because the white settlers promised to stay to the east of the Appalachian Mountains. By 1770 almost 15,000 white settlers were living in the west. The two Simons were in this group: they met each other and became close friends. Later Simon Girty decided to spend the rest of his life helping the natives, while Simon Kenton decided to help the white settlers. You will learn more about them later.

The American Revolution 1776-1783

The time line of the American Revolution on page 62 begins in 1774 when representatives from all thirteen colonies met in Philadelphia. In the next chapter, you will learn how they organized themselves as the *Continental Congress* and signed the *Declaration of Independence*. This declaration announced that they were ready to fight for their freedom from Great Britain.

The map on page 64 shows the places in the Ohio Country that were important in the war. About 2 million people from Europe lived in North America in 1776. About 45,000 of them lived in the area south of the Ohio River that we call West Virginia and Kentucky. Only a few hundred of them lived to the north of this river. The British had forts at Cahokia and Kaskaskia along the Mississippi River in Illinois, at Vincennes in Indiana, at Detroit in Michigan, and at Fort Pitt in western Pennsylvania.

George Rogers Clark

In 1774 George Rogers Clark moved to Kentucky from his boyhood home near Williamsburg, Virginia. He was soon placed in charge of the Kentucky **militia** (citizens who become soldiers in times of fighting). In June 1777, Clark sent spies to study the British forts at Kaskaskia and Cahokia on the Mississippi River. When the spies returned to Kentucky, Clark decided that he could capture these places if he had 350 soldiers.

By June 1778, Clark had found only 178 frontiersmen to help him, including Simon Kenton. Many of these men had relatives or friends who had been killed or captured by the natives. They were eager to punish the natives. After a short time for training, they moved down the Ohio River and across the southern tip of Illinois without being discovered by the British.

On July 4, 1778, Clark's army surprised the fort at Kaskaskia, and it surrendered without firing a shot. The people of Kaskaskia sent word to their friends at Cahokia that Clark's army treated them well. A few weeks later when Clark and his followers rode to Cahokia, the people of that town surrendered without firing a shot. Clark encouraged all the natives and French people living in the area to help the American cause.

This is an artist's idea of George Rogers Clark and his men marching to Vincennes. Are these men "marching"? How would you describe their movement?

When the British at Fort Detroit learned about the loss of Cahokia and Kaskaskia, they decided to strengthen the fort at Vincennes on the Wabash River. They hoped that hundreds of natives would help them to recapture these places. George Rogers Clark learned of this plan and decided that his best defense was to attack. On the rainy day of February 5, 1779, he set out with about one hundred Americans and thirty French settlers of the area to capture Vincennes.

What kind of weather do you have in your county in February? Do you like to sleep outdoors during the winter? For seventeen days, George Rogers Clark led his followers through snow, rain, and high water across the area we call the State of Illinois. The picture on the previous page is an artist's idea of this difficult trip.

On the night of February 22, the temperature dropped below freezing and the wet soldiers had no shelter. The next day French people living in the village around the fort at Vincennes secretly welcomed Clark and his army with food, blankets, and ammunition. George Rogers Clark arranged his men around the fort and told them to fire their guns in such a way that the British would think they were surrounded and out-numbered. When the British surrendered to Clark and his men on February 24, they were amazed to learn how a few tired men had fooled them. Not one of the Americans was lost!

George Rogers Clark was promoted to the rank of Brigadier General in the Army of Virginia and led men in several battles in the area that is now Ohio. Clark County was named in his honor, and you can visit George Rogers Clark Park to the west of Springfield, Ohio. But neither Virginia nor the United States ever paid him for all of his own money he spent to feed and clothe his "army."

Fort McIntosh and Fort Laurens

Early in the Revolution, General George Washington decided that the Americans needed a line of forts between Fort Pitt and Fort Detroit. In the autumn of 1778, Lachlan McIntosh led a group of men from Fort Pitt to begin construction. They built the first fort near Logstown, on the Ohio River, and called it Fort McIntosh. Next the soldiers built a fort on the Tuscarawas River, near the north boundary of present Tuscarawas County, and named it Fort Laurens, which is French for Lawrence.

Fort Laurens was so far from Fort Pitt, and the American army in the area was so small, that the natives were able to steal most of the supplies sent to it. In February 1779, natives, led by Simon Girty, surrounded Fort Laurens and very nearly starved the defenders. While his men were forced to eat their shoes and the skins of animals, the commanding officer decided to try to fool the natives. Under a flag of truce, he gave the natives a barrel of flour

to make them think that there was more than enough food in the fort. The natives left the area, and the Americans were saved. Today you can visit Fort Laurens State Memorial.

The Massacre at Gnadenhutten

In 1781 the British army entered the peaceful Delaware towns along the Tuscarawas River. They forced the Delawares to move to Wyandot lands along the Sandusky River. They took the Zeisbergers and their friends to Fort Detroit to be tried as spies but later set them free.

The Americans defeated the British at Yorktown, Virginia in October 1781, but the Revolution continued in the Ohio Country. During the winter of 1782, there was not enough food at Upper Sandusky for both the Wyandots and the Delawares. The British allowed about 150 of the

Delawares to return to their villages along the Tuscarawas River to gather corn, beans, and squash from their gardens.

Early in March 1782, David Williamson led one hundred British soldiers from Fort Pitt into the Ohio Country. They were to punish natives who were attacking white settlers. On March 8, they found 100 of the peaceful Delawares gathering food at Gnadenhutten. Because these Moravian Delawares had learned to trust the Americans, they gave up their weapons when Williamson asked for them. The soldiers then forced the natives to kneel together in one of the buildings, smashed their heads, and burned the building over them. Only two boys managed to escape to warn the other Delawares at Schoenbrunn and Salem. The picture above shows a part of the reconstructed village of Schoenbrunn you can visit today near New Philadelphia in Tuscarawas County. You can also visit a museum at the site of Gnadenhutten and learn more about the Christian natives who died there.

69

William Crawford

When the other natives learned of the **massacre** (mass killing) at Gnadenhutten, they attacked white settlements in many places in the West. The British did all they could to encourage these attacks. By May 1782, the soldiers at Fort Pitt were demanding that the natives be punished for trying to "get even" for the massacre. In an election between Colonels David Williamson and William Crawford, Crawford was chosen to lead an attack on the native villages along the Sandusky River. Crawford thought the idea was a mistake, but the soldiers insisted on acting quickly and several hundred men set out on horseback.

Early in June, as the Americans were approaching the Sandusky River, they came upon a large group of angry natives. Both sides camped for the night and built large bonfires. During the night, Simon Girty left the native side with a white flag of truce. He told Colonel Crawford that the Delawares were about to surround the Americans, but there was one chance of escape through a swampy area. The Americans did escape from the trap, but they could not agree on what to do next. Within a few days many of them were dead. William Crawford was captured and burned to death on June 13, 1782. Crawford County is named in his honor.

The British signed a treaty of peace with the Americans in 1783 and left the Ohio Country. Simon Girty fled to Canada where he died in 1818. He was considered a traitor to the American cause, but he was a hero in the eyes of the British. The Americans soon forgot about the natives who had helped them in the war and treated them all as enemies. In spite of the treaty, the British continued to help the natives fight against the American settlers who came into the Ohio Country after 1783.

Let's Review Part 3

New Words

massacre
militia
translator

New Things to Do

Divide the class into two groups, with one half representing the natives and the other half representing the American. Re-read the sections above under the headings *The Mission at Gnadenhutten, The Massacre at Gnadenhutten,* and *William Crawford.* Each group should develop reasons why its side was "right" in this situation. Each group should choose two or three representatives to meet with the other side in front of the class to argue the situation before the class. After you hear the discussion between the representatives, write a short statement about what you think of the situation.

What have we learned?

The natives of North America led useful lives long before the people of Europe knew they existed. They believed that the Great Spirit created the land for them to enjoy, and they lived in harmony with nature.

During the 17th century, French and British explorers learned that North America had many animals with beautiful furs. French and British traders soon began to buy furs from the Native Americans. When the natives began to kill animals to sell the furs to the Europeans, they also began to kill each other to control the fur trade.

From 1754 to 1763, the French, British, and natives in North America were fighting each other for control of the fur trade. When the French lost this war, the British gained control of the Ohio Country. As more and more people from Europe moved to America, the natives who once lived along the Atlantic Coast were forced to move westward into the Ohio Country.

By 1770 people living in the colonies along the Atlantic Coast began to think about freeing themselves from British rule. In 1776 they declared their freedom, and the American Revolution spread westward into the Ohio Country. George Rogers Clark was the most important American military leader in the west. The war ended in 1783, and people from the East Coast began to pour into the Ohio Country, as you will learn in the next chapter.

Map Projects

Find the following places on your map of Ohio

Place	County
East Liverpool	Columbiana
Fort Laurens	Tuscarawas
Kelleys Island	Erie
Maumee River	Lucas to Defiance
Ohio River	Columbiana to Hamilton
Perrysburg	Wood
Sandusky River	Ottawa to Wyandot
Tuscarawas River	Coshocton to Summit

Find the following places on your map of the United States.

Place	State
Cahokia & Kaskaskia	Illinois
Detroit	Michigan
Great Lakes	Ohio, Michigan, Wisconsin, Minnesota
Philadelphia	Pennsylvania
Pittsburgh	Pennsylvania
Williamsburg	Virginia

Trace the route of Cartier as well as you can. Trace the route of LaSalle as well as you can. See map on page 3.

Find the following places on your map of the world.

Place	Continent
England	Europe
France	Europe
North Ireland	Europe
San Salvador	Caribbean Sea
Scotland	Europe
Spain	Europe
Wales	Europe
Quebec	Canada

Books to Read

The following books will help you understand what happened in the Ohio Country during the 18th century. Your library may have other books about this period of time.

Beaver Skins and Mountain Men, by Carl Burger, explains how the demand for beaver skins in Europe led to the exploration of North America.

The Frontiersmen, by Allan W. Eckert, pages 3-7, 11-12, 19-21, 119-123 tells the stories of Tecumseh and Blue Jacket as boys.

Fur Trappers and Traders, by Beatrice Siegel, tells how Europeans got furs from the Native Americans.

The Lenape: Indians of North America, by Robert S. Grumet, tells the history of the Lenape from the earliest days to the present. The white settlers called these people Delawares.

Long Knife, by James Alexander Thom, is an interesting story about George Rogers Clark. Chapters 3 through 13 tell about the capture of Kaskaskia. Chapters 24 and 25 tell about the capture of Vincennes.

Panther in the Sky, by James Alexander Thom, pages 13-189, tells the story of the first twelve years of Tecumseh's life.

Chapter 5

How did the Americans displace the natives?

Let's learn...

- **about establishment of the Northwest Territory.**

- **how Ohio was divided for settlement.**

- **how the natives tried to defend themselves.**

In 1776 thirteen colonies on the east coast of North America were controlled by the British king. Their only **responsibilities** (things they had to do) were to pay taxes and produce cotton, tobacco, lumber, fish, and furs for the merchants of Great Britain. In this chapter, you will learn how a desire for **independence** (freedom) led the leaders of the colonies to take responsibility for meeting many challenges. You will also learn how events on the East Coast affected the natives and the settlers in the Ohio Country. The time line on the next page will help you keep track of important events.

The time line on the next page will help you keep track of important events.

Part 1

How was the Northwest Territory established?

Each of the thirteen colonies was ruled by a **governor** (official in charge) from Great Britain. Each colony also elected **representatives** (people who act for a group) to work with its governor to deal with local problems. The people of Massachusetts, Rhode Island, and Connecticut also organized themselves into towns and solved local problems through *town meetings*. By 1770 some leaders of the northern colonies wanted independence. Many leaders of the southern colonies wanted to remain a part of the British Empire.

By 1774 leaders in all the colonies were so angry about British control of their lives that they agreed to meet together in Philadelphia. This was the first meeting of leaders of all the colonies. They decided to organize themselves into a **congress** (law-making group). During the next two years, they met several times to discuss the problems of British control. On July 4, 1776, the members of Congress signed the *Declaration of Independence*. Each one took personal responsibility for independence by signing his name below these words: "...we ... pledge to each other our lives, our fortunes, and our sacred honor."

While the thirteen colonies were fighting the American Revolution, the *Continental Congress* was learning to work as a team. They represented about 2 million people who lived in an area of 500,000 square miles (1,295,000 sq. km.). Each part of the area had different resources and problems. The only forms of travel were on foot, on horse back, or in a sailboat.

Congress worked for more than one year to write a plan of cooperation, which they called *The Articles of Confederation*. Four more years passed before all thirteen colonies agreed to cooperate with the plan. As the colonies gained independence from Great Britain, the Native Americans lost more of their freedoms.

The Goals of Government

Government is a system of rules and regulations that people agree to follow in order to live together in peace. The three basic goals of government are:
1. to provide a situation free of **turmoil** (trouble),

Time Line of Northwest Territory Before 1800

Years	Location	Events
1774	Philadelphia	Continental Congress organized
1776	Philadelphia	Declaration of Independence
1783	Philadelphia	Treaty to end American Revolution
1785	Philadelphia	Public Land Act adopted by Congress
1785	Philadelphia	Virginia Military District established
1787	Philadelphia	Northwest Ordinance adopted
1787	Ohio Country	Survey of the Seven Ranges
1788	Marietta	Ohio Company established first town in Northwest Territory
1788	Marietta	Arthur St. Clair named Governor
1788	Columbia	Benjamin Stites made settlement
1788	Losantiville	Mathias Denman made settlement
1789	North Bend	John Cleves Symmes made settlement
1790	Cincinnati	Fort Wahington built
1790	Cincinnati	St. Clair changed name of Losantiville
1790	Western Ohio	Josiah Harmar defeated by Little Turtle
1791	Western Ohio	St. Clair defeated by Little Turtle
1794	Fort Recovery	Anthony Wayne defeated Little Turtle
1794	Fallen Tinbers	Anthony Wayne defeated Blue Jacket
1795	Darke County	Treaty of GreeneVille signed
1796	Western Reserve	Moses Cleaveland surveyed Cleveland
1796	Fire Lands	Set aside for people from Connecticut
1803	Ohio	Made the 17th state

2. to keep records of all government actions including the ownership of property, and
3. to raise **taxes** (money) to pay for the first two services.

Turmoil may arise from many directions. If the government cannot raise money to operate a military system to prevent outsiders from breaking in, the government will be destroyed. If it cannot raise money to police its citizens and protect the ownership of property, there will be **chaos** (confusion and loss of personal rights).

Ownership of land has always been one of the greatest desires of people in the United States. Poor records of land ownership created turmoil between the colonies and within each of them. For example, between 1600 and 1750 CE, the Kings of England gave many individuals large pieces of land in the American colonies, but no one kept accurate records of how the pieces fitted together. The situation was something like trying to put together a jigsaw puzzle when the pieces do not match. As a result, there were many arguments about who owned what land. The Continental Congress tried to deal with these problems.

The Ohio Country in 1776

"Who owned Ohio in 1776?" This sounds like an easy question, but it is not easy to answer. You have learned that the Native Americans believed that the Great Spirit created the land for them to use and enjoy. The French said that it belonged to them because of claims made by LaSalle and Celeron. The British said it was theirs because they had won the French and Indian War. In addition, several of the American colonies said that British kings had given them parts of the Ohio Country.

When the American Colonies declared war on Great Britain, they had no money and no way to raise money by taxes. The only thing of value was the land they claimed to the west of the Appalachian Mountains. For this reason, the colonies paid their soldiers with promises of land. Those who served a long time were promised more land than those who served a short time. Officers were promised more land than the men who served under them. But no one really knew who owned what the various colonies were promising.

One of the hardest problems the Congress faced was to decide the exact **boundaries** (limits) of each of the thirteen colonies. The map on the next page shows the United States in 1783. The "wiggly" solid lines you see on this map are rivers. Rivers seem to be exact boundaries, but they can change their routes in times of flooding. The dashed lines you see represent boundaries that are easy to draw on a map, but may be very hard to find on the ground. Many of the straight dashed-lines

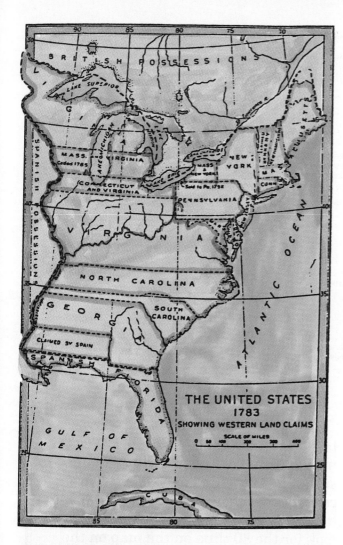

Which states are now in the area marked "Virginia" on this map?

you see are lines of **latitude** (north-south position) and **longitude** (east-west position). These words are explained in the box on the next page.

As you can see, Virginia claimed all the present states of West Virginia, Kentucky, Ohio, Indiana, Illinois, Michigan, and Wisconsin, and a part of Minnesota.

Connecticut and Massachusetts claimed parts of the same land. These overlapping claims did not cause problems until people wanted to move to the West.

The Continental Congress finally agreed that each state would have to give up its claim to lands west of the Appalachian Mountains. Since 15,000 people already lived in the area we call West Virginia and Kentucky, it was agreed that Virginia should keep that area until it could be made into a state.

Public Land Act of 1785

In 1785 the Congress adopted a solution to the problem of lands in the West. It was called the *Public Land Act*. Even before the end of the Revolution, Thomas Jefferson and a few others were trying to decide how to create new land parcels in the West. They wanted parcels that would be almost square and yet fit the shape of Earth. Their problem was like the one you have when you try to wrap a ball-shaped object in a piece of paper. No matter how hard you try, you cannot do this neatly.

The diagram on page 79 shows the Public Land pattern used since about 1830, and the box on the same page explains a part of the system. Ohio was the first area to be **surveyed** (measured accurately on the ground) under the Public Land Act. The map on page 81 shows the most important land survey systems in Ohio. Since many parts of our state were divided before 1830, you may live in an area where the land is divided in a different way. The Public Land

Where in the world are you?

In order to tell someone exactly where you are in the world, you must tell them the latitude and longitude of your position. The diagram on this page shows the meaning of these words.

Each straight east-west line represents a **parallel** of latitude (parallel lines never meet). The equator of the earth is called 0° latitude. All people standing on the line marked 40° North can say that they have the same latitude. Incidentally, the highway known as United States Route 40, that runs across Ohio, is close to this parallel of latitude.

Each line connecting the north and south poles represents a **meridian** (true north-south line) of longitude. When the system of latitude and longitude was invented, England was one of the most powerful nations in the world. The English people, therefore, said that longitude should

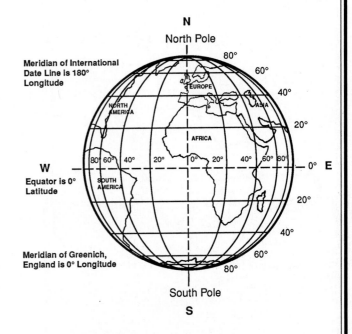

be measured from *Greenwich*, a town in their country. Today all the people standing on the line marked 80° West can say that they have the same longitude west of Greenwich. If you look for the 80° line on the map on the previous page, you can see that it is a short distance to the east of the east boundary of our state.

Today you can buy an instrument that will tell you the latitude and longitude of your position very accurately. You can hold this instrument in your hand, and you can buy it for less than the cost of some automobiles.

The Subdivision of Land under the Public Land Survey

The Public Land Survey divides very large areas of land into three sets of almost square blocks, as you can see on this page. Three sides of the largest blocks are 24 miles long. The north side is somewhat shorter because of the curvature of Earth. The east-west lines are lines of latitude. The north-south lines are shown as meridians, which is another name for lines of longitude.

Each of the 24-mile blocks is divided into sixteen blocks. Three sides of each of these block is 6 miles long, and the north side is somewhat shorter. Each of these six-mile blocks is called a **township** of the Public Land Survey. In some counties of Ohio, these six-mile blocks have a unit of government that is also called a *township*, which you will learn about later.

As you can see, each of the six-mile blocks is divided again into thirty-six smaller blocks called **sections**. Most of the sections are one-mile squares. Many settlers in Ohio bought *whole sections* of 640 acres. Others bought *half-sections* of 320 acres or *quarter-sections* of 160 acres.

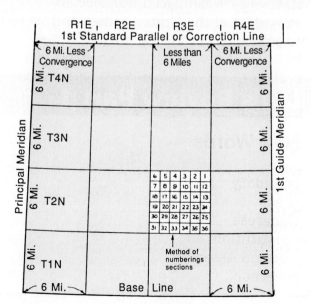

Survey has guided the pattern of land ownership almost everywhere west of the Appalachian Mountains.

Northwest Ordinance of 1787

The members of the Continental Congress worked two more years to create a form of government for the vast area to be subdivided by the Public Land Act. On

Left: The Public Land Survey created almost square parcels of land on the ball-shaped surface of the Earth. Why are the northern boundaries marked "6 Mi. Less Convergence?"

July 13, 1787, they adopted *An* **Ordinance** *(law) for the Government of the Territory of the United States Northwest of the River Ohio.* This is usually called the Northwest Ordinance.

The Northwest Ordinance created a framework of government for people moving to new lands in the west. It provided three forms of government related to the number of people in the territory. In the earliest days of settlement, a group of leaders would be appointed by Congress to govern a particular area. After the population of the area reached 5,000 *men*, they could elect a **General Assembly** (law-making body) to work with the leaders appointed by Congress. After the population of the area reached a total of 60,000, the voters could ask Congress to form a new state that would be equal in power with the original thirteen states.

The wording of the Northwest Ordinance — and of most laws — is very complicated. The ordinance was divided into thirteen short *sections*. The last section had six parts, which included the following ideas.

1. Faith in God, honesty, and education are the bases of good government and the happiness of people. For this reason, schools and other means of education must be encouraged.

2. The natives must be treated fairly. Their lands must never be taken without their agreement. Their private lives and freedom must not be disturbed, except in "just and lawful wars." Everything possible shall be done to have "peace and friendship with them."

3. The area northwest of the Ohio River should someday be divided into three, four, or five states. In fact, the states of Ohio, Indiana, Illinois, Michigan, and Wisconsin were formed from the area.

4. The last article said that there would be no slavery in the territory.

On September 28, 1787, the Congress approved of a **Constitution** (most important laws), but four additional years passed before all thirteen states agreed to it. George Washington was elected President of the United States and served two terms from 1789 to 1797.

Let's Review Part 1

New Words

boundary
chaos
Congress
constitution
General Assembly
governor

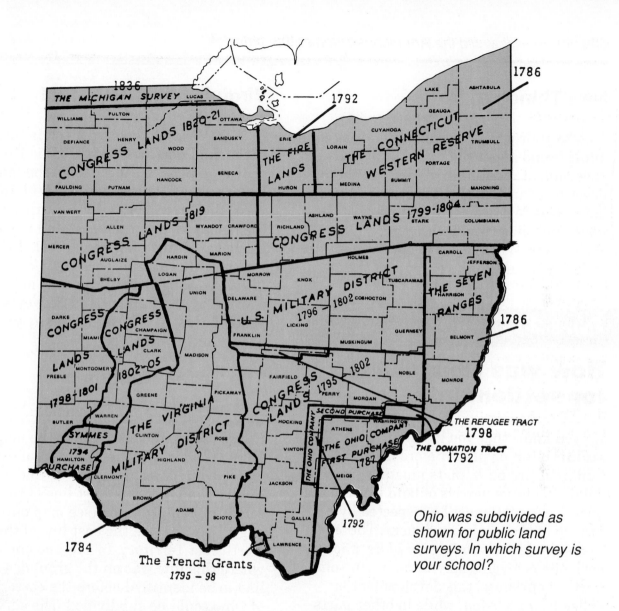

Ohio was subdivided as shown for public land surveys. In which survey is your school?

independence
latitude
longitude
meridian
ordinance (law)
parallel
representative

responsible
section (land)
survey (land)
taxes
township
turmoil

New Things to Do

Talk to your parents, grandparents, or an adult friend about the three basic goals of government mentioned above. Ask them to describe examples of these goals in their daily lives. Write down a summary of their ideas and share them with your classmates. Which goals of government are most important to the parents of the class?

Part 2

How was Ohio divided for settlement?

Do you know that you live in a **subdivision** or **plat**? Before new buildings are built, plats must be drawn to subdivide large parcels of land into smaller ones. Each plan must be inspected by a branch of the local government. These plans are called *subdivision plats*, and each one is given a special name. In some parts of our state, this development is called a *subdivision*, while in other parts it is called a *plat*. The map on the next page is an example of a plat. Most housing subdivisions cover areas from one acre to two hundred acres (1/2 to 100 hectares). We will discuss only the "subdivisions" of Ohio that were made before we became a state.

Virginia Military District

In 1778 Virginia gave up its claim to most of the land northwest of the Ohio River as shown on page 77. It did keep the land between the Little Miami River on the west, the Ohio River on the south, and the Scioto River on the east and north, as shown on the map on page 81. Today we know this area as the *Virginia Military District*. This area was not covered by the Public Land Survey, so people living in it have had many problems about land ownership.

The Seven Ranges

Can you see an area labeled *The Seven Ranges* along the east side of the map on page 81? This was the first part of the entire United States surveyed under the Public Land Act. The west line of the colony of Pennsylvania (see map on page 77) was to be the east line of the Northwest Territory. In 1785 no one knew where this line was on the ground, so it had to be identified before the eastern part of Ohio could be subdivided. The survey of the Seven Ranges was begun where the northern shore of the Ohio River crossed the western boundary of Pennsylvania. Today this starting point is marked by a monument at the southeast corner of Columbiana County. One of the people who worked on this project was Israel Ludlow, whom you will learn about later in this chapter. Today you can visit the original Federal Land Office in Steubenville and learn how early settlers bought land.

Rufus Putnam and The Ohio Company

Shortly after the end of the Revolutionary War, a group of New England soldiers and officers began to meet in Boston, Massachusetts to plan new lives for themselves in the Ohio Country. They formed *The Ohio Company of Associates* and chose Rufus Putnam as their leader.

Congress sold this company almost one million acres for about ten cents an acre. As you can see on page 81, this land was along the Ohio River to the southwest of the Seven Ranges.

On December 3, 1787, twenty-two men, including a master ship builder and his helpers, left their homes in Massachusetts. An artist made the picture on the next page to save the scene for history. These men followed valleys of the Appalachian Mountains southeastward to a point on a stream that flows into the Ohio River near

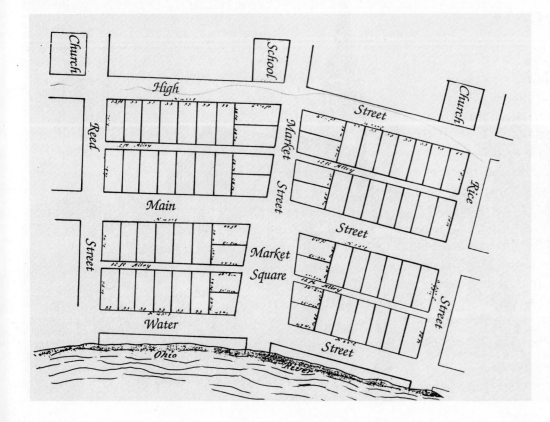

This subdivision was made in 1829. It was named "Nassau". Are there any streets in your town that have the names of the streets shown?

Fort Pitt. At this place, they built flatboats to float downstream to their new homes. On January 1, 1788, a second group of men, women, and children left Massachusetts to join the boat-builders in Pennsylvania. On April 7, 1788, forty-eight people reached the mouth of the Muskingum River and established the town of *Marietta*. They chose this name to honor Marie Antoinette, the Queen of France, because France had helped the Americans win independence from Great Britain. Later that year, Arthur St.Clair arrived to serve as Governor of the Northwest Territory.

An artist drew this picture as members of The Ohio Company were leaving Massachusetts to come to Ohio. How would you feel about moving 700 miles under the conditions shown?

An artist made this drawing of Campus Martius in Marietta. On the basis of what you have learned about southeastern Ohio, what did the artist leave out of the picture?

The settlers built a log fort to protect themselves from the natives and called it *Campus Martius*, meaning "A Field of War." Today you can visit the Campus Martius Museum at Marietta and see a part of Rufus Putnam's house. This house is the only part of the fort still standing. The picture above shows an artist's idea of Campus Martius.

Before the settlers could create homes and farms for themselves, the land had to be divided by the Public Land Survey. Rufus Putnam was the surveyor in charge of this work. The land was very hilly, and the work was done as quickly as possible. For these reasons, the surveying was not as accurate as the diagram on page 79.

The Symmes Purchase

In 1785 a band of Shawnees stole some horses from an army post in Northern Kentucky. Simon Kenton, whom you learned about in Chapter 4, guided Benjamin Stites and several soldiers into the Ohio Country to retake the horses. On the way back to the post, they traveled through the area between the Great Miami and Little Miami Rivers. When Stites returned to his home in New Jersey, he talked about the fine land to John Cleves Symmes, his representative to Congress. Symmes traveled west to visit the area. He then decided to organize a company to buy the land. The *Symmes Purchase* is in the southwest corner of the map on page 81.

Symmes and several partners wanted to buy a million acres of land at "two-thirds dollars per acre" or 67 cents. Eventually, they were able to purchase about 330,000 acres, from the Ohio River northward as far as present Lebanon, in Warren County. This area became known as both the *Symmes Purchase* and the *Miami Purchase*. Before Symmes could sell the land, he had to survey it in accord with the Public Land Act. But the system he used was different from any other part of Ohio or the United States.

In 1788 Symmes led a group of settlers down the Ohio River to the land between the Miami Rivers. When they stopped to rest at Marietta, Symmes asked Israel Ludlow to move west with him. Ludlow was put in charge of laying out the section lines in the land between the Miami Rivers. He also laid out several of the towns in the region, and you can find streets named for him in these towns.

Benjamin Stites was the first to buy land from Symmes. In October of 1788, he led a group of twenty men, four women, and two children, to make a settlement near the mouth of the Little Miami River. They traveled on flatboats, similar to the one you can see in the picture on page 25. When they landed, they used the wood in the boats to build houses. Their town of *Columbia* later became part of Cincinnati.

The second settlement was made by Mathias Denman, Robert Patterson, and Israel Ludlow. Denman bought 800 acres opposite the mouth of the Licking River and had Ludlow survey a town they called *Losantiville*. Two years later, it was changed to *Cincinnati*. On December 28, 1788, Patterson led eleven families, plus twenty-four single men, to the planned town. In January 1789, the Symmes party arrived at Losantiville but then continued downstream about fifteen miles. When they landed, Symmes established the town of *North Bend*. Today North Bend is a village of about 600 people.

A few years later, Robert Patterson and his family established another town about fifty miles north of Cincinnati. They named it

Dayton in honor of Jonathan Dayton, who was a partner of Symmes.

Connecticut Western Reserve

The map on page 77 shows that Connecticut claimed ownership of a narrow strip of land extending from the Atlantic Ocean to the Mississippi River. In 1780 Connecticut offered to give up the western part of the claim if it could keep 120 miles westward from the boundary of Pennsylvania. This tract became known as the *Western Reserve of Connecticut*. Today it is called the *Western Reserve*. In 1795 the State of Connecticut sold 3 million acres of this land to the *Connecticut Land Company* for $1,200,000. You can see this land in the northeast corner of the map on page 81.

The Connecticut Land Company was made up of about fifty men, one of whom was Moses Cleaveland. In the spring of 1796, the Company sent Cleaveland and several helpers to survey the Western Reserve for settlement. The pattern of subdivision they used was based on tracts of land five miles on each side. They did not divide these areas into one-mile *sections*.

Cleaveland and his helpers surveyed a large area during the summer and autumn months, including a town at the mouth of the Cuyahoga River. He then returned to Connecticut and never again traveled west. By the end of 1797, all of the land

east of the Cuyahoga had been surveyed and was being sold to settlers. The town grew to become the city of Cleveland. It

This is an artist's idea of a family traveling from Connecticut to the Western Reserve about 1817. How does this picture of travel differ from the one on page 84?

was named for Moses Cleaveland, but the spelling was changed for some unknown reason.

The Fire Lands

You will notice that the west end of the Connecticut Reserve on the map on page 81 is named *The Fire Lands*. During the American Revolution, several towns in Connecticut were burned by British raiders, and the people living in these towns suffered greatly. In 1792 Connecticut decided to give these sufferers 500,000 acres in the west end of its Reserve. The pattern of land subdivision in this area, which covers Erie and Huron Counties, is different from all others. The picture on the previous page is an artist's idea of a family moving from Connecticut to the Fire Lands.

Other Subdivisions of Ohio

As you can see from the map on page 81, we have discussed surveys of about one-half the area of Ohio. Most of the other half is labeled *Congress Land* or *U.S. Military District*. These areas were surveyed as shown on page 79.

There are several small areas with special names, but we will only look at *The Refugee Tract*. Do you know what a **refugee** is? It is sad to say, but there are millions of refugees in the world today. They are forced to move from their homelands because of war, hunger, or disease. At the end of the War of 1812, Ohio was involved with two kinds of refugees. One group was forced to flee to Canada from Ohio, and the other group was welcomed to Ohio as refugees from Canada. Simon Girty and a few others, who had helped the natives against the settlers, were forced to flee to the north. Some people in Canada, who had done all they could to help the Americans, were forced to flee to the south. The United States gave the refugees from Canada land in *The Refugee Tract*. Today you can ride through this tract on Interstate Highway 70 in Fairfield and Licking Counties and on Refugee Road in Columbus.

Let's Review Part 2

New Words

plat (land)
refugee
subdivision (land)

New Things to Do

1. Find your county on the map on page 81. Which Public Land Survey(s) cover(s) your county?

2. Look at the map of the United States on page 3. Explain why some of the state boundary lines "wiggly", why some are parallels of latitude, and why some are meridians of longitude.

3. Pretend that you live on the East Coast in 1790 and that your family is going to move to the Ohio Country. Make a list of all the things your family will need along the way and during the first year in the west. Now decide which things on the list you may be able to make or find along the way and/or at your new home. Next, decide which items you would like to take from your present home but may not be able to fit into the wagon. When you have made your list of things to take as short as possible, compare your list with those of your classmates.

Part 3

How did the natives defend themselves?

What would you — or your parents — do if a neighbor began to build a new house on your land? The first thing you might do is tell the neighbor to stop. If this did not work, you would have to hire a lawyer and ask a court to settle the argument. The natives tried to stop the Americans from moving into the Ohio Country. Since they could not "go to court", they had to fight to protect their lands. The British controlled all of the St. Lawrence River Valley and most of the Great Lakes area, and they were eager to help the natives attack the American settlers.

Governor Arthur St. Clair

Shortly after he reached Marietta, Arthur St. Clair divided the Northwest Territory into two parts. He named the area east of the Scioto and Cuyahoga Rivers *Washington County* and made Marietta the seat of government. He named all of the rest of the territory *Hamilton County* and made Losantiville the seat of government.

St. Clair moved to Losantiville in December 1789. He did not like this name so he changed it to *Cincinnati*. At the close of the Revolution, a group of American officers, including Arthur St. Clair, organized the *Society of The Cincinnati*. This name honored Lucius Cincinnatus, a citizen-soldier of ancient Rome.

Battles with The Natives

In 1785 Congress sent soldiers to guard Marietta. They built a log fort and named it for Josiah Harmar. Four years later, the three settlements between the Miami Rivers needed protection. Congress sent a small group of soldiers to protect these settlers, and they built *Fort Washington* at Cincinnati.

In the autumn of 1790, St. Clair ordered Josiah Harmar to lead troops northward from Fort Washington to punish the natives who were attacking the new settlements. Harmar led about 1,450 men, plus several hundred women and children *camp followers*. This poorly trained army traveled up the valley of the Great Miami River. They crossed the divide to the Wabash River and reached a point near present Fort Wayne, Indiana, as shown in the map on the next page. A surprise attack by the Miamis, under Chief Little Turtle, killed many of the Americans. Those who escaped fled back to Fort Washington.

In the autumn of 1791, St. Clair himself led a group of 2,700 poorly-trained men and many camp followers northward to punish the natives. About 25 miles north of Cincinnati, he paused for a few days to build Fort Hamilton in present Butler County. About 50 miles farther north, he built Fort Jefferson in present Darke County. Both forts are shown on the map on the next page. By the time St. Clair's army reached a point just west of present Mercer County, almost one-half of his soldiers had run away. The Miamis and other tribes, under Little Turtle, attacked again. They killed 613 American troops and wounded 237 more. Many camp followers were also killed or wounded. Unfortunately for the natives, every

battle they won made the whites more determined to crush them.

Anthony Wayne

Anthony Wayne was an important military leader in the American Revolution. Because of his daring acts during that war, he was often called *Mad Anthony*. He was also a good friend of George Washington. In 1792 President Washington sent Anthony Wayne to Cincinnati to deal with the natives. Wayne spent eighteen months training an army. In the autumn of 1793, he led his men and camp followers northward from Fort Washington into present Darke County, where he built *Fort GreeneVille* to protect his line of supplies. Wayne moved to a point near the site of St.Clair's defeat and built *Fort Recovery*. Simon Kenton, whom you learned about in Chapter 4, urged Wayne to attack the natives immediately, but Wayne wanted to be careful. He spent the winter at Fort GreeneVille, the site of present Greenville in Darke County. The natives attacked Fort Recovery in the Spring of 1794 but fell back after losing many warriors.

Battle of Fallen Timbers: Shortly after the battle at Fort Recovery, Wayne moved his army northward and built Fort Defiance where the Auglaize River empties into the Maumee. Of course, the natives watched everything that the Americans did and reported to the British at Fort Detroit. The British expected Wayne to

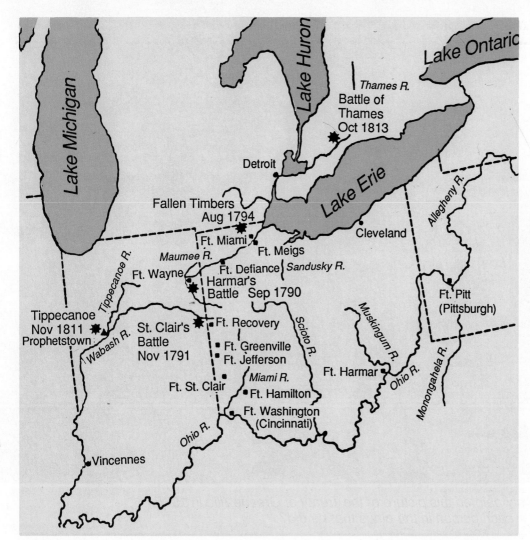

This map shows military sites in the Ohio Country between 1790 and 1814. Why are most of the places west of the Scioto River?

attack Fort Detroit, so they built Fort Miami near the present city of Maumee.

Little Turtle was again asked to be the leader of the natives. When he thought about the battle at Fort Recovery, he told the other chiefs not to fight. When they refused his advice, Little Turtle said that he would stay with his people and fight but not as the leader. The chiefs named

Blue Jacket to be their leader and Tecumseh to be his assistant.

About the middle of August 1794, Wayne's army moved down-stream along the Maumee River. At a point near the southern edge of present Lucas County, there was a large area that had once been covered by tall trees. A great wind had blown down many of these trees. The

Howard Chandler Christy painted this picture of the Treaty of GreeneVille in 1945. Why did the artist show each person in the place that he did?

natives waited for Wayne among the fallen trees. Wayne let them wait for several days and then tricked them into leaving their shelter. Wayne's army attacked and the natives ran to Fort Miami for protection, but the British closed the gates against them.

The Treaty of GreeneVille

When the British refused to help them at the Battle of Fallen Timbers, Blue Jacket and Tecumseh knew that they could not continue fighting. A few months later, Anthony Wayne demanded that leaders of all the tribes in the area appear at Fort GreeneVille to sign another treaty. By the end of July, 1795, more than 1,100 natives

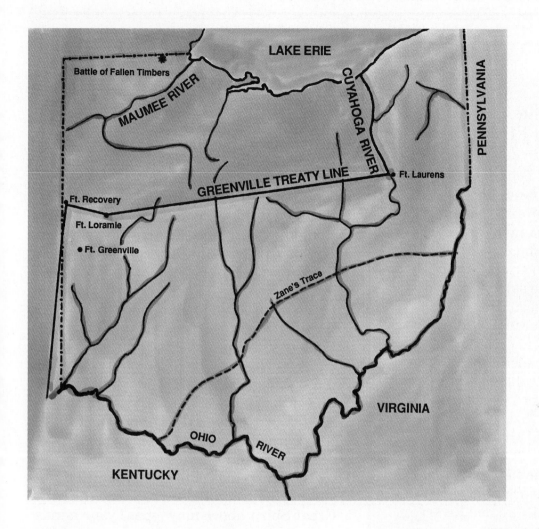

The map shows: LAKE ERIE, Battle of Fallen Timbers, MAUMEE RIVER, CUYAHOGA RIVER, PENNSYLVANIA, GREENVILLE TREATY LINE, Ft. Laurens, Ft. Recovery, Ft. Loramie, Ft. Greenville, Zane's Trace, VIRGINIA, OHIO RIVER, KENTUCKY

The Treaty of GreeneVille was supposed to separate the natives from the settlers "for all times." Is your county north, south, or on the treaty line?

gathered around the fort. Tecumseh refused to go and told the chiefs that he would not sign another treaty.

Anthony Wayne wanted to be certain that every chief at GreeneVille knew both what the Americans wanted from them, and what they would be given in payment. To identify them, Wayne had an artist make a colored drawing of each chief. The picture on the previous page is the best-known

painting of the signing of the treaty. It was created by Howard Chandler Christy, a native of Ohio, about 150 years after the event. You can see the original small painting in the Garst Museum in Greenville. A short time later, Mr. Christy made a very large copy to hang in our state capitol.

The Treaty of GreeneVille described a new boundary between lands that the

GreeneVille Boundary Line

"The general boundary line between the lands of the United States and the lands of the said Indian tribes shall begin at the mouth of the Cuyahoga River and run thence up the same to the portage between the Tuscarawas branch of the Muskingum [River], thence down that branch to the crossing place above Fort Laurens, thence westwardly to a fork of that branch of the Great Miami [River] running into the Ohio, at or near which stood Loramie's store and where commenced the portage between the [Maumee River] and St. Mary's River ...; thence a westerly course to Fort Recovery ...; thence southerly in a direct line [in present Indiana] to the Ohio [River], so as to intersect that river opposite the mouth of the [Kentucky] River."

Americans would occupy and lands of the natives. You should look at the map on previous page as you read the description in the box on this page.

If you look at the maps on pages 81 and 93 you can see how the Treaty of GreeneVille affected the Connecticut Western Reserve. The treaty said that the Delaware, Wyandot, Ottawa, and Chippewa tribes would have to leave the area east of the Cuyahoga River, but they could continue to live "in peace" to the west of it.

In payment for giving up more than two-thirds of the area of present Ohio, the United States promised to give each of the tribes at GreeneVille $1,666 in trade goods plus $825 in cash once every year. Wayne closed the treaty meeting by saying:
"I now ... pray to the Great Spirit that the peace now established may be permanent and that it now holds us together in bonds of friendship until time shall be no more. I also pray that the Great Spirit above may [open] your minds and ... your eyes to your true happiness, that your children may learn to **cultivate** (farm) the earth and enjoy the fruits of peace and industry."[1]

Effects on The Natives

Think back to the problem of a neighbor building on your land. If a court orders that the building be torn down, will your parents be happy? Will the neighbor be happy? The whites were very happy when the Treaty of GreeneVille was signed. People throughout Ohio and the eastern states thought that it would now be safe to live in the Northwest Territory. As you will learn in the next chapter, the natives suffered even more because the Americans did not obey the *Treaty of GreeneVille.*

Let's Review Part 3

New Words

cultivate

New Things to Do

Divide your class into three groups to discuss the following topics.

1. Pretend that one group is the tribe of natives that defeated Josiah Harmar in 1790. You have just learned the Arthur St.Clair is leading an army to battle with you again. Plan how to deal with this situation.

2. Pretend that the second group is the tribe that defeated Arthur St.Clair in 1791. You hear that Anthony Wayne is bringing a bigger and better army to battle you again. Plan how to deal with this situation.

3. Pretend that the third group is Blue Jacket six months after the Battle of

Fallen Timbers. What will you advise your people to do? Bring the class together to discuss the decisions of the three groups.

What have we learned?

During the American Revolution, only a few white traders lived in the Ohio Country. As soon as the war ended, thousands of people from the East Coast began moving west to receive the free land in payment for their service in the war. The Ohio Country became the place where many of the ideas of self-government were developed, including the Public Land Survey of 1785 and the Northwest Ordinance of 1787. These ideas were very important as the United States grew from a population of about 3 million in 1776 to almost 250 million by the end of the 20th century.

The Native Americans tried to resist the movement of settlers into the Ohio Country. They won some battles but learned that they could not keep the Americans out of their lands. In the next chapter, you will learn how Ohio became a state, and how the natives made one last attempt to save their lands in the War of 1812.

Foot note [1]: Eckert: *The Frontiersmen,* pp. 413-414

Map Projects

Find the following places on your map of Ohio.

Place	County
Auglaize River	Defiance to Van Wert
Campus Martius	Washington
Cuyahoga River	Cuyahoga to Geauga
Fallen Timbers	Lucas
Fire Lands	Erie & Huron
Fort Defiance	Defiance
Fort Hamilton	Butler
Fort Jefferson	Darke
Fort Meigs	Wood
Fort Recovery	Mercer
Greenville	Darke
Little Miami River	Clermont to Greene
Marietta	Washington
Maumee City	Lucas
Maumee River	Lucas to Paulding
Muskingum River	Washington to Coshocton
North Bend	Hamilton

Books to Read

The following books will help you understand what was happening in the Ohio Country as the early settlers came. Your public library may have other books on this subject.

The Battle of Fallen Timbers, by John Tribbel, tells how the native tribes in the Ohio Country tried to work together to keep out the white settlers.

Blue Jacket, by Allan W. Eckert, is a biography of the white man who became the leader of the natives at the Battle of Fallen Timbers.

Daniel Boone and The Opening of The Ohio Country, by Seamus Cavan, explains how Daniel Boone helped to make the Ohio Country safe for settlement.

The Old Wilderness Road: An American Journey, by William O. Steele, tells the story of four early explorers of the lands west of the Appalachian Mountains. It explains how their discoveries encouraged other people on the East Coast to move westward.

Chapter 6

What happened during the earliest years of Ohio?

Let's learn...

- about problems the United States faced.

- how Ohio became a state.

- about the War of 1812 in the West.

What do you think of when you see, or hear, the word **frontier** (outer limit). Today you know more about the frontiers of space, medicine, and computers than your grandparents could have dreamed of when they were your age. In the year 1800, the Ohio Country was on the *frontier* of the United States. By that year, almost everyone on the East Coast knew about the Ohio Country. Thousands of people had moved here, were in the process of moving here, or were dreaming of moving to what they thought was the "Promised Land."

Have you seen pictures on television of California? Of Africa? Of China? Of men walking on the moon? Today you know more about these far off places than Congress knew about the Ohio Country in 1800. At that time it took two weeks, or more, for a person to travel from New York to Cincinnati to deliver a message.

In this chapter, we will look at some of the problems of organizing our nation in its earliest years. We will then look at the steps taken to create the State of Ohio and the role of Ohio in the War of 1812. The time line on the next page outlines the events we will discuss.

Part 1

What problems did the United States face?

You could spend years studying the problems faced by the thirteen original states after they were free from Great Britain. The greatest problem was that no group of people had ever tried to organize a government by themselves!

In 1776 almost all nations of Europe were ruled by men who had the title of *king, prince,* or *emperor.* A few nations were ruled by women who had the title of *queen* or *princess.* Many of these rulers said that they ruled by *Divine Right* which meant that they thought God made them the ruler. The leaders of the American colonies wrote the Declaration of Independence to tell the British king that they wanted to rule themselves. But they had no pattern to follow!

In 1776 the native tribes of North America were among the few groups in the world who ruled themselves. Between 1776 and 1787, representatives of the Continental Congress met many times with leaders of the Iroquois and Lenape tribes. The Americans learned how each tribe governed itself by discussions among its members. They learned how leaders of several tribes met together to make decisions for the common good and recorded these decisions in *wampum.* The Americans learned one surprising thing — that native *women* made many decisions for the tribes! For example, the chiefs of the tribes were usually men, but they were often chosen by councils of women!

Role of Women

In the 18th century, there were few places where women had any political rights. Even the queens were usually controlled by councils of men. Our Declaration of

Time Line from American Revolution Through the War of 1812

Date	Location	Event
1774	Philadelphia	First meeting of Continental Congress
1776	Boston	Abigail Adams "Remember the Ladies" letter
1776-1787	Boston	Meetings of American leaders with native tribes
1787	Philadelphia	Congress created Northwest Territory
1788	Marietta	Arthur St. Clair Governor of Northwest Territory
1795	GreenVille	Treaty of GreeneVille signed
1799	Chillicothe	First meeting of General Assembly of Ohio
1799	Philadelphia	Territory of Indiana created by Congress
1803	Chillicothe	Ohio became 17th state
1811	Indiana	Tecumseh's plan to defeat Americans
1811	New Madrid, Missouri	Greatest earthquake struck United States
1812	Northern Ohio	War of 1812
1813	Canada	Tecumseh died

Independence, Northwest Ordinance, and Constitution were written by men. They borrowed many ideas from the Native Americans, but they gave women no role in the new government.

One American woman is remembered for her attempts to influence the Continental Congress through her husband. Abigail Smith Adams cared for her family in Massachusetts while her husband, John, helped to write the *Declaration of Independence*. Many of their letters to each other have been saved. One of Abigail's letter is now called *Remember the Ladies* (see next page).

John Adams was not able to persuade the Continental Congress to even mention women in the Constitution of the United

Parts of Abigail Adams' "Remember the Ladies" Letter

(Note: This wording and spelling is by Abigail.)

I long to hear that you have declared an independency — and by the way in the new Code of Laws which I suppose it will be necessary for you to make I desire you would Remember the Ladies, and be more generous and favourable to them than your ancesters. Do not put such unlimited power into the hands of the Husbands. Remember all Men would be tyrants if they could. If perticular care and attention is not paid to the Ladies we are determined to [stir up] a Rebellion, and will not hold ourselves bound by any Laws in which we have no voice, or Representation....

{From: Phyllis Lee Levin, Abigail Adams, p.82}

States. You will learn more about the struggle of women to gain political rights in later chapters.

Role of Slavery

Of all the problems facing the Continental Congress, the most difficult was *slavery*. Most of the leaders of the northern colonies wanted to **abolish** (end) slavery. Most of the leaders of the southern colonies said they could not exist without slaves.

What do people do who know that they must work together but cannot agree on a difficult subject? The only way the representatives could go forward with plans for the new government was to **compromise** (reach agreement by "give and take") on this question.

The members of the Congress dealt with slavery in two ways as they wrote the *Northwest Ordinance*. To satisfy the North, they agreed that there would be no slavery in the Ohio Country. To satisfy the South, they agreed that slave owners could enter the territory to capture run-aways. Later when they wrote the *Constitution*, which every state had to agree to, they did not mention slavery! In this book, we will refer to the slaves, and all their descendants, as *African-Americans*, as explained in the box on the next page.

Why We Use The Term African-Americans

"...Black people wherever they are, come from the land called Africa. We have been called by many different names — colored, Negro, Black, etc. Most people are known by the land which they or their ancestors lived in or come from. Germans are called Germans because there is a land named Germany. ...Now look at a map. Is there a land called Colorland? Negroland? Blackland? No. There is a land named Africa, which is where we came from. So in our book we shall refer to ourselves as...Africans in America."

From Preface to *Lessons in History — A Celebration of Blackness* (Elementary Edition), by Jawanza Kunjufu, African-American Images, Chicago, Illinois}

Let's Review Part 1

New Words

abolish
compromise
frontier

New Things to Do

Talk to the oldest woman you know who was born in the United States and/or the oldest African-American person you know. Ask her/him about how the roles of women and/or African-Americans have changed during her/his lifetime. Have a class discussion about what each one learns from these talks.

Part 2

How did Ohio become a state?

In 1787 the Northwest Ordinance laid out a plan for creating local government in the Ohio Country. As soon as 5000 *men* — women were not counted — lived in the territory, they could organize a *General Assembly* to work with Governor Arthur St.Clair. The assembly could send a representative to Congress to speak for the people of the territory. When a total of 60,000 people lived in the area, they could ask Congress to let them create a new state. William Henry Harrison, whom you read about in Chapters 1 and 5, played an important role in Ohio becoming a state.

William Henry Harrison

William Henry Harrison was born in 1773 at Berkeley Plantation, near Petersboro,

101

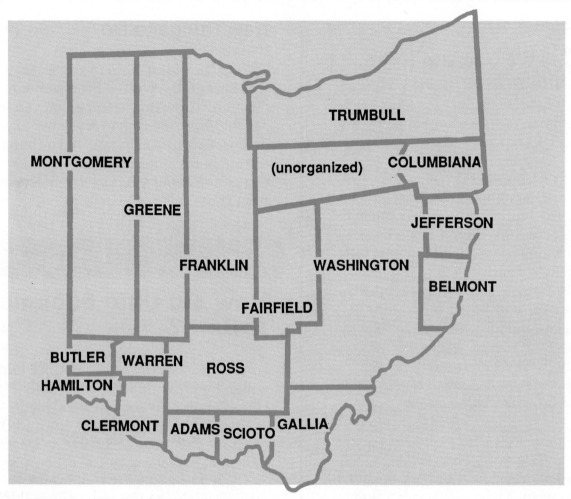

MONTGOMERY

GREENE

TRUMBULL

(unorganized)

COLUMBIANA

JEFFERSON

FRANKLIN

WASHINGTON

BELMONT

FAIRFIELD

BUTLER   WARREN   ROSS

HAMILTON

CLERMONT   ADAMS   SCIOTO   GALLIA

When Ohio became a state in 1803, there were seventeen counties.
Where is your county on this map?

Virginia. You can visit this house today. He began to study medicine but joined the United States Army when he was 21 years old. He was sent to Fort Washington in Cincinnati, where he became Anthony Wayne's assistant. He was with Wayne at the Battle of Fallen Timbers and at the Treaty of GreeneVille. You can see him — without a hat — near the right edge of the picture on page 92.

William Henry Harrison left the army in 1798 to become *Secretary* of the Northwest Territory under Governor St.Clair. In 1799 the General Assembly elected him as its first representative to

Congress. By 1800 the population of the territory was growing so fast that Congress created the *Indiana Territory* to cover all the lands to the west of the Great Miami River. Harrison was appointed Governor of this new territory. You will learn more of him later in this chapter.

Steps toward Statehood

The United States **census** (count of people) of 1800 found 45,365 people living in the area we call *Ohio*, including 337 African-Americans. The census did not count Native Americans because they were not taxed by the government. This growing population made it necessary to create more counties out of the original two — Washington and Hamilton. The map on the previous page shows that in 1802 there were seventeen counties and one "unorganized" area in the land we call Ohio. If you look back to page 93, you can see how some of these counties were related to the boundary of the Treaty of GreeneVille.

Early in 1802, representatives of the seventeen counties asked Congress to make them part of a new state to be called *Ohio*. On April 30, Congress gave them permission to take the following steps.

1. Voters in the seventeen counties would elect representatives to meet at Chillicothe in Ross County. At this meeting, they would choose a name for the new state and write a constitution.

2. Section 16 of every Public Land township (see diagram on page 79) would be set aside for schools.

3. Congress would give the new state the salt springs in the area we now know as Licking County.

In November 1802, representatives of the seventeen counties met in Chillicothe to write a constitution. They adopted the name *Ohio* for their new state and sent the proposed constitution to Congress. These early meetings were held in the building shown on the next page. Later the General Assembly met in this same building from 1803 to 1810 and from 1812 to 1816. Today the oldest newspaper in Ohio, the *Chillicothe Gazette*, occupies a building built from the same plans as this first capitol.

On February 19, 1803, Congress passed an act that made Ohio the seventeenth state of the United States of America, and President Thomas Jefferson signed it into law. In this act, Congress established the boundaries of Ohio and approved our first state constitution. You will learn more about this constitution in Chapter 11.

This building in Chillicothe was the first capitol of Ohio. How does the capitol differ from the building on the right edge of this picture?

The new government of Ohio faced many challenges as thousands of people came to find new homes for themselves. These new-comers thought that they would be safe because the problem of the Native Americans had been solved by the Treaty of GreeneVille. You will soon learn that they were wrong.

Let's Review Part 2

New Words

census

New Things to Do

Pretend that your school has just been built, and you are in the first class to attend it. Also pretend that your class has been elected to draw up a set of "laws" to operate the school. Divide your class into several committees to think about different activities that must be considered. Have each committee make up five laws relating to one of these activities. Have each committee report to the class as a whole and then an open discussion about each committee report. How does this activity relate to what happened in Chillicothe, Ohio in 1802?

Part 3

How did the War of 1812 affect Ohio?

In Chapter 5, you read Anthony Wayne's words after the natives signed the Treaty of GreeneVille. He said "I now...pray to the Great Spirit that the peace now established may be permanent and that it now holds us together in bonds of friendship until time shall be no more." How long will it be until "time shall be no more?" If Wayne could have guessed how many settlers would be moving into Ohio, he might have said, "...until you natives shall be no more." At the same time, British traders continued to roam through the area north and west of the treaty line. They encouraged the natives to attack the Americans. In 1810 there were 228,861 white and 1,899 African-American settlers living in Ohio.

Tecumseh

By 1800 Tecumseh was one of the most important leaders of the natives, but he was not a chief. He traveled throughout Ohio encouraging the natives and spying on the settlers. He wore a disguise to spy inside Fort Washington in Cincinnati. He was accepted as a guest in the homes of some leaders of Ohio, as you can read about in the box on the next page.

Tecumseh allowed only one white artist to paint his picture. This was made from the original. How would you describe Tecumseh from this picture, if you did not know that he was a leader of the Shawnees?

Tecumseh was respected by many leaders of Ohio, but he did not trust them. Nor did Tecumseh trust the British after they had closed the gates of Fort Miami during the Battle of Fallen Timbers. He especially hated William Henry Harrison who was governor of the Territory of Indiana.

Two Important Homes Visited by Tecumseh

In 1782 James Galloway entered the Ohio Country as a member of the Kentucky militia under George Rogers Clark. He returned with his family in 1797 to settle in Greene County near the birthplace of Tecumseh. A year later, he built the house shown below, which now stands on the grounds of the Green County Historical Society in downtown Xenia. Tecumseh visited the Galloways many times between 1798 and 1810, and he almost married Rebecca Galloway.

Tecumseh was also welcomed in the home of Thomas and Eleanor Worthington near Chillicothe. Thomas Worthington helped to establish the State of Ohio, and he served as its fourth governor (1814-1818). In Chapter 3, you learned that the *Adena* people were named for the Worthington home. You can visit this house today, as shown on the next page. Now look back to the picture on the Great Seal of Ohio, shown on page 4: the view on it is the scene Tecumseh saw when he visited Adena!

THE JAMES GALLOWAY CABIN (1798)

GREENE COUNTY HISTORICAL SOCIETY

The James Galloway house is now in downtown Xenia. What did pioneer people use to fill the spaces between logs?

Adena was the home of Thomas and Eleanor Worthington in Ross County. How is this house related to the Great Seal of Ohio?

Harrison set up his headquarters at Vincennes, on the Wabash River (see the map on page 91, and he built *Grouseland* to use as both home and office. You can visit this building today. Between 1800 and 1810, Harrison forced the natives to sign one treaty after another. Each treaty made them give up more of their "homeland" in the area we know as the State of Indiana.

Tecumseh's Plan

During these years, Tecumseh developed a plan for all the tribes living west of the Appalachian Mountains to unite against the American settlers. He then traveled through the area we know as Ohio, Michigan, Indiana, Illinois, and Wisconsin to encourage the natives to fight together against the Americans. He also encouraged them to move to a new town on the west bank of the Wabash River near the Tippecanoe River (see the map on page 91).

Tecumseh's last trip began in May, 1811 with a stop at Vincennes to talk to General Harrison. For the next six *moons* (four-week periods as we measure time), Tecumseh traveled through the area we know as Kentucky, Tennessee, Mississippi, and Alabama. He encouraged the tribes to unite in one big attack on the Americans. Each chief was given a bundle of sticks and told to break one stick on the night of each full moon. When the last stick was broken, they were to watch for a great sign from *Moneto* (the Shawnee name for God). When this came, they were to attack the settlers living near them.

The Prophet

Tecumseh's younger brother was born in 1772 and given the name *Lalawethika*, meaning He-Makes-A-Loud-Noise. He lost an eye in an accident when he was young and later became an alcoholic. His people did not like him. In 1805 "Loud Noise" told the people that he received a **vision** (unexpected idea) of the future. This experience led him to give up alcohol and to change his name to *Tenskwatawa*, meaning He-Opens-The-Door.

Today we would say that Tecumseh was **psychic**, because he had ways of knowing

William Henry Harrison and other war leaders were often honored by statutes of them on horseback.Why were military leaders often shown on horses?

about future events that are hidden from most people. He did not like to show this power so he often had his brother speak for him. The Americans did not know about this arrangement, so they called Tenskwatawa *The Prophet*. Tenskwatawa enjoyed this position, and each time one of Tecumseh's prophecies came true, he accepted the credit.

The Battle of Tippecanoe

Each time Tecumseh traveled, he left Tenskwatawa in charge of the growing village at the mouth of the Tippecanoe River. The Americans called it *Prophet's Town*. Time after time, Tecumseh warned his brother that the natives in the village must wait for the great sign before attacking Harrison at Vincennes. He also told Tenskwatawa to lead the people away to safety if Harrison should attack their town before the great sign appeared.

Traders and scouts warned Harrison about the natives gathering at Tippecanoe. He decided to lead a large army to a place near Prophet's Town and try to get the natives to attack before Tecumseh returned. On November 5, 1811, Harrison ordered his army to make camp just south of the Tippecanoe River. No protection was built, but the soldiers were told to sleep in their uniforms with loaded rifles beside them. Guards were posted all around the camp.

On the day Harrison's army made camp, Tenskwatawa prayed to Moneto for help. That night he had a dream of a knife going through Harrison's heart and killing him.

He told the war chiefs that this dream meant that they should attack Harrison. Some chiefs wanted to attack in the night. Others wanted to obey Tecumseh and move away from Prophet's Town. Tenskwatawa decided to send representatives to Harrison to discuss the situation. The Prophet's men met with Harrison, spied on his camp, and returned to their town.

No one today knows what happened in the Prophet's Town that night. We do know that, before dawn on November 7, 1811, the natives attacked what they thought was Harrison's sleeping army. The Americans awoke quickly and killed many of the natives. The rest of the warriors fled with their women and children. Harrison's troops destroyed the village but did not chase the fleeing natives. A short time later, Tecumseh returned to the banks of the Wabash River. When he learned what happened, he was very angry with his brother.

The New Madrid Earthquake

A few days before December 6, 1811, every chief who agreed to help Tecumseh threw away his last stick. On December 6, all of the region within 500 miles of the small town of New Madrid, in the southeastern corner of the state of Missouri, shook violently. Some buildings in Ohio were destroyed. The course of the Mississippi River near New Madrid shifted by several miles, and a block of earth sank in Western

Fort Meigs was important during the War of 1812. Today you can visit a reconstruction of the fort. Why is a place like this recreated?

Tennessee to create Reelfoot Lake. This was the greatest earthquake on record in North America. If the natives had all attacked the settlers on that day, they might have changed the history of the United States! On that day, Tecumseh and a few friends were near the spot where Loud Noise had made the decision to attack Harrison. Suddenly, they were knocked down by the shaking of the ground. A short time later, Tecumseh and the natives who remained with him moved to Canada to gain protection from the British army.

The War of 1812

Although the British signed a treaty in 1783 to end the American Revolution, they could not accept defeat by the former colonies. As a result, British officers in Canada continued to encourage natives to attack Americans. British ships attacked merchant ships of the United States on the

Photo Opposite Page: The reconstruction of Commodore Perry's ship Niagara contains a few pieces of material from the original ship. Why are there so many ropes or cables?

111

high seas. Because of these actions, on June 18, 1812, the United States declared war on Great Britain. William Henry Harrison was appointed commander of American troops in the West.

The British appointed Tecumseh to be the leader of all the natives fighting against the Americans in the West. They quickly moved across the Detroit River and captured Fort Detroit. To meet this threat, William Henry Harrison built a new fort on the south side of the Maumee River. He named it *Fort Meigs* in honor of the Governor of Ohio, Return J. Meigs. The British fired heavy guns at the fort. The warriors, under Tecumseh, surrounded it and cut off all supplies, but they could not capture it. The picture on page 110 shows the rebuilt Fort Meigs you can visit at Perrysburg in Wood County.

Battle of Lake Erie

Oliver Hazzard Perry, an officer of the United States Navy, was given orders to protect settlements along Lake Erie. He built a few small ships at Presque Isle, which is on the shore of Lake Erie just east of the Ohio-Pennsylvania border. On September 10, 1813, Perry's ships defeated the British ships at Put-in-Bay of South Bass Island (Ottawa County). This victory ended British control of the Great Lakes. Perry notified General Harrison by writing a note on the back of an old envelope:

DEAR GENERAL: We have met the enemy and they are ours — two ships, two brigs, one schooner and a sloop. Yours with great respect and esteem, OLIVER HAZZARD PERRY

During the battle, Perry lost his command ship, the *Lawrence*, but moved to the *Niagara*. At the end of the war, Perry sailed his ships back to Presque Isle and sank them in the bay. Today you can visit Erie, Pennsylvania — which includes Presque Isle — and see the reconstructed ship *Niagara* shown on the previous page.

In 1857 William H. Powell, an Ohio artist, created a very large painting to show his idea of the battle. His picture, which you can see on the next page, shows Perry moving from the badly-damaged *Lawrence* to the *Niagara*. The original painting hangs in the Ohio Capitol. Later Powell painted a similar picture for the Smithsonian Institution in Washington, DC.

Battle of the Thames

With the British Navy driven from Lake Erie, the Americans took control of Fort Detroit. On October 4, 1813, Harrison's army prepared to attack the British base on the Thames River in Canada. This place is shown on the map on page 91. The frightened British commander left Tecumseh and his warriors to fight while he fled to the east. Before the battle,

The original painting of Perry's victory at Put-in-Bay hangs in the Ohio State Capitol. What was William H. Powell trying to show in this picture?

Tecumseh told his friends that he would die in the fighting that was to come. The Americans attacked on October 5th and quickly defeated the native warriors.

Tecumseh was killed in the first round of fighting. A Shawnee **legend** (respected story) says that he was wearing a disguise so the Americans could not recognize him

During the 1830's, Native Americans were assigned to live in these reservations in northwest Ohio. Which counties of Ohio were named for the native tribes assigned to the reservations shown?

and destroy his body. According to the same legend, during the night of October 5-6, Shawnee warriors found Tecumseh's body. They carried it away and buried it with great honor in a place that they would long remember, but the Americans could not find. The picture of Tecumseh on page 105 is a copy of the only **portrait** (painted image) he permitted anyone to make of him.

By the end of 1814, peace came to Ohio. On January 2 of that year, the natives signed another treaty with the United States. As part of this treaty, the Native Americans who wanted to continue living in Ohio agreed to stay on the **reservations** (places set aside) shown on the map on the previous page. On December 24, 1814, the British agreed to terms of peace, and Ohio and the United States were ready for a long period of tremendous growth. In 1895 the people of Cincinnati honored their fellow citizen by dedicating the statue of General Harrison that you see on page 108.

Let's Review Part 3

New Words

legend
portrait
psychic
reservation (land)
vision

New Things to Do

1. Divide the class into two groups. Have one group pretend that they are Tecumseh. Make a list of instructions for his brother to carry out in the village at Tippecanoe while he is traveling. Have the other group pretend that they are The Prophet. Make up a list of reasons why he did not follow the instructions of Tecumseh. Share the lists with the class and have a discussion about how Tecumseh should treat his brother after the destruction of the village.

2. Look at the picture on page 113 and pretend that you are the young man in the boat next to Oliver H. Perry. Write a letter to a friend about your experience in the battle of Lake Erie.

What have we learned?

This chapter has covered a period of about thirty years, from the close of the Revolutionary War in 1783 to the close of the War of 1812. During that short period, a small new nation, called the United States of America, accomplished many things. It set up a system for surveying and governing the western lands, which were much larger than the original states. It adopted a constitution that has served well for more than 200 years. It also added the states of Vermont, Kentucky, Tennessee, and Ohio to the original thirteen.

The census of 1800 found more than 45,000 men, plus thousands of women and children, living in the Ohio Country. By taking the steps required by the Northwest Ordinance, Ohio became a state in 1803. The temporary peace created by the Treaty of GreeneVille encouraged more people to migrate from the East Coast. As a result, the population of our state reached almost 230,000 by 1810.

Each success for the Americans meant another defeat for the natives. In their last attempt to drive the Americans out of Ohio, the natives helped the British during the War of 1812. After this, all fighting between natives and Americans was to the west of Ohio.

Map Projects

Find the following places on your map of Ohio

Place	County
Fort Meigs	Wood
South Bass Island	Ottawa

Find the following places on your map of the United States

Place	State
New Madrid	Missouri
Presque Isle at Erie	Pennsylvania
Tippecanoe River	Indiana

Books to Read

The following books will help you understand the early days of our state. Your library may have other books on this subject.

Frontier Home, by Raymond Bial, uses many color photographs to describe life in pioneer times.

The Frontiersmen, by Allan Eckert, is a biography of Tecumseh that tells the story of his relationship to the Galloway family.

How The Settlers Lived, by George and Ellen Laycock, tells the story, with many drawings, of many early settlements in Ohio.

Log Cabin in The Woods, by Joanne Landers Henry, describes the life of a boy in Indiana in the year 1830.

Shh! We're Writing The Constitution, by Jean Fritz, uses clever cartoons to explain how the Constitution of The United States was written.

Tecumseh, Shawnee Rebel, by Robert Cwiklik, explains how Tecumseh tried to organize the native tribes to defeat the settlers.

Chapter 7

How did travel change during the 19th century?

Let's learn...

- **how our lives are related to movement.**

- **how highways were developed.**

- **how waterways were improved.**

- **how railroads became important.**

The history of human life is a story of *movement*. Thousands of years ago, tribes of people moved to find food; small groups moved to trade goods; armies moved to conquer. These same activities are taking place in the world today. For example, think about all the activities you take part in during an "average" day. Almost all of

117

them — except perhaps *thinking* — involve *movement*. When you move away from your home, you need some form of *transportation*. In this chapter, you will learn how changing forms of transportation affected the people of Ohio during the 19th century. The time line on the next page will help you keep track of events.

Part 1

How does movement affect our lives?

Before you learn how transportation influenced the development of our state, you must understand how it affects your daily life. What forms of transportation can you use? If you walk or ride a bicycle, you provide your own transportation. If you ride a bus, you must be at the bus stop on time, you must have the money to pay for the ride, and you must want to go somewhere close to a bus stop. If you cannot provide your own transportation, you must have someone else move you in an automobile. Every trip you make involves an **origin** (place from which you start), a **destination** (place to which you are going), a route or **right-of-way** over which you travel, and a cost measured in terms of time, money, and/or energy. In this part, you will learn about these ideas.

Origins and Destinations

Every trip you make has an *origin* and a *destination*. Every place is a destination for people who want to go to it and an *origin* for people who want to leave it. Wherever you are right now was the destination of the last trip you made. It will be the origin of the next trip you make. Another word for *destination* is **central place**. Your home is a very small *central place* because it attracts only your family and a few visitors or delivery people. Your school is a larger central place because it attracts hundreds of people every school day. A large amusement or sports center may attract thousands of people. The more people attracted to a particular destination, the more important it is as a *central place*.

Right-of-Way

Have you ever taken a "short cut" while going from an origin to a destination? Has it been across a neighbor's yard? Did any one tell you that you shouldn't do that? The scholarly way of asking this last question is: "Did you have the *right-of-way*?" In other words, "Did you have permission to travel over land owned by someone else?"

Every form of travel is related to particular parcels of land, or rights-of-way, in special ways. Airports are large open parcels of land with special places for people to change from travel through the air to travel on the ground. Boat harbors are

Time Line of Transportation in Ohio

Year	Location	Event
1803	Ohio	Ohio became 17th state of United States
1803	Travel by land	Walking, riding horse back, riding and moving goods in wagons pulled by horses, mules, or oxen
1803	Travel by water	Canoes, flatboats, sailboats
1811	Ohio River	First steamboat on Ohio River — *New Orleans*
1819	Wheeling, Virginia	National Road completed to Ohio River
1821	New York State	Erie Canal opened across New York
1825	Ohio	Work began on Ohio and Erie Canal and on Miami Canal
1830	Ohio	Work began on building turnpikes
1834	Ohio	Travel from Portsmouth to Cleveland on Ohio and Erie Canal
1835	Ohio and Michigan	Erie and Kalamazoo Railroad in operation
1845	Ohio	Travel from Toledo to Cincinnati on Miami and Erie Canal
1900	Ohio	Remaining turnpikes became free roads

parcels of land that touch rivers or lakes where people can change from travel by water to travel by land. Railroad tracks are built on long, narrow strips of land so that people or goods can move from one **station** (stopping place) to another on a *train*. Highways are also built on long, narrow strips of land that anyone can use to travel from place to place by walking, bicycle, automobile, or bus.

119

The Economics of Movement

Do you get an *allowance* — that is some amount of money to spend each week? When you ask your parents to buy something for you, do they ever say, "We can't afford that!"? If you have had one of these experiences, you have learned something about **economics**! You are also using the ideas of economics each time you decide how to use your money, how to "spend" each hour, or how to use your talents. In each case, you answer the question, "How can I get the greatest benefit from what I put into the situation?"

An important question in transportation is: "How can I go from one point to another in the most economical way?" To answer this question, you must think about three things: the route you will follow, the vehicle you will use, and the time and energy you will need to make the trip. If you have plenty of time and personal energy, you can walk across the United States, as dozens of people have done in recent years. If you have very little time and plenty of energy — in the form of money — you can travel in a supersonic airplane.

The Native Americans solved the economics of travel in the only way they could. For most trips they walked. If they were near a river or lake, they used time and energy to build a canoe because they knew that they could travel on water with less energy than needed for walking.

The earliest settlers in Ohio also walked. If they could afford to buy a horse, they could save personal energy by riding on it. They could also use animals — horses, mules, or oxen — to pull loaded wagons. Canoes were of little use to them, but they could build *flatboats* to travel downstream on the larger rivers. (You can see a flatboat on page 25. They could use sailboats to travel on open water. By 1900, Americans were still walking or using animals to travel short distances. In the next three parts, you will learn how new forms of rights-of-way and new vehicles were developed during the 19th century. Each new form made it possible to travel farther and faster in less time and with less personal energy.

Let's Review Part 1

New Words

destination
central place
economics
origin
right-of-way
station (railroad/bus)

New Things to Do

1. Keep a record of every trip you make during one week. Write down each origin and destination, how you traveled, and how long it took. Ask an adult you live with to do the same thing for his/her trips for one week. Write a short report on the differences you find between your trips and the adult's trips.

2. Draw lines on a piece of paper to create four columns. In the left column, list each of the things you would like to do during the next week. In the second column, list the forms of transportation you will need to do each thing. In the third column, list who will have to provide the transportation for each activity. In the fourth column, list what each activity will "cost" in terms of both time and money. Write a short statement about the "economics" of what you hope to do.

Part 2

How were highways developed?

Have you ever walked *Indian file* with friends, that is, one behind another in a single line? How wide a right-of-way do you need to travel this way? Many of the earliest explorers and fur traders in the Ohio Country used the narrow trails created by animals or the natives. Most of these trails were "twisty" because the people or animals who made them followed the *path of least resistance*. This means they went by the easiest route for walking.

As thousands of settlers came into the Ohio Country after the Treaty of GreeneVille, the trails had to be widened. In addition, new roads had to be *opened*. This means the travelers cut down trees so they could move through the forest. But they did not have the energy to remove the tree stumps or build bridges.

In 1800 the settlers in the Ohio Country traveled over land as people of other parts of the world had moved for hundreds of years. By 1900 Ohio had thousands of miles of *highways*, but travel over land had scarcely changed during the century. There are several kinds of highways, but the two most important are *streets* and *roads*. Highways in cities and towns are usually called streets. Highways in country areas are usually called roads. Sometimes we will use the word highways to mean roads, sometimes to mean streets, and sometimes both of these. In this part, you will learn how the foundation was laid for our present system of highways.

Zane's Trace

The map on page 64 shows Fort Pitt — which was the beginning of the city of Pittsburgh — and Philadelphia. Both of these towns were in the State of Pennsylvania, but they were separated by the Appalachian Mountains. In 1800 the easiest way to move goods from Pittsburgh to Philadelphia was on flatboats down the Ohio River to the Mississippi River and on to New Orleans. At New Orleans, the goods were put on sailing ships bound for Philadelphia and other towns along the East Coast. The easiest way to move goods from Philadelphia to Pittsburgh was across the mountains, because it was too hard to travel up the rivers.

But how did the flatboat operators travel from New Orleans back to Pittsburgh,

Zane's Trace and the Natchez Trace formed a walking route between Natchez and Pittsburgh. Why did more people walk from Natchez to Pittsburgh than in the other direction?

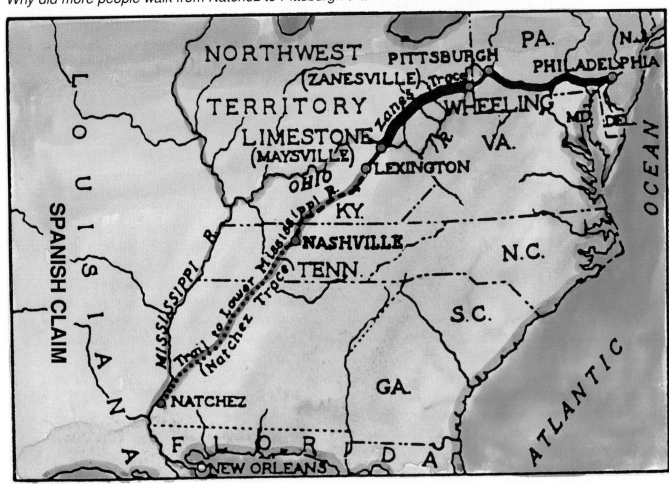

Wheeling, Marietta, or Cincinnati? Most of them walked, and a few rode horses, but there was no road! Congress hired Ebenezer Zane to open a road from Pittsburgh to Wheeling, in what was then the state of Virginia. In 1797 Congress hired Zane to continue this road from Bridgeport in Belmont County opposite Wheeling, to the Ohio River near Aberdeen in Brown County. This second part of Zane's work — known as *Zane's Trace* — became the first planned road in Ohio. You can see this route on the map on the previous page.

Zane and his helpers cut a path through the forest wide enough for a person to travel on horseback. They built ferries to help travelers cross the Scioto, Muskingum, and Hocking Rivers. In payment for their labor, the workers were given large parcels of land. Zane chose land for himself where the city of Zanesville now stands in Muskingum County.

The Natchez Trace

Zane's Trace, from Pittsburgh to Aberdeen, became part of a much longer road. In 1801 President Thomas Jefferson ordered the United States Army to create a road from Natchez, on the lower Mississippi River, to Nashville, Tennessee. This road was called the *Natchez Trace*. Finally a road was opened from Nashville to Maysville, Kentucky across the Ohio River

from Aberdeen. The map on the previous page shows the entire route. Between 1960 and 1990, Congress voted money to build a modern highway along the Natchez Trace. Today you can travel easily from Natchez to Nashville and think about the walk that thousands of boatmen from Ohio once made.

The National Road

In 1806 Congress decided to build a road from the Potomac River in Maryland to the Ohio River at Wheeling. You can see the *National Road*, as it was called, on the map on the next page. This road did not reach Wheeling until 1818. By that time, Indiana and Illinois were states. Congress then decided the road should be built across these new states to the Mississippi River. In 1840 you could travel west on the National Road to Vandalia, Illinois, but no more of it was built in the 19th century.

In 1925 the National Road was renamed *United States Route 40*. Between 1940 and 1960, the state of Ohio rebuilt long portions of this road as four-lane, divided highways. You can still travel on portions of the original National Road in Muskingum, Guernsey, and Belmont Counties. You can still see a few of the unusual "Z" bridges that were built during the 1830s, like the one shown on the next page.

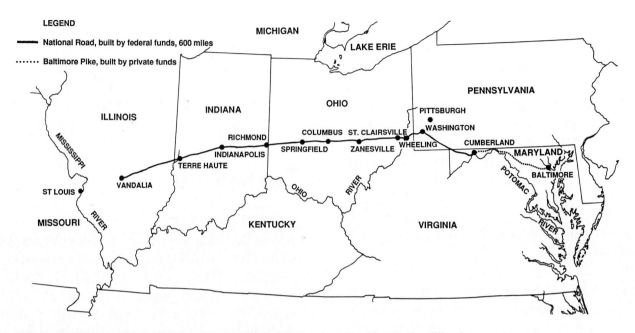

The National Road was built from Cumberland, Maryland to Vandalia, Illinois. Why isn't West Virginia shown on this map?

A few of the "Z" bridges of the National Road are still standing. How fast did wagons move across these bridges? How fast could an automobile move across one of them?

Today *Interstate Highway 70* carries almost all the traffic that once used U.S. 40. The *National Road / Zane Gray Museum* in Muskingum County, near the Norwich Interchange of I-70, explains the interesting history of Zane's Trace and the National Road.

Need for New Roads

As you can see from the census numbers in Appendix B on page 383, in 1820 the population of Ohio was 581,434 people. By 1830 the population had jumped to 937,903. Because of this increase, many

Before 1920 almost all rural roads looked like this in the Spring. What kind of modern vehicle might be able to travel on a road like this?

new towns were established and many older towns grew to become cities. At the same time, many farmers were raising larger amounts of food that had to be moved to the towns. Thousands of miles of new highways had to be opened to meet the increasing demands for travel. This means that new *rights-of-way* were created, but most of the roads looked like what you can see above.

By 1830 the total cost, in time and energy, of moving over the dirt roads was so great that people were willing to pay **tolls**

125

Why Do We Have to Pay Tolls?

Have you ever paid money to ride on a public bus? Have you ever seen your parents stop on a bridge, at a tunnel, or along a highway to pay money for driving there? If so, you know that you must pay a special fee to use some parts of the highway system. Most of this system is paid for by taxes that you will learn about in Chapter 15. Certain parts of it are very expensive to build, but save travelers large amounts of time and energy. To gain these advantages, people are willing to pay extra money, or *tolls*, to use them.

Toll roads are often called **turnpikes**. The word "turnpike" came to us from the old toll roads of England. The company that paved a road had the right to build gates across it from one to two miles apart. In some cases the "gates" were just long poles, that reminded the English people of the *pikes* or *lances* that their armies had once used for fighting. When a traveler paid the toll, the gate keeper would open the gate, or "turn the pike."

(special fees) for better roads. Private companies were encouraged to build **pavements** (hard surfaces) on public rights-of-way. As payment for their work, the companies were given permission to charge travelers for use of the improved roads. The box on this page explains the situation. These new pavements greatly reduced the cost of moving people and goods. The picture on the next page shows a pavement made of split trees.

About 1890, the Ohio General Assembly passed a law that said each county should buy the toll roads within its boundaries and make them free. In many places today, there are roads that older people call "pikes". For example, there is a "Wooster Pike" in Hamilton County and a "Wooster Pike" in Cuyahoga County: both were toll roads that led to Wooster, the county seat of Wayne County. During the 1920s, these two roads became parts of State Route 3.

Highway Vehicles

The picture on page 84 shows a **freight** wagon leaving Massachusetts for the Ohio Country. (*Freight* is anything that is moved except people.) Wagons like this were used throughout the 19th century. They were pulled by as many as eight or ten horses, mules, or oxen. During the spring of each year, when rains turned the roads into mud, several wagons would travel together so the drivers could help each other solve the problem shown on the previous page.

A few "corduroy" roads and "plank" roads were built in Ohio. What will happen to a road like this within a few years?

People traveled in stage coaches like the one shown on page 129. Beginning about 1816, stage coach companies offered regular service between our state capital at Columbus and the county seats of Ohio. Taverns were built along the stage routes to provide food and shelter for the passengers and for the horses that pulled the coaches. Today you can eat and/or sleep in the old taverns listed on page 128. The picture on page 130 shows the *Golden Lamb* at Lebanon, the county seat of Warren County. This is the oldest continuously operating inn in our state. The picture on

page 130 shows *Dunham Tavern* near downtown Cleveland. This was built in 1824 and served as a tavern and inn until 1857. Today it is an interesting museum of life in the 19th century.

By 1900 there were a few hundred miles of paved roads in Ohio that had once been toll roads. There were more than 4 million people in the state, but few of them traveled long distances on the highways. Most of them traveled by water and/or railroad, as you will learn in the next two parts.

Early 19th Century Inns You Can Visit Today

Estab.	County	Location	Name	Rest.	Rooms
1804	Adams	West Union	Olde Wayside Inn	Yes	
1850	Athens	Albany	Albany House		Yes
1825	Brown	Ripley	Baird House		Yes
1837	Columbiana	Hanoverton	The Spread Eagle	Yes	Yes
1839	Cuyahoga	Brecksville	Ye Olde Stage House	Yes	
1844	Erie	Sandusky	Wagner's 1844 Inn		Yes
1845	Erie	Milan	The Milan Inn	Yes	
1831	Franklin	Worthington	Old Worthington Inn	Yes	Yes
1850	Franklin	Columbus	A Very Small Hotel		Yes
1842	Geauga	East of Welshfield	Welshfield Inn	Yes	
1810	Hamilton	Loveland	The 20 Mile House	Yes	
1830	Harrison	Cadiz	Family Tree Inn		Yes
1840	Hocking	Logan	Inn at Cedar Falls		Yes
1798	Lake	Unionville	The Old Tavern	Yes	
1812	Lake	Painesville	Rider's Tavern	Yes	Yes
1812	Licking	Granville	Buxton Inn	Yes	Yes
1850	Licking	Granville	Granville Manor		Yes
1818	Lucas	Waterville	Columbian House	Yes	
1828	Lucas	Waterville	Columbian House	Yes	
1836	Lucas	Maumee	Governor's Inn	Yes	
1837	Madison	Lafayette	Red Brick Tavern	Yes	
1836	Meigs	Pomeroy	Holly Hill Inn		Yes
1830	Miami	Tipp City	Willow Tree Inn		Yes
1804	Montgomery	Germantown	Florentine Hotel	Yes	
1830	Preble	West Alexandria	Twin Creek B & B		Yes
1820	Richland	Mansfield	Malabar Inn	Yes	
1820	Ross	Chillicothe	Old McDill-Anderson		Yes
1817	Tuscarawas	Zoar	Inn at Cowger House		Yes
1818	Wayne	Smithville	Smithville Inn	Yes	
1849	Wayne	Wooster	Howey House		Yes
1903	Warren	Lebanon	Golden Lamb	Yes	Yes

From: AAA Ohio Tour Book, and Bed & Breakfasts and Country Inns

Let's Review Part 2

New Words

freight
pavement
toll
turnpike

New Things to Do

Write a short description of your trip from home to school. Explain the form of transportation you use for each part of the trip. Describe each highway over which you travel, including the number of lanes, the kind of surface, whether or not it has

Stage coaches were the intercity "buses" of the 19th century. How do the safety features of this stage coach compare to those of a modern automobile?

The Golden Lamb, at Lebanon, is the oldest inn in Ohio.
Why were places like this so important in the 19th century?

Dunham Tavern was about three miles east of the center of Cleveland in 1824.
How long would it take to travel this distance in bad weather?

curves and/or hills, what kinds of buildings are along it, and other things that you can see. Try to guess how old each highway is. Could anything you see have been in place in 1900?

Part 3

How were waterways improved?

As you have learned, the early explorers and fur traders used canoes to travel along rivers and lakes, but these vehicles were not useful to the settlers. Many of the settlers in southern Ohio moved down the Ohio River on *rafts* or *flatboats*. By 1820 people could move on the Ohio River and Lake Erie in steam-powered boats. By 1845 they could move from the Ohio River to Lake Erie on two man-made waterways. In this part, you will learn how travel by water was improved during the 19th century.

We must first pause to discuss some questions about water. If you carry a bucket of water out to the street in front of your house and pour the water onto the street, which way will it flow? You will see a very important fact of science: "Water runs down hill!" As you learned in Chapter 2, water falling to the north of the divide shown on page 24 flows to the St. Lawrence River. There is so much

water in the Great Lakes that they never "run dry."

Water falling to the south of the divide runs to the Ohio River. Every summer during the 19th century, more water "ran out" of the Ohio River into the Mississippi River than fell in the Ohio Valley as rain. This means that there was very little water for transportation. What would you think of a situation in which animals pulling wagons across the bed of the Ohio River interfered with boats trying to move on the water? This really happened!

Rafts and Flatboats

Have you ever watched leaves or sticks float on a stream or on water flowing in a gutter or drain? Early settlers made floating platforms, called *rafts*, that moved like the leaves and sticks. These were made by trimming the branches from several cut trees and tying the trunks together with vines. You can see a raft near the center of the picture on the next page. Rafts were easy to make, cost very little money, and could carry much larger loads than canoes. But they could not be steered like canoes, and they could not move upstream.

Flatboats were platforms made of sawed lumber, and they had boards along the edges to keep water off the platform or *deck*. Some were as large as two school classrooms end-to-end and had shelters for

The riverfront at Portsmouth was a busy place in 1886.
What would the railways on the bank of the river be used for?

people and animals. They could be steered by means of crude rudders. Sometimes a sail was used to speed movement downstream. You can see a flatboat on the Ohio River in the picture on page 25.

Throughout the 19th century, flatboats were the least expensive form of river transportation to go downstream, but they could not be moved upstream easily. When settlers reached their destinations downstream, they took the boats apart and used the wood to build houses. Later,

thousands of flatboats were used to carry farm products and other goods to New Orleans, Louisiana. The boats were sold there for lumber.

Many of the settlers in northern Ohio traveled across Lake Erie on sailing ships. Boats operating on open water, such as Lake Erie, need harbors where they can find protection during storms or in freezing weather. The only natural harbors in Ohio were Sandusky Bay and Maumee Bay. All other harbors were man-made.

Steamboats

While living in New York in 1807, Robert Fulton invented the first successful steam-powered boat in America. A few years later, he moved to Pittsburgh. In 1811 Fulton and a partner built the *New Orleans*, the first steamboat to operate on the Ohio River. This great invention made it possible to carry from five to ten times as much freight as the largest flat boat. In addition, steamboats could move upstream against the current of the river. The *New Orleans* passed Cincinnati on October 27, 1811 on its way to the city of New Orleans. A few weeks later, it passed near New Madrid, Missouri just as the great earthquake was changing the landscape.

Each year after 1811, steamboats became more important for moving people and goods on the river. The picture on the opposite page is a view of the waterfront at Portsmouth, in Scioto County, in 1886. You will notice that the closest boat carried United States mail. By 1820 steamboats were also operating on Lake Erie.

The Erie Canal in New York

When Ohio became a state, it was a frontier wilderness compared to the countries of Europe. But the roads in Europe were not much better than those in Ohio. During the last half of the 18th century, the people of England, France, and Germany began to build **canals** (man-made waterways) to improve their transportation systems. Soon after the War of 1812, citizens of the United States began to ask for canals.

Between 1800 and 1820, the population of the United States jumped from about 5 million to almost 10 million. Cities along the East Coast began to grow rapidly. Farmers in western New York State wanted to sell their food crops to the cities, but they could not move their products over the poor roads. Thousands of **immigrants** (people moving to the United States from other nations) wanted to move from the East Coast to the Ohio Country. The State of New York finally decided to build a new transportation system to solve these problems. In 1817 it began work on the *Erie Canal* to connect the Hudson River near Albany to Lake Erie at Buffalo. When the canal was finished, immigrants could travel by water across the Atlantic Ocean, up the Hudson River, across the Erie Canal and Lake Erie to Ohio. The canal boats were pulled by horses or mules walking along a *towpath*.

The Canals of Ohio

As soon as people in Ohio learned about the Erie Canal, they wanted canals for our state. But it was much easier to *talk* about canals than to build them. After five years of argument, the General Assembly decided to build two canals. The first was to run from the mouth of the Scioto River

Many miles of canals were built in Ohio between 1825 and 1850. How are the lakes on this map related to the canals?

at Portsmouth, to the mouth of the Cuyahoga River at Cleveland. The second was to run from Cincinnati to Dayton, but later it was extended to the Maumee River at Toledo. The map above shows these two canals and all the other canals built in Ohio by 1850.

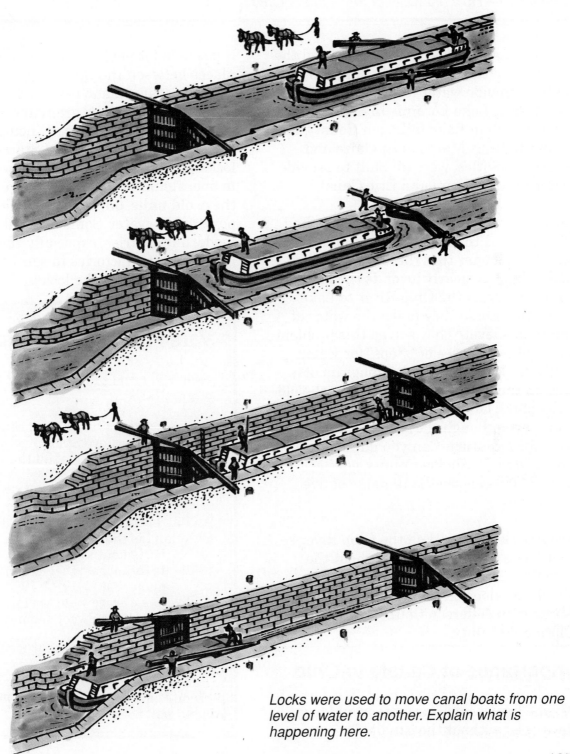

Locks were used to move canal boats from one level of water to another. Explain what is happening here.

Buckeye Lake in Fairfield County, and the Portage Lakes in Summit County were built to provide water for the Ohio and Erie Canal. Lake Loramie in Shelby County, Indian Lake in Logan County, and Grand Lake St.Marys in Auglaize and Mercer Counties, were all built to provide water for the Miami and Erie Canal.

Because water runs downhill, canals had to be built so that the water could not "run out." This meant that the water surface had to be very nearly level. Is the land of Ohio level from the Ohio River to Lake Erie? How could they make the water of the canals level? They solved this problem by building a series of "steps" for water, called **locks**. You can see a diagram of a lock on the previous page. Many of the old locks of the Ohio canals can still be seen today, even though they have not been used for a century. Can you guess how *Lockington*, in Shelby County, got its name? You can see the remains of five locks there.

Today locks are used on the Ohio River so that boats can operate throughout the year. You can see them in operation at six places along this river between Stratton in Jefferson County, and Chilo in Clermont County.

Importance of Canals to Ohio

No one knows how our state would have developed without the canals. They made it possible for people to settle in many places between the Ohio River and Lake Erie. They also made it possible for farmers to send their grain and animals to Cleveland, Columbus, Cincinnati, and the big cities of the United States. The locks provided water falls that were used to operate mills. You can still see some of these old mills, but they are no longer powered by water. Some of our large, modern industries, especially the paper-making factories in southwestern Ohio, were built at the locks.

Verse from A Canal Song

(Words shown [ ] are simplified from original.)

There's a little silver ribbon runs across
    the Buckeye State,
'Tis the dearest place of all the earth
    to me,
For upon its [quiet] surface I was born
    some years ago
And its beauty, [glory], always do I see.
Cleveland is the northern end and
    Portsmouth is the south,
While its [branches] they are many,
    many, Pal
And where e'er we went we took along
    our Home Sweet, Home,
    you know,
In those [pleasant] days upon the
    old canal.

From: Pearl R. Nye papers of Ohio Historical Society

Three kinds of boats were used on the canals: passenger boats, freight boats, and *combination* boats that carried both freight and passengers. Some boats were owned by families that lived on them, as you can see below. Very few boats operated on the canals after 1890 and none after 1913. The verse from a canal song, in the box on the previous page, will give you an idea of how people felt about the canals.

Some families lived on canal boats.
What would be the advantages and disadvantages of living like this?

You can ride on canal boats like the St. Helena at Canal Fulton in three places in Ohio. Why were all canal boats built as low as this one?

The Canals Today

You will be surprised to find how many miles of the old canals you can see today! In fact, you can take canal boat rides near Piqua in Miami County, at Roscoe Village in Coshocton County, and at Canal Fulton in Stark County. The picture above shows the boat at Canal Fulton. You can see water in several miles of the Ohio Canal in

the Cuyahoga National Recreation Area in Cuyahoga and Summit Counties. All of the lakes that were built to provide water for the canals are now used for recreation.

In the towns that grew up along the canals, you can find names that include *port, lock,* or *canal.* You can find city streets and country roads named Canal or Lock in places where you can no longer see the canal. In addition, several state highways run along the old waterways.

But just as the canal system of Ohio was being completed in 1845, entrepreneurs were beginning to build a better form of transportation that took business from the canals. In the next part, you will learn how railroads changed our state during the last half of the 19th century.

Let's Review Part 3

New Words

canal
lock (canal)
immigrant

New Things to Do

1. Take a large bucket filled with water out to a sidewalk, driveway, or street near your home. Pour small amounts of water onto the pavement in various places to get a feel for how water behaves on different slopes.

2. Experiment with blocks of wood and/or toy boats in a bath tub containing three or four inches of water. How does the object react when you make small waves? How hard is it to move the object across the tub? Write a short description of what it might be like to travel on a raft or flatboat.

Part 4

How did railroads become important?

Soon after steamboats were built, inventors tried to use steam to move vehicles over land. Because the highways were in such poor condition, they found it easier to make vehicles that moved over roads made of iron rails. In 1828 the Baltimore and Ohio Railroad operated the first passenger train in America near Baltimore, Maryland. By 1845, when the last canal was completed in Ohio, there were a few short railroads operating in our state.

Railroads were easier to build than canals, and they could be built in places where canals could not go. For 100 years, railroad trains were pulled by steam-powered **locomotives** (self-moving machines). In the earliest days, the wood for fuel and water for steam were taken from woods, creeks, and ponds along the route. Later it was found that coal was a better fuel. In 1835 the Erie and Kalamazoo [Michigan] Railroad operated the first train in Ohio, which you can see on the next page.

By 1839 there were fifteen miles of railroad track in Ohio — all in Erie County. By 1851 there were 788 miles of track in Ohio, and ten years later there were more than 3,000 miles. The map on the next page shows where these lines were. Today you can see the first engine to operate on the Cincinnati, Hamilton & Dayton Railroad in 1851. It is in the museum at Carillon Park in Dayton. By 1871 a person living in Ohio could travel by railroad to the East Coast, the West Coast, the Gulf Coast, or the Canadian border of the United States.

How fast do you travel? Very few people can walk four miles in one hour. On a bicycle, you may go twenty-five miles in an hour — if the route is not too hilly. You can go much faster in an automobile. In 1850 you could travel about two miles an hour in a canal boat or ten miles an hour in a railroad car! Even the slow freight trains were much faster than ox carts moving over dirt roads. By 1860 railroad trains

The earliest rail passenger cars looked very much like stage coaches. Judging from the size of the people, how long is this entire train?

More than 2,000 miles of railroad were built between 1851 and 1861.
Where is your home on this map? If it is on one of the rail lines, is there still a railroad there today?

moved at more than twenty miles per hour! But some people thought that human bodies could not stand such a high speed! By 1900 Ohio had one of the biggest and best rail systems in the United States, and this system had great influence on the development of our state.

Let's Review Part 4

New Words

locomotive

New Things to Do

1. Look in the "yellow pages" of your telephone directory under the heading of Railroads. Make a list of the railroads you find and their addresses. If you can find no listings, go to your local library and ask to see the *Business Yellow Pages*. Try to find the local offices and railroad tracks on a map of your county.

2. In 1900 almost every town in Ohio had a railroad station. You can still see many of these today being used for other purposes. Try to find one of these stations near where you live. Write a short report on what you find.

What have we learned?

When Ohio became a state in 1803, people were traveling from place to place in ways they had used for thousands of years. They walked or used animals to travel over land, and they sailed, rowed, or floated to travel over water. During the 19th century, many thousands of miles of highways were opened, but very few miles could be used in all kinds of weather.

By 1820 steam-powered boats improved travel for people living along Lake Erie and the Ohio River, but river travel needed enough water to float the boats. Between 1825 and 1845, travel improved greatly for people who lived near one of the new canals.

Steam engines that could move from place to place made it possible to build railroads that could operate in all kinds of weather at "high" speeds. Throughout the 19th century, the people of Ohio worked to improve their transportation system. Throughout the century, some part of almost every trip was made over unpaved roads, but canals and/or railroads greatly reduced the time and energy needed to move longer distances. These new forms of transportation helped to improve the overall economics of our state. In Chapter 13, you will learn about a new form of transportation that was created near the end of the 19th century — automobiles!

Map Projects

Find the following places on your map of Ohio.

Place	County
Buckeye Lake	Fairfield & Perry
Grand Lake St.Marys	Auglaize & Mercer
Hamilton	Butler
Indian Lake	Logan
Lake Loramie	Shelby
Maumee Bay	Lucas
Miami & Erie Canal	Hamilton to Lucas
Middletown	Butler
National Road	Belmont to Preble
Ohio Canal	Scioto to Cuyahoga
Portage Lakes	Summit
Portsmouth	Scioto
Roscoe Village	Coshocton
Sandusky Bay	Erie
Toledo	Lucas
Zane's Trace	Belmont to Brown

Find the following places on your map of the United States.

Place	States
Baltimore	Maryland
Erie Canal	New York State
Kalamazoo	Michigan
Natchez Trace	Mississippi to Tennessee
New Orleans	Louisiana
Philadelphia	Pennsylvania

Books to Read

The following books will help you understand the forms of transportation discussed in this chapter. Your library may have other books on these subjects.

General

Transport on Land, Road, and Railroad, by Eryl Daies, is a short history of the inventions that changed how we move.

Canals

The Erie Canal, by Ralph K. Andrist, is set in New York State, but many settlers of Northern Ohio used it to get to their new homes.

Story of America's Canals, by Ray Spangenburg, tells the story of building and traveling on canals from ancient times to the present.

Steamboats

Steamboat in A Cornfield, John Hartford, has many photographs and a short story of a steamboat that was left in a cornfield when the water of the Ohio River suddenly dropped.

West by Steamboat, by Tim McNeese, is the story of steamboats moving immigrants into the Ohio Country.

Railroads

Railroads: The Great American Adventure, by Charlton Ogburn, is a well-illustrated, popular story of the development of railroads in the United States.

The Spectacular Trains: A History of Rail Transportation, by John Everds, traces the story of American railroads from the earliest days to 1990.

Train, by John Coiley, is a beautifully illustrated story of how railroads came into existence and how they operate today.

Wheels Across America, by Clarence P. Hornung, has an interesting collection of pictures of land transportation in the United States. Two pictures in this chapter are from this book.

Chapter 8

How did people live during the 19th century?

Let's learn...

- **how events in Europe affected Ohio.**

- **how slavery affected Ohio.**

- **about everyday life in rural places.**

- **about religious groups that came to Ohio.**

Peace came to Ohio at the close of the War of 1812, and this made our state attractive to new settlers. In this chapter, you will learn how wars and famines in Europe, and conflicts over slavery, encouraged millions of people to move into Ohio during the 19th century. The table below shows how the population of Ohio grew during this century. The time line on the next page will help you understand the events that took place.

Ohio Population Growth During the 19th Century

Census Year	Total Population	White Population	African-American Population
1800	45,365	45,028	337
1810	230,760	228,861	1,899
1820	581,434	576,711	4,723
1830	937,903	928,329	9,574
1840	1,519,467	1,502,122	17,345
1850	1,980,329	1,955,060	25,279
1860	2,339,511	2,302,808	36,673
1870	2,665,260	2,601,946	63,213
1880	3,198,062	3,117,920	79,900
1890	3,672,316	3,584,805	87,113
1900	4,157,545	4,060,204	96,901

The United States Bureau of the Census counts the people of our nation every ten years. Why did the population of Ohio increase so much from 1800 to 1810?

Part 1

How did events in Europe affect Ohio?

In Chapters 5 and 6, you learned how the people of the United States learned to rule themselves after gaining freedom from Great Britain. Their success encouraged many people in Europe to seek freedom too. In this part, you will learn about the **migrations** (movements of large numbers of people) from some of the countries of Europe shown on the map on page 148. Was one of your **ancestors** (grandparents, great-grandparents...) a part of this migration?

France

More than any other nation, France helped the American Colonies win their freedom. When the people of France saw that it was possible to gain freedom from a king, they joined together to take control of their country. This led to almost twenty-five years of turmoil in France.

In 1790 a group of French people planned to escape from this turmoil. They paid money to a salesman in France to buy land in the Ohio Country. When they arrived in the United States, they learned that the salesman had stolen their money. To rescue them, Congress gave them land on

Time Line of Groups Migrating to Ohio

Years	Event
	Native Americans
1795	Forced to move north and east of Treaty of GreeneVille Line
1815	Forced to move into reservations in northwestern Ohio
1840	Forced to move west of the Mississippi River
	People from Europe
1619-1800	From England and Germany came to colonies on East Coast
1790	From France
1801-1900	From Great Britain (England, Ireland, Scotland, Wales)
1814	Refugees from Canada (discussed in Chapter 5)
1840-1900	From Germany
1845-1900	From Ireland
1870-1900	From Italy
1880-1920	From eastern and southeastern Europe
1880-1920	Jews from Russia and eastern Europe
	People from Africa
1620-1808	Slaves brought from Africa to North America
1808-1861	Slaves brought illegally from Africa to United States
1820-1865	Underground railroad in operation
1861-1865	Civil War
1865	Slaves freed at close of Civil War
	Religious Communities
1524	Swiss Brethren organized in Europe
1681	William Penn established Pennsylvania for Society of Friends (Quakers)
1800	Mennonites and Amish move to Ohio
1774	Ann Lee forms Millennium Church of United Believers in the Second Coming of Christ in England — later called Shakers
1787	Ann Lee and Shakers migrate to New York
1806-1910	Shaker community in Warren County
1806-1912	Shaker community in Montgomery County
1822-1889	Shaker community in Cuyahoga County
1824-1907	Shaker community in Hamilton County
1817-1898	Society of Separates operate community of Zoar in Tuscarawas County

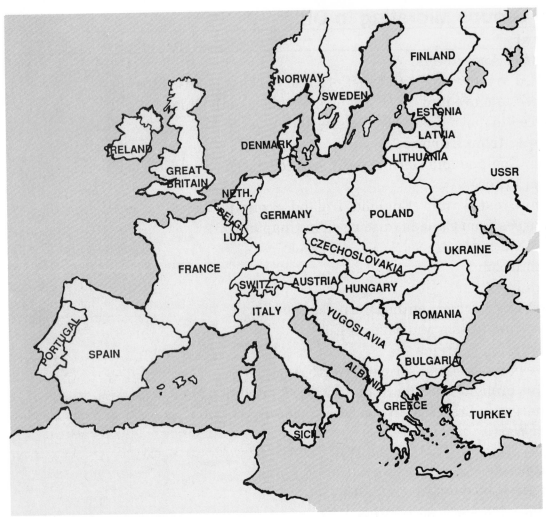

This map shows the nations of Europe in 1939. Name the people who came to Ohio from Great Britain?

the Ohio River just west of The Ohio Company, as shown on page 81.

Some of the French refugees crossed the Appalachian Mountains and created a town on the north shore of the Ohio River. They named this place *Gallipolis*, which meant "city of the Gauls." (*Gaul* was the ancient Roman name for the area we call

France.) By mistake, they actually settled on land owned by The Ohio Company. A short time later, Congress gave the remaining French people land near the mouth of the Scioto River. This second parcel is labeled *The French Grant* on the map on page 81. Few other French people migrated to Ohio.

Great Britain

During the 19th century in Great Britain, a few families were very wealthy, but most people were very poor. Some wealthy families bought land and/or set up businesses in the United States. They sent educated people to manage these businesses. Many more poor Welsh, Scottish, Scotch-Irish, and English people migrated to the United States and Ohio in the hope of finding better lives.

Germany

For several hundred years, the nation we know as Germany was divided into small states. These states fought with each other constantly, and the ordinary people suffered greatly. In order to escape from this turmoil, thousands of German people came to the American Colonies before 1776.

The turmoil in Germany continued through most of the 19th century. In addition, several times during the century, German farmers could not produce enough food to feed all the people. These times of **famine** (starvation) also encouraged millions of Germans to cross the Atlantic Ocean, and tens of thousands of them settled in Ohio. Many of these people were skilled craftsmen, and most were willing and eager to work.

Ireland

In the 19th century, Ireland was a very poor country whose main food was potatoes. In 1845 there was not enough rain for the potatoes to grow so the people were starving. Because of this, tens of thousands of unskilled Irish people migrated to America and Ohio. What kind of work can people do if they have no education and no skills? Most of the men became the laborers who built the canals, roads, and railroads you learned about in Chapter 7. The women went to work in factories and/or washed clothes for other people. Many Americans had no respect for these people, as the following story shows.

If a slave fell into the water while working on a boat on the Ohio River, the captain would stop the boat because the slave was valuable "property". If an Irishman fell into the water, the boat kept going because the captain thought the Irish were of little value.

Italy

At the time of the American Revolution, the ordinary people in Italy were very poor and had no freedom. The country was divided into many small *states* that were always fighting. During the 1870s, there was so much fighting that tens of thousands of people moved to America, and many settled in Ohio. By 1900 the largest cities of Ohio had areas called *Little Italy*

Streets of all big cities looked like this in the 19th century. How many different activities can you see in this picture?

that were filled with Italian immigrants. In 1895 an artist sketched the scene above in an Italian neighborhood of a big city.

Russia

During the 15th and 16th centuries, Christian people of Western Europe **persecuted** (badly hurt) the Jewish people who lived in their nations. The rulers of Russia were more **tolerant** (they treated the Jews better). As a result, many thousands of Jewish people moved from Western Europe to Russia.

Throughout history, the common people of Russia lived almost as slaves of their rulers and of the rich families who owned

150

all the land. Near the end of the 19th century, the Russian leaders began to persecute the Jews, and the Jews began to flee to America. Between 1880 and 1920, more than two million Jewish people left their homes in Eastern Europe to come to the United States. After 1920 a small group of *Communists* seized control of Russia and created the *Union of Soviet Socialist Republics* (USSR). The Communists would not allow anyone to leave the country. Today a very large number of Jewish people living in Ohio are descendents of the people who escaped before 1920.

Living conditions were very crowded on sailing ships. Why are these people dressed as they are?

Travel from Europe to Ohio

How long would it take you to cross the Atlantic Ocean today? Before you can answer this question, you must ask, "How will I travel?" If you go by supersonic transport, it will take less than three hours. If you go by ordinary jet plane, it will take about eight hours. If you go by fast ship, it will take five or six days. If you go by freight ship, it may take fourteen days.

In the days of sailing ships, crossing the Atlantic Ocean was a slow and unpleasant experience. The picture on the previous page is an artist's idea of such travel. As you can see, even the wealthy people in the picture traveled in crowded conditions, and everyone suffered equally when the sea was rough. The poorest people traveled under conditions that were little better than those of the slaves who were carried from Africa to America. Of course, the Europeans were not chained in one place on the ships like the slaves shown in the picture on this page.

Immigrants, who had no money for travel, could come to the United States only as **indentured** servants. This meant that they *sold* the first three to seven years of their lives in America in exchange for the cost of travel. The *sponsor*, who paid the cost of travel, agreed to provide food, clothing and shelter, and sometimes small wages. Indentured women often took care

Slave traders bought human beings in Africa and sold them in North America. How did living conditions of these slaves compare with conditions of the people shown on page 151?

of children, cooked, and did housework for their sponsors, or worked in factories owned by their sponsors. Indentured men worked for their sponsors on farms, in mines, at lumbering and other kinds of heavy labor. Indentured boys worked as **apprentices** (learner-helpers) to skilled craftsmen.

What was it like to travel from Europe to Ohio 150 years ago? The boxes on the next pages give **excerpts** (short quotations) from the diary of the leader of a group from Switzerland. These Swiss people paid for their transportation, so they traveled under better conditions than indentured people. Most immigrants had experiences like those described.

Excerpts from The Diary of Matthias Durst

(Page numbers refer to *New Glarus 1845-1970*.)

On April 16, 1845, 196 people left their homes in Switzerland because economic conditions were very difficult. They traveled by boat to the Netherlands. On May 13 the group got onto a sailing ship, and the ship left Amsterdam for America. After fifteen days at sea, Matthias Durst wrote:

On the 28th [of April] we felt and saw the consequences of our fate. On this day we had to mourn two victims. The first ...after having suffered many deaths for several days gave up the spirit at 3 o'clock in the afternoon. She was bound in a coarse linen cloth with three buckets of sand placed at her feet to [make her] sink better. (p. 53)

After a bad storm he wrote:

In the morning of the 16th [of June] there was complete calm. We did not move from the spot, and so it went all day. We longed for wind but in vain. On the 17th we had better wind again, and on the 18th things went fine. ...We had that much more reason for longing to reach shore as soon as possible as on this day our main staple potatoes, have given out... There would have been potatoes for many more days if they were healthy. But in the beginning...

we did not receive any, only to let them rot, because when one gets down to the [bottom] of the ship one's nose is filled with such a [smell] that one is almost [made ill]... (p. 63)

On the 27th day of June he wrote:

The most joyful day of the whole sea voyage! ...At about 11 o'clock the shout of joy rang out: Land! (p.71)

Three days later the ship dropped anchor in the harbor of Baltimore, Maryland. A few days after that, the people of Switzerland traveled by railroad and canal to Pittsburgh. On July 11th they boarded a steamboat to travel down the Ohio River. Mr. Durst described the river trip as follows:

It went quite well until about 10 o'clock [PM], then we stopped and started again on the morning of the 12th. [Before] noon our ship ran into another steamboat so that we believed everything was in splinters. We learned later that it was done intentionally because of a [argument]; it is supposedly not rare that they greet one another in this manner so as to do damage to each other's ships. Luckily our ship remained the victor but it too was damaged some. It is inexcusable of the crew to undertake such a daring venture and to endanger the lives of the 250 people who were on our ship. It is said to be forbidden under penalty of 500 dollars but

This boat was built in Cincinnati in 1861 and burned in 1865. Why were there so many people on this boat?

The Story of the Steamboat Sultana

The steamboat *Sultana*, shown in the picture above, was built in Cincinnati to carry about 250 passengers. It began operating just as the Civil War started in April 1861. It was used by the United States Army all through the war. In April 1865 the *Sultana* went to Vicksburg, Mississippi to remove soldiers who had been wounded or were prisoners of the Confederate Army. Almost 1,900 soldiers were crowded onto the boat, and it started up the Mississippi River to take them home. On April 27, at a point just north of Memphis, Tennessee the *Sultana* exploded. Someone took a black-and-white photograph, and an artist added the color you see. Almost 1,500 people died in this accident.

From: Display at The Cincinnati Historical Society Museum.

they do not care about that. (p.99)

The immigrants reached Cincinnati, Ohio, about 2 AM on July 18th, and Mr. Durst went sight-seeing later that day. The population of the city at that time was about 72,000. The following note from the diary will show you what a stranger thought about the largest city in Ohio.

Today I looked around some of the town. It is one of the most beautiful and largest in the [United States]. The streets are wide and paved, on both sides are walkways with cloths stretched over them and they all cross at right angles. The houses, all built of brick, in which [wealth] is apparent. (p. 109)

Many steamboat accidents were far worse than the one mentioned by Mr. Durst. For example, the picture on the previous page shows the destruction of a steamboat made in Cincinnati. You can read the story of this accident in the box below the picture.

Let's Review Part 1

New Words

ancestor
apprentice
excerpt
famine
indentured
migration

persecute
tolerant

New Things to Do

1. Go to the information about Ohio counties on page 381 (Appendix A) and copy the names of counties related to the French language. Also copy the meanings of these names. Locate these counties on your map of Ohio.

2. Many family names are related to the countries from which migrants came to the United States. For example: Names that begin with *Mc—* or *Mac—* are usually from Scotland. Names that begin with *O'—* are usually from Ireland. Names that begin with *Sch—* are usually from Germany. Use your telephone directory and count the number of names that begin with each of these three sets of letters. If you can identify names of people that came from the country of your ancestors, count these names also.

Part 2

How did slavery affect Ohio?

As you have learned, slavery created difficult problems for the founders of the United States. Most of the representatives from the southern states owned slaves.

Many representatives from the northern states wanted to **abolish** (wipe out) slavery. In 1808 Congress passed a law making it illegal to bring more people from Africa as slaves. But slave traders ignored this law and brought almost 250,000 more men, women, and children to our country between 1808 and 1861.

The argument over slavery grew as families from the East Coast moved westward.

How A Run-Away Slave Defended Himself

Ad White, a [run-away] from Kentucky...made his way to the place of [safety], and thinking he was far enough away [from the South], had quietly settled down on the farm of Udney Hyde, near Mechanicsburg [in Champaign County]. His master had tracked him to the farm of Hyde and obtained a [court order] for his arrest.... Ben Churchill, with eight others, undertook his capture. Ad was...a powerful man...and had [said he would never] return to slavery alive....Ad slept in the loft of Hyde's barn...and one person only [could enter] at a time.

Here [Ad] had...a rifle, a double-barreled shotgun, revolver, knife and axe, and had the steady nerve and skill to use them... Churchill and party arrived at Hyde's and found [Ad] in his [loft]....

Deputy-Marshall Elliott, of Cincinnati, [made] the first and only attempt to enter where White was, and as his body passed above the floor of the loft he held a shotgun before him, perhaps to protect himself, but [surely] to scare White. But White was not to be scared away...and, quick as thought, the sharp crack of a rifle rang out on the air, and Elliott dropped to the floor, not killed.... [The slave owner sued Udney Hyde for protecting a fugitive slave. Mr. Hyde was found guilty of this crime, and he was required to pay the slave owner $1,000 to "purchase" Ad.]

...Ad White was [told] of his freedom, and at once returned to Mechanicsburg, where, in 1881, he was still [living], borne down by hard work and age, but ever [enjoying] the memory of those who gave him shelter and protection...

Quoted in Howe: Vol. 1, pp. 384-6, from Beer's *History of Clark County*.

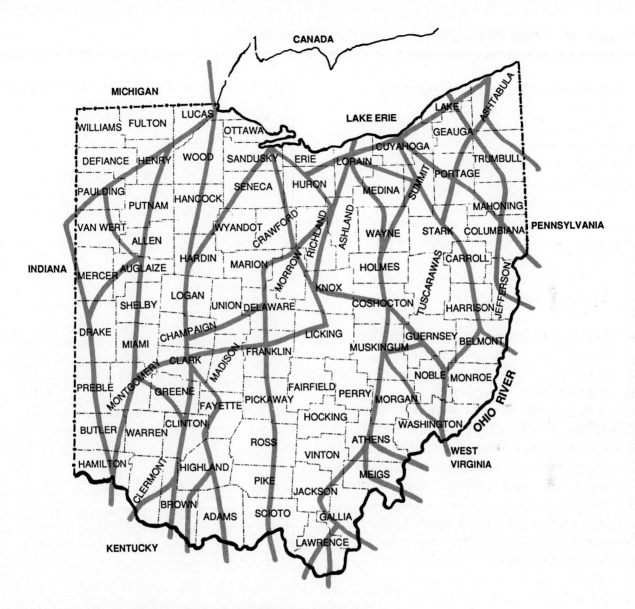

No one ever made an official map of the Underground Railroad.
Where is your home in relation to a line of the Underground Railroad?

Since the Northwest Ordinance prohibited slavery in Ohio, many slaves tried to escape into Ohio. But as you have learned, the Northwest Ordinance permitted owners of escaping slaves to enter Ohio to recapture their "property." This combination of laws led to many conflicts similar to the one described in the box on the previous page.

157

The Underground Railroad

Have you ever seen a railroad that had no tracks and no locomotives? The *Underground Railroad* connected hundreds of "safe" houses, called *stations*, scattered across Pennsylvania, Ohio, Indiana, and Illinois. The owners of these houses broke the law by helping run-away slaves escape to Canada. The map on the previous page shows the "railroads" that operated in Ohio.

The Reverend John Rankin and his wife, Jane Lowry Rankin, lived in Brown County on the edge of a high hill above the Ohio River town of Ripley. Their house could be seen from the Kentucky side of the river, and they kept a lamp burning in a window every night. Their home was the first stop on the Underground Railroad for about 2,000 escaping slaves. You can visit the house today. The Rankins had several helpers, including John Percial Parker, a freed slave whom you can learn about in the box on this page.

Levi Coffin, his wife, Catherine White Coffin, and their friends operated another important *railroad*. The Coffins were members of the *Religious Society of Friends* — people who are often called *Quakers*. Throughout the United States, the *Friends* helped slaves escape from the South. The picture on the next page is one of the best-known scenes of a station. It was painted in 1891 by Charles T. Webber,

John Percial Parker, Freedman

John Percial Parker was born into slavery in Norfolk, Virginia in 1827. He was sold at least twice before being taken to Mobile, Alabama, where he became a skilled iron worker. He was so skilled that he was able to earn money to buy his freedom in 1845. Three years later, Parker married Miranda Boulden of Cincinnati, and in 1856 they moved their family to Ripley, Ohio. He built a factory in Ripley to make things from iron. In 1886 it was the third largest factory in Ripley with 10 workers. The eight Parker children grew up to be very successful people.

The most important time of John Parker's life was the period from 1856 to 1865. During those years, he helped the Rankins move run-away slaves into the Underground Railroad. Slave owners put up a reward for anyone who could capture or kill Parker. But he continued to cross the Ohio River many times to help hundreds of escaping slaves. He died in Ripley in 1900.

Based on: The Cincinnati Enquirer, v.153, no.303, 2/8/94, page C-1 and Howe, v. 1, p. 339

In this picture of a station on the Underground Railroad, Levi Coffin is the white man in the wagon, and Catherine Coffin is the white woman in the center of the picture. How were all these run-aways hidden in the wagon?

an Ohio artist. Webber was born in 1821, and he knew how the Underground Railroad operated. He wanted to keep alive the memory of what African-Americans had once been forced to do.

The Civil War

After almost 200 years of argument between the Northern and Southern States, seven states of the South decided to create their own nation. They organized the *Confederate States of America* (CSA) and tried to take control of army and navy bases of the United States in the South. Because the counties of Kentucky were divided on the question of slavery, the state did not join the South, but it did not declare war on the CSA. You will learn more about this tragic war when you study

American History. At the end of the war in 1865, all slaves were freed.

A few African-Americans, like John Parker, gained freedom before the Civil War. Some of these *freedmen* were highly skilled craftsmen, and a few became educated in law, medicine, teaching, and preaching. The vast majority of freed *Negroes* — as they were then called — were very poor. Most of them settled in the cities of the North where they found work as laborers or as house servants. They often lived together in areas that were called *ghettos*. During the 15 years between 1865 and 1880, 40,000 former slaves moved into Ohio. The table on page 146 shows how the total number of African-American citizens of Ohio increased from fewer that 400 in 1800 to almost 100,000 in 1900.

Let's Review Part 2

New Words

abolish

New Things to Do

Find two or three classmates who have family backgrounds like yours — that is, ancestors who came from the same country, from the same county of Appalachia, from slavery, or from the same religion. Do research by talking to your older relatives and by reading. Try to learn how your ancestors were treated where they once lived, and why they came to the United States and/or Ohio. Share what you learn with your classmates.

Part 3

How did people live in rural areas?

If you look at the census information in Appendix B, you can see that in 1800 everyone lived in **rural** areas, that is, on farms and in towns having fewer than 1,500 people. By 1900 only one-half of the people of Ohio lived in rural places.

Life on Farms

Have you visited a *historic village* to learn how people lived in rural areas during the 19th century? The table on the next page gives information about the largest places in Ohio. Almost every county has a historical society, and many have museums of 19th-century life.

Throughout the 19th century, people who lived on farms had to do many things for themselves that we now pay someone to do for us. Their first houses were built from logs, and they had only the simplest of furniture. Some families got water for themselves and their animals from a **well** (a hole dug down to a supply of ground water), or from a **spring** (water running from an opening in a hillside). Some families had a **cistern** (a large stone-lined pit) to store rain water that fell on the roof of the house and/or barn. Their toilets were outdoor *privies* that had to be located so that the human wastes would not pollute the water supply. The picture on page 162 is an artist's idea of a farm during the 19th century.

Wood was the most important fuel. In the earliest days, a wood-burning fireplace was used for heating, cooking, and for lighting the cabin at night. Later, animal fat was cooked to make candles for lighting. By 1870, families could buy cast-iron stoves for heating and cooking, and oil lamps for light. Families in southeastern Ohio

19th Century Village Museums in Ohio

County	Name of Place	What You Can See
Coshocton	Roscoe Village	Many original canal town buildings still in use
Defiance	Au Glaize Village	19th century village and farm
Erie, Huron, Seneca, and Sandusky	Historic Lyme Village	5 buildings from 1817 to 1890
Franklin	Ohio Village	15 relocated buildings in the form of a 19th century village
Fulton	Sauder Farm and Craft Village	Large collection of buildings and crafts of 19th century
Geauga	Century Village	20 buildings from the 19th century Western Reserve area
Hamilton	Sharon Woods Village	10 relocated buildings in the form of a 19th centuries village
Montgomery	Carillon Historical Park	Buildings and crafts of the 19th and early 20th centuries
Summit	Hale Farm and Village	Many 19th century buildings arranged as a village
Warren	Caesar Creek Pioneer Village	About 15 relocated log houses arranged as a village

were among the first people in the United States to use coal to heat their homes and/or cook.

In the earliest days, there were two sources of energy for doing farm work: human effort and animals. The picture on page 163 shows how human energy was used to make flour by pounding on grain. The picture on page 164 shows an animal-powered *mill* for grinding grain. By 1850 farmers could buy wind-powered machines to do a few of the jobs that once required human labor.

Throughout the 19th century and into the 20th century farm families used few items they could not make themselves. Can you explain how the children got water out of the well?

During the first half of the 19th century, every farm had a vegetable garden, fruit trees, chickens to provide eggs and meat, and cows or goats to provide milk for family use. Food had to be **preserved** (saved) for winter use. Meat was smoked or packed in salt. Vegetables and fruits were cooked and stored in glass jars. Potatoes, other root crops, and grain were stored in rat-proof containers. Milk was used to make cheese. In addition, most farms raised some crops and animals to sell in the nearest town.

Farm life was lonely and difficult. Neighbors helped each other with the hardest jobs, such as building houses and barns, harvesting, and preparing food for the winter. A trip of five miles required at least two hours, because the only forms of transportation were walking, riding horseback, or riding in a horse-drawn wagon, buggy, or sled. Going to town was an important event because the farmers could sell their products and buy hardware, cloth, sugar, salt, spices, coffee, and tea. Going to church provided a chance to meet friends as well as to worship God. The *County Fair* was a big social event each summer as people "showed off" the things they had grown or made.

Life In Small Towns

Small towns were very important to the economy of the 19th century. They served as exchange points where the food raised on surrounding farms could be shipped to the cities, and the goods produced in the cities could be distributed to the farms.

Living conditions in small towns were much like those on the farms. While farm families usually had more than 50 acres of land, people living in towns seldom had more than one acre. The town lots were big enough so that the owners could have a few fruit trees, raise vegetables — and often chickens — for their own use.

People who lived in the towns were usually craftsmen or **merchants** (people who buy and sell goods). The craftsmen included dress makers, shoe makers, carpenters, blacksmiths, wagon makers, mill operators, tin smiths, and furniture

A large amount of human energy was needed to grind grain in a device like this. How might pre-historic people have made a device like this?

An animal was tied to the end of the pole and made to walk in a circle to grind grain. Why are there two platforms at the post?

makers. Merchants bought food from nearby farms and either sold it to the town people or hauled it to a larger city. They bought things in the city that could not be made in the town and sold them to the people living in and around the town.

Many towns were along creeks that could be dammed to provide water power to operate a mill. The town water supply might be the mill pond, a well in the market area, or cisterns in every yard. Some people earned their living by selling water, which they carried in barrels on water wagons from a nearby pond to the houses of the town.

Circuit Riders

Do you know what a *circuit* is? This word is closely related to *circle*, because a circuit forms a closed loop. When new parts of Ohio were opened to settlement, there were very few doctors, lawyers, teachers, or religious leaders to serve the settlers. The judges of a county had to *ride circuit*, that is, go from place to place to settle conflicts. Lawyers rode circuit

with the judges to help people solve
legal problems.

Education was a problem for people in
rural areas. In some cases, teachers
created *boarding schools* in towns.
Children lived near the school for four or
five days a week and spent weekends at
their homes. Later, when there were
enough people in an area, they worked
together to build a school and to hire a
teacher for their children. But many
children had to walk long distances.

Many people in rural areas wanted
religious leaders to help them worship
God, to marry them, and to pray at time
of death. Since few rural areas could
afford full-time religious leaders,
these men also *rode circuit*.

Johnny Appleseed

John Chapman was one of the best known
men in Ohio during the first half of the
19th century. Even today, he is part of the
legend of our state. No one really knows
why he spent his life traveling around
Ohio and nearby areas. He traveled from
farm to farm and town to town. In a sense,
he was a traveling newspaper, because he
told people what was happening in other
parts of the state. But most importantly,
everywhere he went, he planted apple
trees. He planted so many of these trees,
in so many places, for so many years, that
everyone called him *Johnny Appleseed*.

*Johnny Appleseed planted thousands of apple
trees in Ohio. What do you do with the seeds
from apples you eat?*

The picture on this page shows how an
artist thought he looked. You can visit his
grave in Ashland, the county seat of
Ashland County.

By the end of the 19th century, many farm
families enjoyed the labor-saving
equipment you can see on page 167. The
largest farms had steam-powered
machinery to do many of the hardest jobs.
The railroads made it possible to move
farm products to the big cities of Ohio and

the East Coast. But life on the small farms did not change much until about 1940 when electricity became available in rural areas.

Let's Review Part 3

New Words

cistern
merchant
preserve
rural
spring (water)
well (water)

New Things to Do

Pretend that you live in the house shown on page 162 in the year 1840. The road shown on the picture leads to a small town five miles away, which is a station on the Underground Railroad. Write a story about how your family might celebrate your tenth birthday.

Part 4

Why did religious groups come to Ohio?

Are you ever told that you are "wrong" about something you believe in? Has another person hurt you because of your

belief? During the 18th and 19th centuries, many of the wars in Europe were about differences in religious beliefs. Several groups of people refused to fight because they believed that everyone should live together in peace. They came to America in the hope of finding that peace. Three of these groups came to Ohio to practice some form of **communal** (shared) living. Each group believed in living by a passage from the Christian Bible that you can read about in Acts 4:32-35.

Mennonites

In 1524 a group of religious people in Switzerland organized themselves as the *Swiss Brethren*. By 1561 almost everyone called them *Mennonites*. During the 17th century, several new ways of farming and manufacturing were developed. Many Mennonites accepted these new ideas, but Jacob Amman opposed them. Mennonites who supported Amman became known as *Amish* people in honor of their leader.

The Mennonites and Amish would not fight in the wars in Europe. When their neighbors attacked them, they fled to England. When the English people began to abuse them, they moved to William Penn's colony of Pennsylvania. Because they believed very strongly in peace, they would not fight in the American Revolution. When patriotic Americans abused them, the Mennonites and Amish moved westward into Ohio.

Today Mennonite and Amish people continue to practice *communal responsibility*. This means that each family owns the land on which it lives and the equipment it uses, but they always help each other in times of need. For example, the picture you will see on the next page shows Amish people in Holmes County helping a neighbor whose barn burned in 1989.

The question about whether new ideas should be accepted or opposed continues to divide the Mennonites and the Amish. Mennonites use electricity in their homes, tractors on their farms, and automobiles to travel. The Amish use only oil or wood or coal for heating and cooking, oil for lighting their homes, and horse-drawn equipment for farming and transportation.

You can see these 19th century household "machines" at the Walcott House Museum at Maumee. What form of energy was used to operate these machines?

When a Amish barn burned in 1989, neighbors worked together to build a new one.
How many people can you count on this picture? How can so many people work so close together?

While riding along a rural road, have you ever seen a sign that says: HORSE-DRAWN VEHICLES AHEAD? Have you seen vehicles like the one on the next page? You can see many such signs and vehicles in Geauga, Holmes, and Wayne Counties in northeastern Ohio, and in Williams and Fulton Counties in northwestern Ohio. Holmes County has the largest number of Amish families of any county in the United States. During the 1980s, a group of Amish families moved from northeastern Ohio to Adams County. Many Mennonites live in Madison and Allen Counties.

Shakers

In 1774 Ann Lee and seven friends moved from England to New York City, because she had a dream that told her ordinary people did not have to live in misery. She believed that they could solve their problems by working together. She had another dream that the world would soon end. A group of people believed her, and together they formed the *Millennium Church of United Believers in the Second Coming of Christ*. A short time later, these believers came to be known as *Shakers*, because their bodies shook when they worshipped God.

Between 1787 and 1896, twenty-four Shaker communities were organized in the eastern United States. As you can see on the time line on page 147, four of these

communities were in Ohio. You can still see buildings of the Warren County community at the *Otterbein Retirement Community* on State Route 63 near State Route 741. The Montgomery County community disappeared completely. The Cuyahoga County community disappeared when the city of *Shaker Heights* was built during the 1920s. Several of the original buildings of the Hamilton County community are still standing, and they may soon be included in a historical park.

The Shakers practiced true communal living. No individual owned anything, and each accepted the discipline of the group. They were hard working people and invented all kinds of devices to make their lives easier. They were the first people to harvest and package seeds of flowers and vegetables to sell in stores. But they did NOT do one thing, and this helped to end their existence — they were so sure that the world was going to end that they did not marry and produce children.

Society of Separates

In 1817 a group of German people wanted to separate themselves from the churches of that time. They migrated to the Tuscarawas River in Ohio. By combining their time, talent, and money, they bought a large area of land on the north boundary of Tuscarawas County. These people called themselves the *Society of Separates*, and named their community *Zoar* from a story in the Bible.

Amish people still use the only form of personal transportation available in the year 1900. What kind of "fuel" is needed to operate this form of transportation?

The members of the Society of Separates owned nothing as individuals. They worked together to build large brick buildings and create excellent farms. In 1898 the peace and harmony of the group ended and the community broke apart. The people living at Zoar sold the land and buildings and divided the money between themselves. The Ohio Historical Society now owns some of the buildings and land, so that we can learn how this form of communal living once existed in Ohio.

Let's Review Part 4

New Words

communal

New Things to Do

Pretend that it is the year 1850, and that you are a reporter for your county newspaper. Do some research in your county library and write a newspaper article about one of the individuals or groups of people discussed in this part.

What have we learned?

Life was not easy in the United States at the beginning of the 19th century. It was very hard in the wilderness of Ohio. At the same time, life was even more difficult for ordinary people in Europe. As a result, millions of people migrated from Europe to seek new lives in the freedom of our new nation and state.

By 1850 Ohio had several large cities and a good transportation system. Because conditions in Europe continued to be bad, hundreds of thousands of people migrated across the ocean in the hope of improving their lives. At the close of the Civil War, African-Americans were freed from slavery in the South and thousands of them migrated to Ohio. By the close of the

century, more than four million people were living in our state.

During the first half of the 19th century, almost every family had to raise at least some of its food. Towns developed as central places where farmers could exchange their crops for goods and services they needed. By the end of the century, Ohio had two of the largest cities in the United States, while fewer than one-half of the people lived in rural areas. In the next chapter, you will learn about the cities that developed during this century.

Map Projects

Find the following places on your map of Ohio.

Place	County
Akron	Summit
Gallipolis	Gallia
Mechanicsburg	Champaign
Salem	Columbiana
Shaker Heights	Cuyahoga
Zoar	Tuscarawas

Find the following places on your map of the world.

Place	Continent
France	Europe
Germany	Europe
Great Britain	Europe
Ireland	Europe
Italy	Europe
Russia	Europe and Asia
Switzerland	Europe

Books to Read

The following books will help you understand the ideas discussed in this chapter. Your library may have other books on these subjects.

Books about Immigrants

Appalachia: The Mountains, the Place, and The People, by Betty L. Toone, explains how immigrants moved into the southeastern part of our state, and how they have lived over the years.

Coming to America, by Albert Robbins, tells why millions of people left their homes in Europe to look for new lives in America.

The Russian Americans, by Paul R. Magocsi, is the story of Russian people who came to America.

Books about Slavery

The African Americans, by Howard Smead, is a short history of people of Africa who were forced into slavery in 1600 AD and their descendants in America today.

Get on Board, The Story of The Underground Railroad, by James Haskins, tells the story of escaping slaves and the people of the North who helped them.

The Story of Harriet Beecher Stowe, by Maureen Ash, has many pictures relating to the woman who did so much to end slavery.

Books about 19th-Century Life

Growing Up Amish, by Richard Ammon, describes how Amish people live today from the point of view of a school girl.

John Chapman: The Man Who Was Johnny Appleseed, by Carol Greene, is the life story of the man who did so much to help people in the rural parts of Ohio.

The Olden Days, by Joe Mathieu, has many pictures of 19th-century life in a small town.

Chapter 9

How did the cities of Ohio develop?

Let's learn...

- **why some settlements grew to become large cities.**

- **how people lived in cities during the 19th century.**

In the last chapter, you learned how the population of Ohio grew from 40,000 in 1800 to more than 4,000,000 in 1900. In 1800 everyone lived on farms or in small towns. By 1900 half the people lived in **urban** places (villages and cities). In this chapter, you will learn how the cities you know today were created out of the dense forests that once covered most of Ohio.

Part 1

Why did some settlements grow into big cities?

In Chapter 5, you learned how the first settlers came into Ohio. You also learned that the companies that bought large areas of land from Congress had plans to create towns. None of them could have dreamed that their towns would become the cities we know today! In 1800 no city of the world had more than 100,000 people. In this part, you will learn about the pattern of activities that changed a wilderness into cities. The diagram on this page will help you understand this process. But the first step must be to learn the meanings of several words.

Meanings of Words

We have been using words like *settlement, town, village,* and *city* without agreeing on what they mean. Now we must look at these and a few related words more closely.

Settlement

Any small group of migrants could create a *settlement* in the Ohio Country. Many such groups had no fixed goal for their journey west. Sooner or later, they became tired of traveling and decided to "settle down" in a

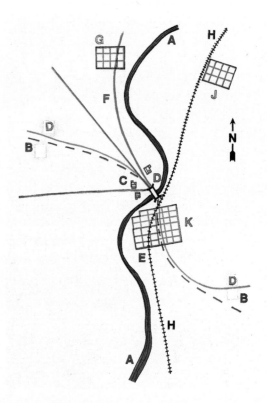

Diagram of early steps in changing a wilderness into a city.

A. Stream
B. Trail created by natives and animals
C. Three friends buy land, divide it into three parts, and build homes close together
D. Turnpike company improves the trail and builds a bridge
E. An entrepreneur lays out a town along the turnpike
F. Second turnpike company builds a new road northward from bridge
G. Another entrepreneur lays out new town along turnpike
H. Two towns compete to have railroad built on that side of stream
J. Third town built along railroad track
K. First town expands

suitable place. They built shelters and tried to create a supply of food. Some of these early settlements disappeared, a few grew to become cities, but many continue to exist today as small groups of buildings near the intersections of roads. The diagram on the previous page shows that three families bought large parcels of land and built their houses close together for protection and help. They chose this location because an old trail crossed a stream at this point. Without any thought for the future, this became the first step in the development of a city.

Town

In some cases, land owners decided to create *towns* that would attract other settlers. In Chapter 5, you learned about Marietta, Cincinnati, and Cleveland. The earliest towns were along the Ohio River and Lake Erie so that new-comers could reach them easily. Later, towns were created along the rivers that empty into the Ohio River and Lake Erie. Still later, towns were created along the canals, turnpikes, and railroads.

The owners of each town created a *subdivision plat* showing streets, house lots, and public places. Certain areas were set aside for a **market** (an open space for selling food and other goods), a school, a church, and perhaps a cemetery. In order to attract people to the town, the owners

advertised in newspapers along the East Coast, and even in Europe.

Not all town developers were completely honest in their advertising. For example, you can turn back to page 83 to see the 1829 plan for the Town of Nassau. This town had a market place and parcels for a school and two churches. Three of the streets led to the Ohio River, and Main Street was part of an important county road. The plat does NOT show that Water Street would be flooded at least once every year, NOR that there was a steep slope from Water Street up to High Street. But people on the East Coast or in Europe did not know this.

Corporations

The first constitution of Ohio said that the General Assembly could create **corporations**. A *corporation* is an organization formed under state laws to act as a **legal** (lawful) body for certain purposes. Most of the companies that make and/or sell the things you buy are private corporations. Some companies use the word in their names, as *General Motors Corporation*. Many other companies use the symbol *Inc.*, which means *Incorporated*. Every village and city of Ohio is a **municipal** corporation, or a *municipality*. Each municipality has exact boundaries that separate it from the surrounding townships or counties. There are two kinds of municipalities in Ohio,

villages and **cities**. A *village* is an incorporated place with fewer than 5,000 people. A *city* is an incorporated place with 5,000 or more people.

Why Some Towns Grew

If every town of Ohio began as a simple plan, why did some grow to become large cities while others did not? We can only look at a few reasons why such development took place. We will first look at three reasons related to geography and then at three reasons related to human behavior.

Location

A *settlement* could be made wherever there was a supply of water, land for farming, and material for building shelters. If the chosen area did not have all three of these resources, the settlement could not survive. If there was a planned town, but only a small area of suitable land, the town was not likely to grow. For example, in Chapter 2, you learned that the southeastern half of Ohio is hilly and has poor soils for agriculture. The early settlements along the rivers in the Southeast did not grow into big cities because the small areas of level land were subject to flooding.

Accessibility

Land has value only if it is **accessible**, that is, if people can get to it. Each settlement and town created during the 19th century was along the best transportation route available at that time. The diagram on page 174 shows that the original trail through the settlement became part of a turnpike, and the turnpike company built a bridge across the stream. Because of this improved accessibility, someone platted a town across the bridge from the original settlement. Next, a road was established on the west side of the stream northward from the bridge. This new road encouraged another person to plat a second town along it.

Each new form of transportation affected the development of towns. When the canals were built, new towns served as central places for farmers sending their products to the big cities. A historical marker in Delphos, on the line between Allen and Van Wert Counties, tells how transportation affected that village. The box on the next page simplifies the message.

When the railroads were built, towns competed with each other to be on the rail lines to improve their accessibility. For example, the next stage of development on the diagram on page 174 was construction by the railroad. Both of the existing towns

During the 19th century, there were many water wheels like this in Ohio. What happens to the water at the bottom of the wheel?

Simplified Message on Historical Marker at Delphos

Delphos was settled and grew as a canal town. It was originally four separate settlements that grew together. The town became a center of activity on the Miami and Erie Canal, second in size only to Fort Wayne, Indiana. The first canal boat passed through Delphos on July 4, 1845.

Farmers from miles around came to load their fruits, vegetables, grain, and animals on the canal boats. When the *Ohio and Indiana Railroad* was built in 1854, from Crestline in Crawford County, Ohio to Fort Wayne, it did not pass through Delphos. As a result, the farmers stopped coming to Delphos and the city stopped growing.

encouraged the railroad company to build on its side of the stream. The company chose to build on the east side, and the first town began to expand. Later, a third town was platted to the north along the railroad track.

Supply of Energy

No settlement could grow without a dependable source of energy beyond that of humans and animals. For this reason, many early settlements were made along streams that could provide water to operate mills like the one shown on the previous page. It took a large amount of human energy and animal energy to build a mill. Once built, the mill could grind grain, saw lumber, and do other heavy work with a very small amount of human effort. Few towns grew if they did not have a mill.

When the canals were opened for transportation, mills were built at many of the locks to use the energy of falling water. You can still see some of these, as shown on this page. By 1825 the energy of *steam* could be used to do much more work than water mills. You will learn about this in the next chapter.

Entrepreneurs

Entrepreneurs are people who get things done, usually for a profit to themselves. They know how to set goals and they work

hard to reach them. No town became a big city unless entrepreneurs worked to make this happen. In the diagram on page 171, some entrepreneurs built the turnpike and bridge, and others built the first town. Still others built the railroad and laid out the other towns. On the other hand, some towns in ideal locations did not grow, because the citizens did not want them to grow.

This building was a water mill at a lock on the Miami and Erie Canal at Tipp City. What kind of energy may this mill use today?

From what you learned about Simon Kenton in earlier chapters, would you say that he was an entrepreneur? Kenton "owned" thousands of acres of land as payment for the many things he did to help George Rogers Clark and the settlers in Kentucky. Because he never stayed in one place for a long time, most of his land in Kentucky was taken by other settlers. In 1801 he decided to settle down with his wife and children on land he owned in what we know as Clark County. He built a mill to grind grain and saw lumber. In 1803 the town of Springfield was platted next to Kenton's land.

Kenton continued to spend most of his time fighting against the natives who did not live by the Treaty of Greenville. As a result, his mill fell into ruins. In 1810 he could not repay money that he owed to other people so he was thrown into jail in Urbana. But he was so popular with the people of the county that they elected him *county jailer*, which means that he was in charge of the jail in which he was a prisoner! The picture on this page makes him look like an entrepreneur, but he seldom wore such clothes.

In the last years of his life, Simon Kenton dressed like this. How would you describe Simon Kenton from this picture?

Politics

Politics can be defined as, "the art of people living together in groups." In order for a town to grow, the people living in it had to work together to create a government. Politics is closely related to the creation of laws, as you will learn in later chapters. It played an important part in the growth of every town in Ohio. For example, the seat of government is almost always the largest town in a county, but who decided where the *county seat* should be? As new, smaller counties were created from larger ones, as shown on page 102, several settlements often competed to be named the county seat. As you can see on the map on the next page, in 1900 two-thirds of the counties had only one or two towns of more than 1,500 population. One of these was always the

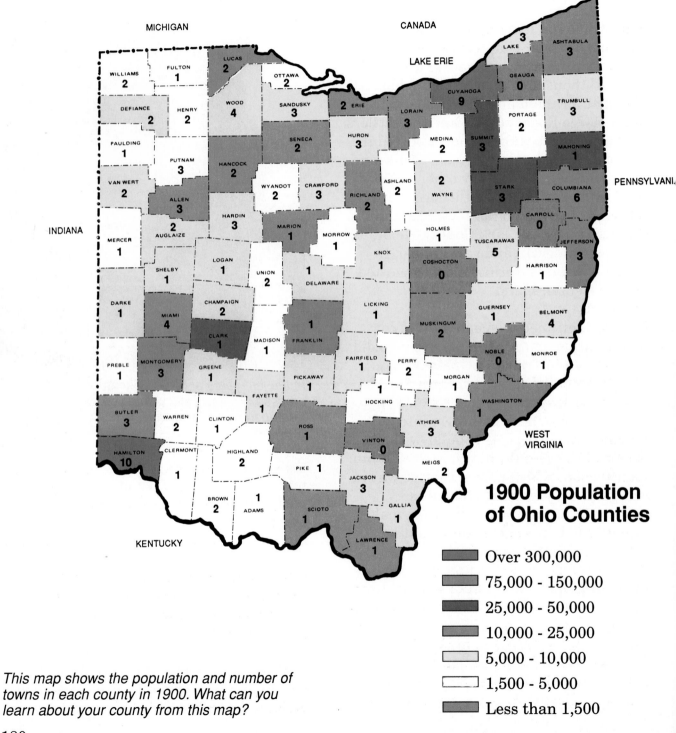

1900 Population of Ohio Counties

	Over 300,000
	75,000 - 150,000
	25,000 - 50,000
	10,000 - 25,000
	5,000 - 10,000
	1,500 - 5,000
	Less than 1,500

This map shows the population and number of towns in each county in 1900. What can you learn about your county from this map?

180

county seat. Even today, there are very few counties where the county seat is not the largest town.

The first town in an area often became the county seat. For example, in 1796 Nathaniel Massie laid out Chillicothe in the wilderness along the Scioto River. When Ross County was formed in 1798, Chillicothe was made the county seat. When Ohio became a state in 1803, Chillicothe was made the first capital because of its central location and easy accessibility. As more and more people moved into northern Ohio, they wanted the seat of government to be closer to them. In 1808 the towns of Putnam and Zanesville, on opposite sides of the Muskingum River, competed to be the new capital. Zanesville won the contest, and today Putnam is part of Zanesville.

When the General Assembly met at Zanesville in 1810, it decided to move the capital even closer to the center of the state. The towns of Delaware, Dublin, Franklinton, and Worthington each wanted the law makers to choose their town. Franklinton was platted in 1797 on the west bank of the Scioto River. When Franklin County was established in 1803, Franklinton was made the county seat. In that same year, James Kilbourne platted the town of Worthington in Franklin County. One of the first buildings Kilbourne built was the church shown on this page. Delaware County was formed

This church was built in the town of Worthington in 1803. Where did the bricks come from to build this church?

from Franklin County in 1808, and the town of Delaware was made the county seat. The town of Dublin was platted in 1818.

With so many places to choose from, how did the General Assembly make a decision? Writers of the *The Ohio Guide* said,

"Dublin was chosen as the capital of the State by a [committee] appointed for that purpose, but political horse trading [cancelled] its selection."

On the basis of this "political horse trading," the General Assembly decided that Franklinton was most attractive for reasons explained in the box below.

How Columbus Became the Capital City of Ohio

In the winter of 1810, four citizens of Franklinton formed a company to establish the State capitol "on the high bank of the Scioto river opposite Franklinton." They offered to give the State two separate pieces of land of ten acres each. One lot was to be for the capitol and the other for the state prison. As one writer said, these leaders of Franklinton felt that "...equal and immediate quarters should be provided alike for the *law makers* and the *law breakers*." They also agreed to spend up to $50,000 to build the capitol and prison.

Adapted from: Howe: Vol. I, p. 619

You can see the first capitol in Columbus on the next page. Today Delaware is still the county seat of Delaware County; Dublin and Worthington are cities in Franklin County; but you cannot find Franklinton on a state map, because it is part of inner-city Columbus.

Boosters

Every settlement that grew to be a big city had entrepreneurs who were also *boosters*. These people were so enthusiastic about the future of the town that they told everyone — far and wide — how wonderful it was. They wrote letters to friends and relatives in Europe and the Eastern States. They had artists make drawings — there were no photographs before 1840 — and they sent copies of these drawings to newspapers and magazines. They tried to show visitors how much better life was in their town than in other places. If there were two towns alike in all ways, except that one had *boosters* and the other did not, the town with *boosters* grew faster! Does your school have a *Boosters Club* that works to support school activities?

How Central Places Grew

Early in the 19th century, some towns were central places because they had mills for grinding grain and/or sawing lumber. Others had blacksmith shops for making ironware. Others had merchants who sold sugar, salt, clothing, and other necessary items. As the economy of an area improved, people were able to produce more goods than they needed for themselves. They also gained some free time for pleasure and recreation. Perhaps they wanted to buy books or rubber boots, or go to a theater — there were no "movies". As soon as entrepreneurs learned that there was a need for such things, some of them tried to supply the need. The town that had the first book store, boot shop, and/or theater attracted customers from a larger area, so it became a larger central place.

As the economy continued to grow, some people wanted to buy better furniture — perhaps a piano, or they wanted to hear an orchestra perform. If entrepreneurs in one of the growing towns satisfied these new wants, that town grew even more. But only a few towns could become very large cities, with large stores, hospitals, and special schools, because not everyone needed such

The building on the right was the first capitol in Columbus. How does this building compare with the capitol in Chillicothe, as shown on page 104?

goods and/or services. In addition to showing the number of towns of 1,500 or more people in 1900, the map on page 180 shows how the population of Ohio was divided among the counties. Cleveland and Cincinnati were, by far, the largest central places in the state. At the same time, Cuyahoga County and Hamilton County had far more towns of over 1,500 population than any other counties.

Patterns of Central Places

Why did the largest cities of Ohio grow in the 50-mile-wide (80-kilometer) diagonal band you can see on page 8? No one *planned* that this should happen. The town of Cincinnati was platted in 1788 because entrepreneurs thought that it was a good location. When Fort Washington was built, Cincinnati became a central place for a large part of the Ohio River Valley. By the 1830s, there were turnpikes leading to Cincinnati from all directions. As the south end of the Miami and Erie Canal, it became the central place for much of western Ohio and eastern Indiana. Because it was a large central place during the 1840s, it became a center of railroad construction, which led to further growth.

In 1795 the Connecticut Land Company bought a large area in northeastern Ohio and had Moses Cleaveland survey it for development. Cleaveland decided to lay out a town at the mouth of the Cuyahoga River, and this town became the central place for all later development in northern Ohio. During the 1820s, Cleveland became even more important as the northern end of the Ohio and Erie Canal. When railroads were built, Cleveland was on the best route between New York and New England in the East and the great farm lands of the Middle West. By 1890 Cleveland was also the center of the petroleum and steel industries of America.

When the state capital was moved to Columbus, that city became the central place for government of our state. Turnpikes were built to connect it to all the county seats, but Columbus never had good transportation by water.

No one *planned* that Columbus should be about mid-way between Cincinnati and Cleveland, but once it happened, more and more people moved back and forth between these three cities. This movement encouraged other entrepreneurs to build towns along the route. As a result, a very large part of the population of our state lives in the yellow band shown on the map on page 8.

Let's Review Part 1

New words

accessible
city
corporation

entrepreneur
legal
market
municipal
politics
town
urban
village

New things to do

Use a map of your county and the "business pages" of your local telephone directory to make a list of the central places in your county. If you live in a very large county, do this for about one-quarter of the area. Note whether each place is a city or village. Write a short report of how these places seem to be related to your county seat.

Part 2

How did people live in cities?

In the last chapter, you learned how people lived in rural areas during the 19th century. Life in the cities was very different. All big cities began as small towns, but as the population increased, people were forced to live very close together. While such conditions seem unpleasant to us today, they were better than the immigrants had known in Europe. In this part, you will learn how life in the cities changed during the 19th century.

Houses

Towns created before 1820 often had *inlots* and *outlots*. People built their houses on

The main street of Lancaster, the county seat of Fairfield County, looked like this in 1846. What would you say the first two buildings on each side of the street were used for?

The main street of Lancaster looked like this in 1886. How many different kinds of horse-drawn vehicles can you see?

the small *inlots* and raised food on the nearby, larger *outlots*. The inlots were usually about 25 feet by 100 feet in size. The first houses were usually made of logs. Even wealthy people, like the Worthingtons of Chillicothe, lived in log houses until they could build brick homes like Adena shown on page 107. When bricks were used, they were made by hand close to the house being built.

By 1850 newer houses were two or three stories high. They often had a store or workshop on the first floor and living space above. The buildings usually covered most of the area of the lots on which they were built. If the town continued to grow, by 1870 many of the buildings were four or five stories high — but no higher because there were no elevators. On the previous page and on this page you can see how the main street of Lancaster, the county seat of Fairfield County, changed as that city grew between 1846 and 1886. You can find buildings like those on this page in almost every old town of Ohio. The picture on the next page shows the fronts, sides, and backs of big-city houses of the 1850s.

During most of the 19th century, houses were lighted by burning candles or oil lamps. By the end of the 19th century, most houses were lighted by burning gas. The rooms were heated by burning wood or coal in a fireplace or cast iron stove. Some people earned their living by going from house to house to sell small amounts of firewood and/or coal. **Soot** (small bits of carbon from burned coal), fumes, and fires were common problems.

In the earliest days, the only sources of water were public wells, streams, and *water wagons* that delivered it from house to house. Sooner or later, the town found it necessary to lay pipes under the streets to carry water to the houses, but there was only one faucet for each house. By 1900 most houses had a faucet for each family.

Human and animal wastes created big problems. In the earliest days, each building lot had one or two outdoor privies like those used in rural areas. During the second half of the 19th century, the larger cities built **sewer** systems by laying pipes underground to carry away the **sewage** (human wastes). But sewers were not useful until the water supplies were large enough to flush out the sewer pipes. The sewage was then flushed into the streams where it created more problems. Large numbers of people died from typhoid fever, typhus, cholera, and dysentery, because no one knew as much as we do now about the bacteria and viruses in sewage.

Transportation Within Cities

When a town reached a population of 3,000 to 4,000, it was too large for people to walk everywhere. Entrepreneurs then provided transportation-for-hire. The earliest **omnibuses** (a Latin word meaning "for everyone") were simple four-wheel, horse-drawn wagons with a few benches for riders to sit on. Riding in an omnibus was a slow and rather painful experience, because the streets were not paved. But riding did save human energy.

During the 1850s and 1860s, entrepreneurs in many towns of Ohio

As the population of Ohio grew during the 19th century, many people lived in houses like these in the largest cities. If each family had two rooms, how many families may have lived in the house closest to the camera?

Columbus, Ohio had a horse-drawn street railway system in the 1870s. Our present capitol was built during the 1860s. Why is this building so much larger than the one on page 183?

built **street railways** by laying tracks in city streets. Horse-drawn wagons could move along these tracks with greater speed and comfort, because the wheels did not bog down in the mud. This form of transportation made it possible for cities to grow even more, because people could live farther from their places of work and shopping. The following table shows how transportation affected Cincinnati.

Year	Area	Population	Transportation
1849	2 sq.miles	110,000	Omnibuses
1870	8 sq.miles	216,000	Street Railways

The picture on this page shows an early streetcar in Columbus, Ohio. In 1890 **inventors** (people who make new things) created electric motors to take the place of horses for moving the streetcars. The larger cities then began to grow rapidly, as you will learn in a later chapter.

Wagons like this were used to deliver milk, baked goods, and other foods to house from 1820 until 1920. How did they keep the milk clean and fresh?

Food

Since walking was the main form of transportation, people had to buy food close to where they lived. They had to buy some types of food almost every day, because there was no refrigeration to prevent spoilage. Every neighborhood had stores that sold canned and dried foods,

fruits and vegetables, and meats, but very few stores sold all of these types of food. Small bakeries sold bread, rolls, and pastries baked in the building. Milk was sold from wagons like that shown above.

By 1850 entrepreneurs were selling blocks of ice to families to keep meats, fruits, vegetables, and milk from spoiling so

For many years, the canals of Ohio were an important source of ice. Would you want to use this ice in a cold drink? Why or why not?

quickly. This ice was taken from the canals and lakes of Ohio during the winter months. The picture above shows how the ice was cut and removed from a canal. After the ice was removed, it had to be hauled to the towns and stored in special buildings to keep it from melting.

Social Conditions

At the beginning of the 19th century, there were no laws regulating working conditions or the general welfare of the people. By 1900, there were a few laws, but men worked long hours at tiring jobs. Because of crowded housing, *saloons* — places that sold alcoholic drinks, food,

and entertainment — were popular for relaxation. Drinking often led to accidents and fights.

Women had very hard lives because they were expected to bear many children under very difficult conditions. They could not vote or own land, and they received no help from the government if they lost their husbands. It was very difficult for a single mother to support her children, as explained in the box on the next page.

Wealthy People

Wealthy people faced all of the problems that ordinary people faced, but they could

190

Excerpts from A Widow's Story

Note! Words in [ ] have been simplified.

In a small room of a [crowded] house on an alley we found a widow who was trying to support herself and a little boy by making vests. Everything about her spoke of better days, and when we stated our business she [turned red] and seemed unwilling to discuss the subject... A pile of woolen vests lay on a table.... Although of [poor] material, they were made...neatly....

"If I work steadily all day, and quite late at night," she said, "I can make fourteen of these a week, but I hardly ever go to bed at all Friday night, as I must have them done by Saturday noon in order to get my pay.... When the time arrives [on Saturday afternoon to have the work examined] I tremble from head to foot with [fear], for the fellow who [examines it is nasty]. If he cannot find a flaw in the work, he will say, 'Can't you make more than a dozen vests a week?...' ... and it [hurts] me so to take abuse from a person so utterly beneath me in every way."

"And what", we asked, "do you get for these vests?" "Only fourteen cents each," was the answer. "Then you make, with all this toil, $1.96 a week?" "Yes, and sometimes even less, and the rent for this room is $2.00 a month." "Then." we suggested, "you have only about $5.50 a month to live on?"

"Not even that, for my [sewing] machine is not yet paid for, and I ought to have $3.00 a month for payments on that. This I have been unable to do lately, for my child has been sick, and I had to buy [special things] for him. I am ashamed," she continued, "to tell you how little we spend on food. ...I would never then have believed that anyone could exist on what I have had to this winter."

Quoted in An Ohio Reader, pp. 153-4 from "Women's Work", Third Annual Report of the Bureau of Labor Statistics, 1879, pp. 267-270

President William Howard Taft was born in this house on the edge of Cincinnati. He is one of the boys you can see. What can you say about the Taft family from this picture?

solve them with less effort. Those who chose to live in the cities bought several small parcels of land so that they could build larger homes and have open space around them. They built cisterns to catch rain water for private water supplies. They hired servants — who were often indentured — to do most of the house work, including carrying the human wastes from "slop jars" used in the houses to outdoor privies. They built their own storage places for food and for ice.

Most of all, wealthy people owned horses and carriages so that they could move to the outskirts of town "to get away from the noise and dirt of the city." When you visit a large city today, you can often find 19th century houses of wealthy people within two miles of the center of town. By 1950, most of these fine houses were in areas considered to be **slums** (run-down housing). In recent years, some of these buildings have been fixed up for modern uses.

The picture above shows the house in which William Howard Taft was born in 1857. This house was built in 1840 on a hilltop about two miles from the heart of Cincinnati. By 1940 it was used as apartments for several low-income families. In 1950 a group that works to **preserve** (save) historic places bought the house and gave it to the National Park Service. The building was then restored to the way it was when young "Billy" Taft lived there, and you can visit it today.

You have learned how steam railroads spread across our state between 1840 and 1900. As soon as a new line was built, entrepreneurs began to create new towns for wealthy people from five to fifteen miles from the centers of the big cities. They advertised: "Live in the country, away from the noise and dirt of the city and be only thirty minutes from your place of work." Glendale, in Hamilton County, was one of the first model towns built in the

United States. It was laid out in 1852, about twelve miles from the center of Cincinnati, for business leaders of that city. The picture below shows how the village looked about 1860. Today the trees are much bigger than those shown, but the buildings are still in use. You can find similar railroad communities around all the large cities of Ohio.

Let's Review Part 2

New words

inventor
omnibus

Glendale, Ohio was established in 1851 as a model community. Why do you think the artist showed a railroad train on this picture?

preserve
sewage
sewer
slum
soot
street railway

New Things to Do

First talk to the oldest person you know about how she/he lived as a child or about what they know about the way their parents lived. Next pretend that you are living in a city of Ohio in the year 1880. Now write a story comparing life in 1880 to your life today.

What have we learned?

Today it is hard to imagine that there were no villages or cities in Ohio 200 years ago. The biggest towns had forts to protect them from the natives. As settlers learned to survive in the Ohio Country, some of them began to create central places for special activities. As more and more immigrants came from Europe, some of the central places grew to meet the needs of the newcomers. By 1900 Ohio had the fourth largest population in the United States, and half the people lived in villages and cities.

Millions of people came to Ohio from Europe and the South to gain freedom and better jobs. While living conditions were not easy for ordinary people in the cities of Ohio, they were far better than the new-comers had known. Some of the buildings of the 19th century are still standing, but the people who first used them would not understand the modern conveniences they now have!

Map Projects

Find the following places on your map of Ohio.

Place	County
Crestline	Crawford
Delaware	Delaware
Delphos	Allen & Van Wert
Dublin	Franklin
Glendale	Hamilton
Lancaster	Fairfield
Worthington	Franklin

Find the following places on your map of the United States.

Place	State
Fort Wayne	Indiana

Books to Read

The best place to learn about the early towns in your county is to read a history of the county written about 1890. Your public library should have this.

Chapter 10

How did industry develop during the 19th century?

Let's learn...

- about the relationship between knowledge, energy, and tools.

- how the industries of Ohio developed.

What do you think of when you hear the word *industry*? Are you an *industrious* person — do you do things that are helpful to other people and to your future life? **Industry** is the economic activity that deals with making and selling goods and services. In 1800 the industry of Ohio was very simple. Farmers raised crops. Water-powered mills ground grain and/or sawed wood. Blacksmiths made things out of iron. Merchants bought and sold goods. By 1900 Ohio was one of the important industrial states of the world.

Four things were needed to bring about this change: knowledge, energy, tools, and raw materials. In Part 1, you will learn about the relationship between knowledge, energy, and tools. In Part 2, you will learn about some important industries that used the raw materials of our state.

Part 1

How are knowledge, energy, and tools related?

There are many ways to gain useful knowledge. For example, have you heard the old saying, "We learn by doing!"? Perhaps after you have "messed up" while trying to "learn by doing", someone has said, "We must learn from our mistakes." In Chapter 7, you learned some ideas about *economics* and thought about the question, "How can I get the greatest benefit from what I put into a situation?" Another way to ask this question is, "How can I do a job most *efficiently*?" The goal of **efficiency** is to use knowledge and tools to create useful results while using the smallest possible amount of energy and raw materials. The box on this page discusses various ways to use knowledge

How Early People in The Ohio Country Cut Down Trees

The Native Americans could cut down small trees with their flint knives. The early settlers used axes and saws made of iron to cut trees of all sizes, but these tools also required large amounts of human energy. The picture on the next page shows that *teamwork* could reduce the energy required of any one worker. But it also shows that knowledge of tree-cutting is very important to safety! In fact, there are so many unsafe things shown in this picture that it must be a *cartoon*.

Since survival depended on raising food as quickly as possible, the early settlers could remove only small trees. They killed large trees by stripping the bark from bands around the trees. These trees would die within a year and fall several years later. But there was no energy available to remove the stumps of trees; therefore, they were left to rot in the ground.

The French settlers at Gallipolis were city people who knew little about survival in the forest. Would you feel safe working with these men? Explain your answer.

and tools to remove trees as related to the picture above.

In addition to forests, the people who bought land in the northwestern corner of Ohio had another great problem: the land was swampy! In fact, a large area was called *The Black Swamp*. The land was so flat that water could not drain away. After the trees were cut, the farmers had to use their knowledge and tools to create drainage systems. As a result of their work, this area now has some of the best farm land in the United States.

Do you ever have good ideas that you do not carry out? If you do not put ideas to use, nothing happens. All of the industrial progress of the 19th century grew out of applying energy to create new tools. The

197

new tools then reduced the human energy needed to create useful items. The box on this page explains how the cycle of knowledge, energy, and tools reduced the work of women in making clothing.

Sources of Energy

As you have learned, the most important sources of energy at the beginning of the 19th century were food and running water. Food has always been the only source of energy for humans and animals: without enough good food, they cannot do useful work. Running water was needed to turn the water wheels that operated machinery in mills. We still use the word *mill* today for factories that grind grain, spin thread, make cloth, saw wood, and make steel, paper, carpets, and other products.

How Creation of Clothing Changed During the 19th Century

In 1800 a pioneer woman had to make clothing for herself and her family while using a long, slow process. First, she had to create fibers either by raising sheep, cutting off the wool and cleaning it, or by raising **flax** plants (the source of linen thread) and breaking them down into thin fibers. Next, she had to spin the wool or linen fibers into thread by using either of the devices shown on the next page. The lower device was a simple tool that required little time or skill to make, but much time and skill to produce thread. The spinning wheel in the upper part was a much better tool, but it required far more knowledge and time to make.

She colored the thread by soaking it in dyes made from berries, leaves, or nuts and then boiling the mixture in a tub. Next, she wove the thread into cloth. She cut the cloth into pieces and sewed them together to form a dress. Buttons were handmade from bone or shell. You can watch people doing these jobs at some of the historic villages listed on page 161.

When machines were created to spin threads and weave cloth, women could no longer afford to spend time and energy creating cloth by the old methods. At first, these machines were operated by water-power, but by 1850 all were steam-powered. Later, when machines were created to cut and sew cloth, many women found that they could not afford the time and effort required to make clothing.

Steam

By 1850 most of the industries of Ohio used steam as their main source of energy. Burning wood was the most important fuel for creating this steam until about 1850. The first railroad trains, including the one on page 140, burned wood. It was not unusual to stop one of these trains and have the workers and passengers pick up wood along the right-of-way. Because of the great demand for wood to make steam, by 1870, the forests were disappearing. Also by 1870, coal replaced wood as an important source of energy for making steam. The picture on the next page shows a coal-burning boiler (on the left) that creates steam for the engine (on the right) used to power the machines in a 19th century factory. By 1900 steam was used to generate electricity.

Coal

The map on page 29 shows where you can find coal in southeastern Ohio. Early in the 19th century, small amounts of coal were mined by digging into a hillside where a bed of coal could be seen. As coal became important for creating steam, land owners began to drill holes into the earth in search of *black gold*, as coal was often called.

Spinning thread was an important part of pioneer life. What does it mean to "spin thread?"

After 1840 almost every factory had a boiler to create steam and an engine to change heat energy into mechanical actions. Where was this boiler made?

At this point, you should look at the geological map on page 17 and the geological time line on page 18-19. The "youngest" layers of rocks in Ohio contain layers of coal. The thinnest layers of coal are about six inches thick, while the thickest layers are several feet. To be useful, a layer of coal had to be at least thirty inches thick so that people could work inside it.

When a useful layer was found, the owner dug a shaft into the ground, built an elevator, and lowered workers down to the coal. As some workers loosened the coal, others loaded it into small railroad cars and rolled them to the elevator. The picture below shows two boys moving a loaded car through a space where coal had been removed earlier. How would you like to work ten hours every day in a space half as high as you are tall, with your only light coming from oil lamps? Many boys began such work before they were 16 and continued until they died 20, 30, or 40 years later. Who would work under such conditions?

Life of a Miner: Very few settlers lived in southeastern Ohio during the 19th century, and the coal mines needed workers. Where did they come from? Most Ohio miners were immigrants who had worked in the mines of England, Wales, Germany, Sweden, Poland, Hungary, and other places in Europe. Many of the miners gladly came as indentured workers because they wanted to enjoy the freedom of the United States.

Because there were very few towns, the mine owners had to build houses for their workers and their families. These *coal towns* were not planned like the ones described in Chapter 9. They were usually built in the cheapest possible way, with

Coal mining was a very hard and dirty job. How thick was the coal layer the boys are working in?

only one *General Store* that was operated by the mine owner. The poem in the box on this page are the words of a song about life in a company town.

From 1870 to 1950, coal was such an important source of energy that people said: "Coal is King!" The graph on the next page shows how coal mining increased in our state around 1900. In Chapter 14, you will learn how coal is mined today.

Petroleum

By the end of the 19th century, **petroleum** was an important source of energy. This natural resource is made up of many useful chemicals. Some of these are the gases we know as *natural gas, propane,* and *butane*. Some are very thick fluids we know as *asphalt* and *paraffin*. We also get *gasoline, kerosene, lubricating oil, heating oil,* and *grease* from petroleum. If you mix

The Company Store

By Isaac Hanna, Engelwood,
Illinois, 1895

Note: Words in [ ] are simplified.

The lot of the miner
    At best is quite hard,
We work for good money,
    Get paid by the card;
We scarcely can live,
    And not a cent more,
Since we're paid off in checks
    On the company store.

Those great coal [companies]
    Are growing apace,
They are making their millions
    By grinding our face;
Unto their high prices
    The people pay toll,

While they pay fifty cents
    For mining their coal.

They keep cutting our wages
    Time after time,
Where we once had a dollar,
    We now have a dime;
While our souls are near [starved],
    And our bodies are sore
We are paid off in checks
    On the company store.

Though hard we may labor
    But little we have;
We are robbed of our rights,
    Though we fought for the slave;
[Company] keeps [grabbing]
    For more and still more;
They will soon own the earth
    Through the company store.

From: Korson: *Coal Dust on the Fiddle,* p.78

Ohio Extractive Industries
Changes in Value of Products

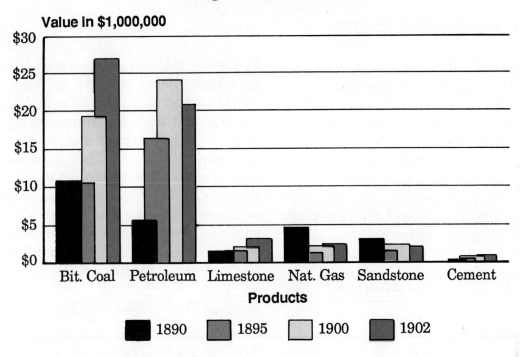

Extractive industries take raw materials out of the earth.
Was limestone or sandstone more important to Ohio around 1900?

asphalt with sand and gravel, you create *asphaltic concrete*, which is widely used to make highways — perhaps you know it as *blacktop*.

You have learned about the importance of salt to the early settlers in Ohio. Today we know that underground deposits of salt are often found with deposits of petroleum. The story in the box on the next page tells how people of southeastern Ohio were sometimes disappointed while drilling

holes for salt water (**brine**), because they found petroleum instead.

In the last chapter, you learned how people used candles and/or oil lamps to light their homes. Farm families made candles and oil by cooking fat from the animals they killed for meat. A very important source of oil needed by people living in cities was the fat, or *blubber*, of whales. Whale oil was so important that thousands of these great sea mammals were killed

The First Oil Well in Ohio

The first oil well in Ohio was drilled in 1814, near Caldwell, the county seat of Noble County, by a man who was hoping to find salt water. When a heavy, smelly, dark-brown fluid came out, he was disappointed and covered the hole. About two years later, another man drilled a well nearby hoping to find salt water. He found salt water mixed with a small amount of oil. This well was still used to obtain salt when the author [Henry Howe] visited it in 1846.

Traveling salesmen, who were also called "peddlers," or "medicine men," would stop at the well and collect the oil. They did this by soaking pieces of cloth in the mixture, and squeezing out the oil. They put this into small bottles and called it *Seneca Oil*. They traveled around the countryside selling it to farmer's wives to cure rheumatism, sprains, and bruises, for which, they said, it was especially useful.

Adapted from: Howe: vol.2, p. 353

each year for this purpose. Sometimes the meat was used for food, but sometimes only the fat was used.

By 1859 when petroleum was discovered at Titusville, Pennsylvania, a short distance east of Ashtabula County, entrepreneurs knew that oil from petroleum could be used in lamps in place of whale oil. The picture on the next page shows a very early oil well, while the picture on page 27 shows a modern one.

Several times we have talked about the differences between the northwestern and southeastern portions of Ohio. As you can see on the map on page 29, they have one thing in common. Both areas have large deposits of petroleum. The story in the box above tells how petroleum was found — but not wanted — in southeastern Ohio. It was discovered in northwestern Ohio at about the same time it was found in the southeastern part of our state, but nothing was done with it for a long time. The box on the next page tells how the work of one man brought wealth to Hancock County.

Within a few years, petroleum wells were being drilled throughout the southeastern and northwestern corners of Ohio. By 1900 Cleveland was the center of the petroleum

How Gas Was Discovered at Findlay

People around Findlay called Charles Oesterlen the "gas fool," because he believed that there was petroleum under Hancock County. After years of trying to persuade people, in 1876 he raised enough money to form a company to drill for gas. The well was a successful one, and "when the gas gushed forth with a panting roar and shot a column of flame sixty feet into the air, people were alarmed for a time."

Findlay was a small and almost unknown town when gas was struck. It took a year for the news of the discovery to spread, so that other companies would drill. In 1886, a well called *Karg* was drilled, and it produced 15 million cubic feet of gas daily. News of this well made Findlay the center of attention in the oil industry.

Adapted from: Howe: vol. 1, p. 872

The first oil well in the United States was at Titusville, Pennsylvania in 1866. Titusville is northeast of Youngstown, Ohio. What is the building made of? What does the shape remind you of?

industry of the United States because it was the home of John D. Rockefeller.

John D. Rockefeller: John Davidson Rockefeller was born in western New York in 1839. By the time he died in 1937, he was one of the richest men in the world.

John's family moved to Strongsville in Cuyahoga County when he was fourteen years old. Four years later, John went into business with a friend, and they became very successful. A short time later, he began to **refine** (make useful) petroleum in Cleveland. By 1865 he and a partner were hauling, refining, and selling petroleum products.

In 1870 John D. Rockefeller organized a new company in Cleveland and named it the *Standard Oil Company*. If you look at the graph on page 203, you can see that petroleum was almost as important as coal to the economy of our state in 1900. Mr. Rockefeller owned almost all of the petroleum of Ohio and a large part of it in the whole world. In the early years, the most important products made from petroleum were *kerosene,* or *lamp oil*, and *lubricating oils* and *grease* to improve the efficiency of machinery. The diesel fuel and heating oil, that are widely used today, are similar to kerosene. By 1900 a very small amount of petroleum was being refined into gasoline for automobiles.

By the end of the 19th century, Ohio had the largest known supply of energy in the United States in the form of coal and petroleum. It was also the home of people who had the knowledge and skills to create many useful products from these resources.

Let's Review Part 1

New Words

brine
efficiency
flax
industry
petroleum
refine

New Things to Do

1. *Tools* are used to help you do all kinds of jobs more easily. Today many tools are operated by electricity, which was not available in the 19th century. Make a list of all the tools in your house that have some iron but do not require electricity. Steel is a form of iron. How does each of these tools make life easier in your family?

2. Read the words of *The Company Store* song again. Write a short explanation of how you would feel if you had to do all your shopping in a store owned by a coal company.

Part 2

How did industries develop?

During the 18th century, inventors in England discovered ways to use the energy of *steam*. This made it possible to work with iron more easily. The machines they created from iron and operated by the energy of steam led to the *Industrial Revolution*. Nations of the world that took part in this revolution became far more wealthy than those that did not.

The transportation system of the United States began to benefit from this revolution early in the 19th century. By the end of that century, Ohio was one of the leading industrial states of the world. During the 19th century, the most important industries of Ohio *manufactured* products related to lumber, agriculture, and mining. **Manufacture** is an interesting word. It is made up of two Latin words that mean "made by hand." Today almost all manufacturing involves machines that make things much faster and more accurately than can be done "by hand." In other words, machines create things more *efficiently*. We will now look at a few of these industries.

Lumber

The great forests of our state were not cleared until there were hundreds of immigrant men to use the saws and axes to cut the trees. In addition to providing a source of energy for making steam, three of the most important uses for wood were building houses, making furniture, and making barrels.

You can still see wood barrels in use in a few places today. Perhaps you know someone who has a barrel that was sawed in half to make a table. During the 19th century, barrels were very important containers for moving all kinds of liquid and solid goods. You have learned that fresh meat was packed with salt to prevent spoilage. What do you think they did with the meat after it was salted? They packed it into *barrels*. Barrels could be rolled along ramps onto and off of wagons, canal boats, river boats, and railroad cars. They were very strong and could be used over and over again.

Agriculture

Agriculture is *the* most important industry! No nation can exist without food. You have learned that almost everyone who came to the Ohio Country during the 18th and early 19th century expected to grow food for themselves. Even those who lived in small towns grew food in their

This kind of plow was used early in the 19th century. What did the farmer do to operate this plow?

large yards. Farming tools were very simple, like the plow shown above. Iron was so expensive that all of this plow was made of wood except the cutting edge.

Corn, wheat, oats, and rye were the most important grains in Ohio. Potatoes and sweet potatoes were the most important vegetables. Apples, grapes, pears, and peaches were the most important fruits.

Sugar was made from sorghum grain. Almost one-half of the farms raised **live stock** (cows, pigs, sheep, and goats) for sale. Many farms in the hilly, southern half of the state grew tobacco on small areas. But towns could not grow until farmers could produce enough food to feed people living in the cities. To produce more food, the farmers needed better tools.

Agricultural Tools

During the 19th century, agriculture became more efficient as entrepreneurs learned to work with steam and iron. During the last half of the 19th century, the city of Springfield in Clark County had the largest factory in the world for making farm machinery, which you can see below. Each smokestack on this picture represents

This factory made Champion farm machinery in Springfield. It was one of the largest factories in the world. If each smoke stack represents one steam engine, how many engines did this factory have?

a large steam engine, like the one on page 200. Each steam engine operated machines needed to form iron into useful shapes. By 1900 most farms had better tools, like the horse-drawn plow shown on the next page. The largest farms had movable steam engines like the one shown on page 211.

Preserving Foods

The biggest problem with the products of agriculture is spoilage. In the pattern of nature, grains, fruits, and vegetables ripen at certain times. They must be picked within a short time, or they will become unusable. After picking, they must be stored in special ways so that they do not spoil. Grains could be stored in cool, dry, insect-proof places for long periods of time. By 1900 large factories in Ohio bought tons of fruits and vegetables from the farmers, and "packed" them in tin cans or glass jars.

Milk and meat spoiled within a few hours if not treated properly. Some factories in small towns bought milk to make cheese that could be stored for a much longer time than milk. Today Amish people still change large amounts of milk into cheese at factories you can visit in Holmes County. Farmers who lived near big cities could walk their animals to meat factories. Farmers who lived near the canals could send their animals to the big cities by boat. In the cities along Lake Erie and the Ohio River, meat was packed into barrels with salt and sent by boat to cities along the East Coast. On page 177 you learned how Delphos changed when a railroad was built to the north of that town. By 1870 entrepreneurs were buying cows and pigs in Ohio, Indiana, Illinois, Iowa, and other midwestern states. They put these animals into railroad cars and shipped them to meat factories in eastern cities.

This kind of plow was used late in the 19th century. Could a poor farmer own a machine like this? Explain your answer.

Candles and Soap

In Part 1, you learned how farm families made candles and oil for their own use. They also made soap from the fat of animals. In 1837, William Procter and James Gamble, whose wives were sisters, decided to make use of the fat from tens of thousands of animals that were being killed. They built a factory to make soap and candles in what is now downtown Cincinnati. This partnership was the beginning of the *Procter & Gamble*

Company, which is one of the largest corporations in the world.

Leather

How many things do you own that are made of leather, that is, the skins of animals? The process of changing the hide of an animal into a piece of leather is a long, slow, smelly process called *tanning*. There were many tanneries in Ohio during the 19th century, but none are in operation now.

210

Today it is hard to imagine the number of uses that people once had for leather, because they had no plastics. If you know anyone who is ninety years old, ask her/him about the uses of leather when she/he was a child. You will get a long list, including shoes, belts to drive machinery, saddles, and harnesses. For many years, Portsmouth in Scioto County was an important center for making leather shoes, but the last factory closed by 1960. The picture on the next page shows a 19th century factory that had a "forest of leather belts" that drove the machines that made goods. These belts were driven by a steam engine like the one on page 200. You can also see a leather belt in the center of the picture below.

Steam engines like this could be moved from place to place. What safety problems can you see in this picture?

All the machines in this factory were driven by leather belts.
What safety problems do you see in this picture?

Mining

Mining means "taking materials of nature out of the ground to use for economic purposes." Materials that are mined cannot be returned to their natural condition. The most important materials mined in Ohio during the 19th century were clay, coal, iron ore, petroleum, salt, and stone. The graph on page 203 shows how the value of some of these products changed around the year 1900. We talked about coal and petroleum as sources of energy earlier in this chapter, and we will now look at the other materials.

Clay and Sand

Clay has little value as you find it in nature. If you mix certain kinds of clay with water, you can form it into many useful shapes. If you heat these shapes in a **kiln** (special oven), you can create products such as dishes, bricks, tiles, and vases. The word pottery has two related meanings: the factory where products are made from clay is a *pottery*, and some of the products are called *pottery*.

Good clay and natural gas were available near the city of East Liverpool, which is on the Ohio River in Columbiana County. In 1848 a factory was opened there to make ordinary household dishes. During the Civil War, Congress made it very expensive to bring good dishes into the United States from other countries. As a result, pottery owners in East Liverpool increased the number of dishes they made and began to make higher-quality products. By 1890, East Liverpool had 18 potteries that employed almost 2,200 workers. You can see one of the largest potteries below. This factory employed 613 workers. Today you can visit the *Pottery Museum* in East Liverpool to learn about this great industry, but very few clay products have been made there since 1950.

The Knowles, Taylor & Knowles Pottery in East Liverpool, Ohio was one of the largest potteries in the world. How many kilns are shown in this picture?

213

Chapter 10 — How did industry develop during the 19th century?

Ceramic materials are made from special clays and/or sands that are mixed with other materials and baked at very high temperatures. The three most widely used ceramic products are porcelain, fire bricks, and glass. You may have special dishes or works of art in your home that are *porcelain*. All of the kilns used to make bricks, pottery, and glass must be lined with *fire bricks*, which are ceramic materials. All boilers used to create steam are also lined with fire bricks.

In some places of the world, archaeologists have found glass objects made thousands of years ago. To make glass, you need special sand and high temperatures that can be closely controlled. Lucas County had good sand but no satisfactory fuel. When natural gas was discovered south of Lucas County, several glass factories were built in northwestern Ohio. Glass factories were also built in Muskingum and Guernsey counties. Most of the products made in Ohio were ordinary bottles, jars, plates, drinking glasses, and window glass, but beautiful objects of art were also created. Today you can visit a museum of glass products at Cambridge, the county seat of Guernsey County. You can see beautiful pieces of both ancient and modern glass artwork at the Toledo Museum of Art.

Iron

You have learned how important iron was to the early settlers. Before 1845, all of the iron used in Ohio was carried across the mountains from the East Coast. This means that it was scarce and expensive. *Blacksmiths* were very important people because they had the tools and knowledge to change iron into useful shapes.

In 1845 geologists exploring in Lawrence County found iron ore. **Ores** are rocks that contain useful metals, such as iron, gold, silver, lead, and copper. Within a few years, geologists found iron ore in Hocking, Jackson, Perry, Scioto, and Vinton Counties. They found the same ore in parts of eastern Kentucky and western West Virginia. Geologists named this entire area the *Hanging Rock Iron Region*.

In order to separate iron from its ore, the ore must be mixed with crushed limestone and heated until it melts. For many years, charcoal was used as the fuel because it burns at a very high temperature when air is blown into it. The Hanging Rock Region had limestone and trees that could be changed into charcoal.

By the time the Civil War broke out in 1861, there were 80 iron furnaces in the Hanging Rock region of Ohio. The Buckeye Furnace in Jackson County, which you can see on page 31, was one of these. For almost forty years, Ohio was the most important source of iron in the United States.

Mahoning County is northeast of the Hanging Rock Iron Region, but it too had a large deposit of iron ore. It also had a large deposit of excellent coal that could be used in place of charcoal. For this reason, Youngstown, the county seat of Mahoning County, became a center of iron making. The picture below shows the Brier Hill Iron Furnace in Mahoning County in 1886. By 1900 most of the iron ore of Ohio was used up. As the supply of iron ore was disappearing in Ohio, geologists found a tremendous supply of iron ore in northeastern Minnesota. Now look at the map on page 3 and try to answer the question, "How could the iron ore from Minnesota and the coal of Ohio be brought together?" The answer is colored blue on the map! The ore could be carried in ships on the Great Lakes, which form the largest inland waterway in the world!

If you look at the map on page 134, you see that Cleveland was located at the northern end of a canal system that served the coal fields of Ohio. Entrepreneurs in that city built a harbor at the mouth of the Cuyahoga River. For many years, lake ships, like that shown on the next page, carried iron ore from Minnesota to Cleveland. Canal boats carried Ohio coal

The Brier Hill Iron Furnace in Mahoning County looked like this in 1886. How was this furnace different from the Buckeye Furnace shown on page 31?

to Cleveland. As a result, that city became one of the great iron-making centers of the world. You will learn more about this in Chapter 14.

Salt

You have learned how important salt once was for preserving meat. Today the United States mines more salt than any other nation, and Ohio is the fourth largest source in the United States. There are huge salt mines far below Lake Erie in Cuyahoga, Lake, and Ashtabula counties. At Rittman in Wayne County, salt is mixed with water deep in the ground and pumped to the surface. Today most salt is used to create other chemicals and to melt ice on highways.

Stone

Stone has been an important building material throughout history. It can be removed from the ground and cut into useful shapes without using iron tools, and it does not decay. Since wood rots quickly when it touches the ground, many of the settlers in Ohio built their houses on stacks of stones set at each corner of the building. As the cities of Ohio grew during the 19th century, almost every house rested on **a foundation** (support) of stone.

If you look back to page 16, you will see a sandstone quarry in north-central Ohio.

The steamship Willis B. Boyer carried iron ore from Minnesota to Ohio for almost fifty years. It is now a museum at Toledo. Why is there a flight of steps?

Many important buildings in Ohio, such as schools, county buildings, and churches were built of sandstone quarried at Berea in Cuyahoga County. Berea sandstone was also used to make mill stones that were used to grind grain in many parts of the world.

You can see the remains of several large limestone quarries in central and western Ohio. When the owners of these quarries stopped removing rock, the pits filled with water. During the last half of the 20th century, scuba diving became a popular sport and several of the water-filled quarries are used for this sport.

Today sand and gravel are the most widely used forms of stone. Most of the 19th century turnpikes you learned about in chapter 7 were paved with sand and gravel. When rock walls were built as foundations for buildings, layers of *mortar* were put between the rocks to make the walls stronger. This mortar was a mixture of sand, water, and *lime*, a product made from limestone. Have you heard older people say that something painted white was "whitewashed?" *Whitewash* is a mixture of lime and water, and it was a popular form of paint for many years.

Since 1880 sand and gravel have been widely used to make two forms of concrete which are very important in our daily lives. You learned about *asphaltic* concrete earlier in this chapter. The other form is *Portland cement* concrete. Today the foundations of almost all buildings are made of Portland cement concrete. Many highways, sidewalks, and walls are also made from this kind of concrete. Portland cement is manufactured in Greene and Muskingum Counties by heating limestone and shale to a very high temperature.

By 1900 many of the cities of Ohio had manufacturing plants. Cleveland and Cincinnati were among the ten largest centers of manufacturing in the United States. If you want to see how the industry of Ohio, and the entire United States, developed during the 19th century, you should visit the *Sauder Farm* and *Craft Museum* at Archbold in Fulton County. If you want to see an even bigger display, you can visit *Greenfield Village* and the *Henry Ford Museum* at Dearborn, Michigan just a few miles north of Toledo on I-75. Plan to spend a full day at each of these three great museums of American history and industry.

Let's Review Part 2

New Words

ceramics
concrete
foundation
kiln
live stock
manufacture
ore

New Things to Do

1. Go to the food storage space in your home or to a food store. Look at the labels on packaged foods. Make a list of twenty kinds of packaged foods together with the name and address of the company that prepared the food. Find each city on one of your maps.

2. Look for an old building in your neighborhood that has a stone foundation, outdoor stairs, and/or decorations. Be careful not to choose things that are made of concrete or metal that looks like stone (you can tap with a small stone to tell the difference). Make a sketch of these items and explain the condition of them.

3. Look at a building foundation, a sidewalk, and a street pavement or driveway made of Portland cement concrete. How are these surfaces
different from the stone items?

What have we learned?

When Ohio became a state in 1803, the living conditions of its citizens were only a little better than those of the Native Americans. But the Americans had three resources that the natives did not have: iron tools, knowledge, and energy resources to create more comfortable lives.

The settlers used their tools to clear the forests for agriculture and to get the natural resources of the earth. Knowledge helped them to develop these natural resources and use the energy of steam. The economic system of the United States encouraged entrepreneurs to use personal energy and money to manufacture new products.

As Ohio became an industrial state, many people had to work at hard physical labor, but a majority of them gained more comfortable lives for themselves. A small number of people gained such great wealth and power that they were able to control parts of the economy.

Map Projects

Find the following places on your map of Ohio.

Place	County
Archbold	Fulton
Berea	Cuyahoga
Caldwell	Noble
East Liverpool	Columbiana
Findlay	Hancock
Hanging Rock Iron Region	Jackson, Lawrence, Perry, Scioto and Vinton
Sauder Farm Museum	Fulton
Springfield	Clark
Strongsville	Cuyahoga

Find the following places on your map of the United States.

Place	State
Greenfield Village	Dearborn, Michigan
Henry Ford Museum	Dearborn, Michigan

Books to Read

From the "yellow pages" of your telephone directory, pick out three industries that are important in your county. Read about these industries in an encyclopedia. Try to find items made by these industries in your local stores.

Chapter 11

What was the role of government during the 19th century?

Let's learn...

- how our nation and state are ruled by laws.

- about schools in the 19th century.

- about social problems in the 19th century.

- about presidents of the United States from Ohio.

In earlier chapters, you learned how representatives from thirteen British colonies learned to work together to rule themselves. They created the first nation in modern times to be organized under the *rule of law*. In this chapter, you will learn how the original laws of our nation and state were established.

In order to enjoy the benefits of rule of law, the people must take part in making the laws. This means that people must be educated to understand the laws and have respect for them. In order to have respect for laws, the people must know that they will be treated fairly. For this reason, you will learn how laws were changed as social problems developed during the 19th century. You will also learn about eight men of Ohio who were elected to the position of President of the United States. The time line on the next page will help you follow events of this chapter.

Part 1

What does it mean to be ruled by laws?

In 1800 most of the people in the world were governed by kings, queens, or other individuals who could do almost anything they wanted to do. Two people who got into exactly the same kind of trouble might receive entirely different punishments. A friend of the ruler might be forgiven, while an enemy might lose his head. The men who worked together to create the United States of America

wanted to establish equal justice for everyone under the *rule of law*. In this part, you will learn how several kinds of laws influence our lives.

Constitution of the United States

The basic idea of the leaders of the thirteen original states was: "The less power government has, the better it is for the people." The constitution they wrote established a government that had three main parts. A **legislative** (law making) branch, called *Congress*, would be elected by the people of each state, and it would have the highest powers. An **executive** (law enforcing) branch would carry out the laws under the leadership of a *President*. A **judicial** branch would make certain that laws were carried out fairly under leadership of the *Supreme Court*. The Constitution gave the new government only the powers outlined in the box on page 223.

The leaders of the Continental Congress completed writing the Constitution of the United States in September 1787, a few weeks after they adopted the Northwest Ordinance. In 1789, the thirteenth state agreed to live under this rule of law, and the first Congress of the United States was elected in 1790.

While the thirteen original states were deciding whether or not to accept the

Time Line of Events in Chapter 11

Year	Event
1783	End of American Revolution
1785	Public Land Act required that Section 16 of each township be used for education, and that one township of each large grant be used for a college
1787	Continental Congress agreed on Constitution
1789	13th state agreed to Constitution
1791	Bill of Rights adopted — First ten amendments
1803	Ohio became 17th state
1804	Ohio University established in Athens County
1824	Miami University established in Butler County
1833	Oberlin College established in Lorain County
1841	William Henry Harrison, President of the United States
1861-1865	Civil War
1862	Congress adopted Morrill Act to create colleges of agriculture and mechanic arts.
1865	African-American slaves set free
1869-1877	Ulysses S. Grant, President of the United States
1873	National Industrial Congress organized in Cleveland Miners National Association organized in Youngstown Women's Christian Temperance League chapter in Highland County
1877-1881	Rutherford B. Hayes, President of the United States
1881	James A. Garfield, President of the United States
1886	American Federation of Labor organized in Columbus
1889-1893	Benjamin Harrison, President of the United States
1890	United Mine Workers Union organized in Columbus
1897-1901	William McKinley, President of the United States
1898	Spanish American War
1901-1904	William H. Taft, Governor of Philippine Islands
1909-1913	William H. Taft, President of the United States
1921-1930	William H. Taft, Chief Justice of U.S. Supreme Court
1921-1923	Warren G. Harding, President of the United States

Outline of The Governments of the United States and Ohio

	United States	Ohio
Constitution adopted	1789	1803 and 1851
(Basic laws)		
Bill of Rights	1791	1803 and 1851
Legislative Branch	Congress	General Assembly
Creates statutory laws		
Upper House	Senate	Senate
Lower House	House of Representatives	House of Representatives
Executive Branch	President	Governor
Carries out laws		
Judicial Branch		
Constitutional law	Supreme Court	Supreme Court
Statutory law	District Courts	Common Pleas Courts
Common law		Common Pleas Courts

constitution, Congress created ten **amendments** (additions or changes) that became known as the *Bill of Rights.* The original states accepted the Bill of Rights in 1791.

First Constitution of Ohio

In Chapter 6, you learned how leaders from seventeen counties met at Chillicothe in 1802 to write a constitution for the State of Ohio. This first constitution still affects our lives, because it guided the development of our state for almost fifty years.

The first three articles of our State Constitution were related to the first three articles of the Constitution of the United States. The first article said that the *General Assembly* would represent the people of Ohio in making laws. The second article described how the *Governor* of Ohio would enforce the laws. The third article described how the *Supreme Court* of the state would see that the laws were enforced fairly. The outline above shows how the three branches of our national and state governments are related in organization.

Constitutional Powers of the Government of the United States

Section 8 of the constitution gave the national government the following powers:

1. To collect taxes to pay for "the common defense and general welfare of the United States."
2. To borrow money.
3. To regulate trade with other nations and between states.
4. To make rules about people from other nations becoming citizens of the United States.
5. To create and control a system of money.
6. To establish a system of post offices.
7. To encourage and protect new ideas.
8. To establish a system of justice under the Supreme Court.
9. To do all things necessary to insure the safety of the nation.
10. To deal with other nations.

Three Forms of Law

In the United States we have three kinds of law: **constitutional law, statutory law,** and **common law**. *Constitutional law* is the most important. Our fifty states are held together by the Constitution of the United States. Each state has its own constitution which cannot conflict with that of the United States. Every constitution must include a way that it can be amended. The United States Constitution was changed only fifteen times during the 19th century. The First Constitution of Ohio was **repealed** (ended) in 1851, and a Second Constitution was adopted. This new constitution was amended several times before 1900.

Statutory laws are much easier to make and to change, but each one must be in harmony with the constitution. Have you ever heard someone say, "There ought to be a law against that!" If the problem has existed for a long time, there probably is a statutory law about it, but it may not be enforced very well. If the problem is caused by new conditions that no one ever thought about, a new statutory law may be needed. For example, in 1890 there were laws about racing horses on city streets, but none about speeding automobiles because no one had ever seen an automobile. As time passes and events change, new statutory laws are created, but sometimes the old laws are not removed. For example, when new laws were created to deal with speeding automobiles, the laws about racing horses were not removed immediately.

Common laws are far older than statutory laws or constitutional laws. They are used to solve problems when there are no written laws to cover a situation. Do you try to use *common sense?* When problems arise that are not described in any law, a judge must try to follow what other judges did in similar cases, or *common law*, to solve them fairly. You can think of the idea of *rule of law* as a house. The box on this page will help you understand this relationship.

How Laws Are Related to The Goals of Government

In Chapter 5, you learned that the three basic goals of government are:
1. to provide a situation free of turmoil.
2. to keep records of all government actions, including ownership of property.
3. to raise taxes to pay for the first two services.
We can now look at some of the ways in which the constitutions of the United States and Ohio dealt with these goals.

When the leaders of the thirteen colonies signed the Declaration of Independence, they had no army or navy to support them. Many of the men who fought in the Revolutionary War belonged to the *militia* of their colony. All militia members were required to provide their own rifles, pistols, and other weapons. For this reason, the Bill of Rights of the United States and Ohio said that citizens could own guns.

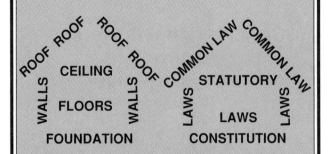

Steps in Building a House

1. A person draws plans to build a new house and gets legal permission to do so.
2. The foundation is built and checked for safety.
3. Walls, floors, and a roof are built on the foundation according to the plans.
4. Unexpected problems arise and the plans are adjusted to solve the problems.

Steps in Creating Rule of Law

1. A group of people agree to create a new government.
2. A *constitution* is written and they agree to live by it.
3. *Statutory laws* are adopted by the legislative body in harmony with the constitution.
4. Unexpected problems arise and decisions are made based on ideas of *common law*.

Very few other nations of the world give citizens this "right." Both Bills of Rights also said that the militia could be called upon to prevent turmoil within the nation and state.

In order to have rule by law, it is absolutely necessary that every unit of government keep accurate written records of everything it does. For this reason, every unit has people who **record** (write down) what the unit does and the money it takes in and/or spends.

Many kinds of records are kept in government offices: some are kept in city offices, some in county offices, and some in state offices. If your parents lived in a city when you were born, your *birth certificate* should be in the records of that city. If they lived in an unincorporated area, your certificate should be in a county office. An official record of the time and place of your birth is important in at least three situations. If you want to find a part-time job while going to school, you must show the employer a copy of your birth certificate to prove your age. If you want to travel to another nation, you must show proof of where you were born to get a **passport** (proof of citizenship). When you want to retire and apply for Social Security benefits, you must show proof of when you were born.

No unit of government can carry out its goals if it cannot raise money in the form of taxes. Even the first two constitutional powers of the United States, listed in the box on page 223, require money to pay for the people and equipment needed to do the work. When you buy stamps to mail letters or birthday cards, you are helping to pay for the sixth service, the postal system. Where does money come from for all these services? It comes from *taxes*. You will learn about the present taxes of our state in Chapter 15.

Second Constitution of Ohio

By 1850 conditions in Ohio had changed so much that leaders of our state felt they could no longer operate efficiently under the First Constitution. The General Assembly could no longer handle the problems of the growing villages and cities. The courts could not provide prompt and fair justice. For these reasons, the people of Ohio voted to call a *Constitutional Convention*. This convention began to work in May 1850 and finished in March 1851. The new constitution was accepted by the voters in June 1851. We still live under this Second Constitution, which you will learn more about in Chapter 15.

When you consider that no group of people had ever decided to set up a new government under the *rule of law*, the leaders of the United States and Ohio did an amazing job in establishing our nation.

Let's Review Part 1

New Words

amendment
common law
executive
judicial
legislative
passport
record (verb)
repeal
statutory law

New Things to Do

Should citizens be permitted to own guns? This is a very serious question in the United States today. If someone in your family has been shot, your parents may belong to a group that is trying to get the government to forbid the sale of guns. If someone in your family is a member of the *National Rifle Association*, you have heard that the Ohio Constitution gives citizens the right to own guns. This difference of opinion has created turmoil for many years. Arrange a class debate on the question: "Should the United States have gun control laws?" Let each class member choose which side he/she wants to be on. Have the members of each group gather arguments to support its side. Then elect two representatives of each side to debate. At the end of the debate, write a statement about what you learned from this experience.

Part 2

How were schools established?

Have you heard that America was once called, "The melting pot of the world?" In earlier chapters, you learned how immigrants from all over Europe came to Ohio. Most of those who could read, write, and speak English were from Great Britain. Many of the others had to go to school to learn the language of America. Schools also taught the immigrants about **citizenship** (taking part in government). For this reason, some people said that the schools *melted* them to fit the American pattern. The early leaders of our nation knew that education was an important part of the idea of rule by law.

Paying for Schools

Does your school system have trouble paying for your education? Today many, many school systems in Ohio have such problems, but most had even greater problems during the 19th century.

You have learned that the early leaders of the United States were well-educated people. They knew that the form of government they were creating would need educated leaders. For this reason, the Public Land Act of 1785 required that Section 16 of every township be used for purposes of public education. It will help if you look back to page 79 to review the plan

for subdividing land. This idea did not work well, so in 1826 the General Assembly sold all the school lands and used the money for public schools. The Public Land Act also said that "one-third of [the income from] all gold, silver, lead and copper mines" would also be used for education. But none of these metals were found in Ohio.

Our Second Constitution gave the General Assembly power to collect taxes to support free public schools. It also said that no public money could be spent for private or church-related schools. The General Assembly then adopted a set of laws to guide the development of what they called "common schools" in Ohio. One part of this

law said that local boards of education should establish "...one or more separate schools for *colored* children, when the whole number [of these children] exceeds thirty...." You must remember that this law was written in 1851 when there were only 25,500 African-Americans living in our entire state.

School Operations

Throughout the 19th century, most of the schools in rural areas were one-room buildings built on small parcels of land. The picture above shows a school in Warren County during the 1840s. Today you can see many schools built between 1880 and 1900 that look like this. Some

You can see this "converted" school house near Williamsburg in Clermont County. What do you think this building was used for at different times?

are in ruins, but others are used for different purposes. The picture above shows how one old school house was changed into an auto service station and roadside stand.

Perhaps thirty children, from 6 to 14 years of age, learned from one teacher. Only a few children went to school beyond age 14. The teacher usually had a high-school education and was paid a small salary plus "room and board." This means that the teacher had a sleeping room and ate with a family that lived near the school. Classes were arranged to permit the children to help on the farms. You can visit one-room school houses at Hale Farm in Summit County and at the Ohio Village in Columbus.

Before 1850, many city schools were private *academies* that charged each student a fee. This means that children from poor families seldom went to school. As immigrants increased the populations of cities, many evening classes helped them learn the English language. Other classes taught them how to become citizens of the United States.

By 1900 almost all city children were attending schools until at least fourteen years of age. Some who went to high school rode on streetcars, but walking was the main form of transportation. Some church groups, and especially the Roman Catholic Church, established schools for their children.

Three Ohio School Teachers

Do you know about the *Three R's* of elementary education — *readin, 'ritin,* and *'rithmetic*? Three young men from Ohio completely changed the teaching of reading, writing, and arithmetic during the 19th century.

William Holmes McGuffey: William McGuffey was two years old in 1802 when his parents moved to Trumbull County. His mother taught him until he was eighteen years of age. He then went to an academy and graduated from college in 1826. Later that year, he began to teach at Miami University in Butler County. His students had so much trouble with the English language that McGuffey wrote six "reading" books for them. These books became so popular that more than 130 million copies were used by several generations of school children all over the United States. Today you can buy reprints of *McGuffey Readers*.

Platt Roger Spencer: Platt Spencer was born in New York State in the same year as William McGuffey. At the age of nine, he became fascinated with writing, but he had no paper. He wrote on birch bark with a quill pen and ink made from berries. He even used a stick to write in sand. Wherever he wrote, he wrote in a beautiful style. In 1810, his family moved to Ashtabula County, and Platt went to school at Conneaut. Before long the teacher was letting him teach his classmates how to write.

When he finished school, Platt Spencer had no trouble finding jobs in which clear writing was important. (Typewriters were not invented until 1869!) When his fellow workers saw his beautiful writing, some of them paid him to teach them how to write. Your grandparents may have learned *Spencerian* handwriting in school!

Joseph Ray: Joseph Ray was born in Cincinnati about ten years later than William McGuffey and Platt Spencer. By the time he was sixteen years old, he was teaching mathematics there. He then went to Ohio University in Athens County.

When Woodward High School was organized in Cincinnati in 1831, Joseph Ray became the first teacher of mathematics. His students had so much trouble with the textbook that he wrote a new one. By the time he retired, he had written fifteen mathematics books that were used all over the United States.

Colleges

The Public Land Act required that land be set aside to pay for colleges. Both the Ohio Company and John Cleves Symmes were supposed to use one township (36 square miles) of their lands for this purpose. The Ohio Company set aside two townships (72 square miles) in what is now Athens County. When the General Assembly met in 1804, it established *Ohio University* on this land.

When Congress sold the land between the Miami Rivers to John Cleves Symmes, he agreed to use one township (36 square miles) for higher education. By the time the General Assembly was ready to create a college in southwestern Ohio, Symmes had sold all of his land. The legislature, therefore, chose a township between the Great Miami River and the Ohio-Indiana border to establish *Miami University*. Miami opened as an academy in 1818 and became a college in 1824.

In 1862 Congress passed what is known as the *Morrill Act* to help each state create

229

a school for "agricultural and mechanic arts." This law led to creation of the Colleges of Engineering and Agriculture at *The Ohio State University*.

As the population of Ohio grew during the second half of the 19th century, several religious groups established colleges in Ohio. While the main purpose of these schools was to educate religious leaders, other students were welcomed. Oberlin College, established in Lorain County in 1833, was the first college in the United States to accept women and African-American students. As you can see on the map on page 157, Oberlin was the only station on the Underground Railroad in Ohio that had six routes.

The people who established the government of the United States knew that the idea of *rule of law* could succeed only if the citizens of the nation could understand and take part in government. For this reason, public education has been important throughout our history.

Let's Review Part 2

New Words

citizenship

New Things to Do

Look at the "yellow pages" of your local telephone directory under the heading of *Schools*. Make a list of ten subjects you could study at these schools. Write a sentence about the school that surprised you most. Write another sentence about why you might like to study at one of the schools.

Part 3

What were the social problems in 1900?

In earlier chapters, you learned about the great changes that took place during the 19th century. Almost everyone had a better life in 1900 than their **ancestors** (grandparents, great-grandparents...) had in 1800, But life was not easy for everyone. We will now look at three problems facing the people of Ohio in the year 1900. As you read this chapter, our nation is still trying to solve these problems.

The Labor Movement

Do you know any one who belongs to a **labor union**? *Unions* were organized so that workers could protect themselves from being **exploited** (unfairly used) by owners of some industries. In the poem, *The Company Store*, on page 157, you

During the last years of the 19th century, working people often felt that they were slaves to the owners of big businesses. How is this picture related to the way workers felt?

learned how owners of coal mines controlled the lives of workers. On page 201 you saw a picture of boys working in a mine. The political cartoon above shows how many workers felt about their jobs. The story in the box on this page will give you some idea about work in factories. Beginning about 1880, the workers of Ohio started *The Labor Movement* that encouraged workers throughout the

Factory Work in The Late 19th Century

People often talk about the rapid growth of women and child labor. It is hard to find girls to do good kitchen work in a home for pay of three to four dollars a week plus food, but many girls work in factories, operating machinery and doing the work of men, for pay of 50 to 75 cents a day. Men doing the same kind of work are paid from $1.50 to $2.00 a day for the same amount of work.

Children are put to work in factories at twelve years of age, and do the work of men by the age of fifteen, but they are paid only 30 to 50 cents a day. They work at these low wages until they are men, and then they are let go to make room for new boys. I have found boys working hard in a room at 120 degrees Fahrenheit.

Adapted from: Fassett, "Labor's Competitors" in *An Ohio Reader*, p. 158.

The Women's Temperance Crusade met outside a saloon in New Vienna, Ohio, to protest the owner selling alcohol to their husbands. What do you think these women were trying to do?

United States to unite to protect their interests.

In 1873 representatives of workers throughout Ohio met in Cleveland to organize the *National Industrial Congress.* In that same year, representatives of coal miners in Ohio met in Youngstown and organized the *Miner's National Association of the United States.* An important activity of the miner's group was to help immigrants become citizens so they could vote for political candidates who promised to help workers.

In 1886 labor representatives from all over the United States met in Columbus, Ohio to organize the *American Federation of Labor.* Four years later, miners from

all parts of the nation met in Columbus to organize the *United Mine Workers.* You will learn more about unions in the next chapter.

Women's Rights

As you have learned, the constitutions of the United States and of Ohio were written by men for men. Women could make few decisions for themselves: they could neither vote nor own land. Oberlin College was a leading school in helping women gain equal rights. For example, Lucy Stone graduated from Oberlin in 1847 and became a leader in the *women's suffrage movement* — **suffrage** is the right to vote.

When women married, they were expected to stay at home and take care of their children. Families often had ten or more children, but many of these died before they reached the age of five years. Some women were lucky enough to have the household equipment you can see on page 167, but many more did not have such "modern" equipment.

Alcoholic husbands created great problems for many women. The *Women's Temperance Crusade* was organized in several counties of south-central Ohio to reduce the evils of alcohol. In December 1873, a speaker from New York met with the women of Hillsborough (now Hillsboro), the county seat of Highland County, to tell them about a plan to stop alcoholism. Fifty women of Hillsborough agreed to work together for this purpose.

As a first step, they wrote letters to owners of places selling alcohol asking them to stop doing so. If the owners did not agree, the women held prayer meetings in front of the places of business. The picture on the previous page shows one of these gatherings at New Vienna, near Hillsborough. Soon women in nearby counties were also trying to reduce the use of alcohol. Women in larger cities, including Columbus and Cincinnati, tried this method, but were not successful in the big cities.

African-Americans

In 1800 almost all African-Americans were slaves. In 1863 President Abraham Lincoln said that all slaves would be freed at the close of the Civil War. Between 1865 and 1870, the constitution of the United States was amended three times to provide equal rights for Africa-Americans. On page 146, you can see how freed slaves moved into Ohio during these same years.

By 1900 almost 100,000 African-Americans lived in Ohio. Almost one-half of them lived in small areas of the seven largest cities. Many of the others lived in the counties of southeastern Ohio where the mining and lumber industries needed unskilled help. The political leaders of the state did little to help them.

The mother of John Mercer Langston was born in slavery in Virginia but was freed before John was born. When she died, four-year-old John and his two brothers moved to Chillicothe, Ohio to live with friends of the family. In 1841 he entered Oberlin College.

While a student at Oberlin, John worked for the rights of African-Americans. He was the first of his race to earn a degree in *theology* ("study of God") from Oberlin. He returned to Virginia and became the first African-American to practice law in that state. Later he was the first African-American elected to represent

Virginia in Congress. He ended his career as head of the law school at Howard University.

New Words

ancestor
exploit
labor union
suffrage

New Things to Do

Choose one of the pictures in this part, and pretend that you are living in the situation shown. Write a letter to a friend about your experience.

Part 4

Which presidents came from Ohio?

Political leaders from Ohio have played important roles in the history of the United States. Many people like to say that our state was the home of eight presidents of the United States! It is true that eight men who served as president spent parts of their lives in Ohio, but several of them also spent many years in other states.

Portrait of William Henry Harrison. This lithograph was made in 1846 from a daguerrotype.

Perhaps you have watched part of a presidential election on television. The system used today is quite different from what it was before we had radio and television. But two things have not changed: it takes very hard work and a large amount of money to be elected.

William Henry Harrison

William Henry Harrison (1773-1841) was the ninth president of the United States, but he served for only a few weeks. You can see a picture of him as president above.

You learned several things about him in Chapters 1 and 6, and saw a picture of him on the previous page and on page 108. At the close of the War of 1812, he was elected to serve in political offices in Hamilton County, in the Ohio General Assembly, and in the United States Senate. He made his home in North Bend, Ohio with his wife, Anna Symmes Harrison. Anna was a daughter of John Cleves Symmes, who established North Bend in 1789.

William Henry Harrison's campaign for the presidency was the first to use advertising "gimmicks" like this. One of the slogans on the ball says, "To guide the ship, we'll trust old Tip." What do you think this meant?

In 1836 the leaders of the *Whig Party* asked Mr. Harrison to run against the Democratic Party candidate, Martin Van Buren. Mr. Van Buren was elected. In 1840, the leaders of the Whig Party again asked Mr. Harrison to run against President Van Buren. This time the Whig Party emphasized Mr. Harrison's role in driving the Native Americans out of Ohio and Indiana. The **slogan** (saying), "Tippecanoe and Tyler too!", reminded voters that General Harrison had won the battle of Tippecanoe. James Tyler was the Whig candidate for vice president. The "buckeye" was adopted as a symbol of the campaign. The picture on this page shows a token of the campaign.

We do not know what kind of president Mr. Harrison would have made. He became ill on the day he started his duties in March 1841 and died a few weeks later. His wife did not even have time to move to Washington.

Ulysses Simpson Grant

Ulysses Simpson Grant (1822-1885) was the eighteenth president of the United States. He served two terms from 1869 to 1877. You can see a picture of him as president on the next page.

Hiram Ulysses Grant was born in 1822 at Point Pleasant, on the Ohio River in Clermont County, in the house shown on the next page. The man in this picture is the doctor who helped Mrs. Grant during the birth of Hiram. You can visit this house today.

Photograph of Ulysses S. Grant during his last year as President of the United States.

In 1823 the Grant family moved to Georgetown, the county seat of Brown County. When asked in later years about his school days, Mr. Grant said that his two men teachers gave more attention to *beatings* than to *books*. As a teenager "Lyss", as he was called, went to an academy at Ripley that was operated by the Rev. John Rankin, whom you learned about in Chapter 8. In 1839 he became a student at the U.S. Military Academy at West Point.

When Hiram Ulysses Grant reported to West Point, the school had no record of him. They were expecting *Ulysses Simpson Grant* (*Simpson* was his mother's family name). Mr. Grant changed his name immediately. He married Julia Dent of Missouri while he was on duty in that state.

Mr. Grant never again lived in Ohio, but in 1855 his parents moved to Covington, Kentucky, which is directly across the Ohio River from Cincinnati. During the Civil War, Mrs. Grant and their children lived with his parents, and he visited the family

President Grant was born in this house at Point Pleasant. The man shown is the physician who helped Mrs. Grant with the birth of Ulysses. If this picture was made when Mr. Grant was 45 years old, how old must the doctor be?

many times. General Grant was an outstanding leader of the United States Army. He brought the war to an end in April 1865 by defeating the Confederate Army under General Robert E. Lee.

At the close of the war, the leaders of both the Democrats and the Republicans — who had once been Whigs — encouraged this famous man to run for president of the United States. Mr. Grant ran as a Republican and was elected. The United States faced many great problems in trying to bring the North and South back together. Ulysses S. Grant had some good ideas about doing this, but too many others in the government were interested only in gaining wealth and power for themselves. He completed his second term as president in 1877 and moved to New York City. Later he wrote the story of his life and finished it just four days before he died in July 1885.

Rutherford Birchard Hayes

Rutherford B. Hayes (1822-1893) was the nineteenth president of the United States, serving from 1877 to 1881. Mr. Hayes, whose picture is on this page was born in Delaware, Ohio in 1822 — just after his father had died. He attended Kenyon College in Knox County and then studied law. He practiced law in Fremont, the county seat of Sandusky County, and later in Cincinnati. He married Lucy Ware Webb who was of great help to him in his activities.

The picture is a lithograph made from a photograph of Rutherford B. Hayes taken about 1877.

Mr. Hayes served in Congress from 1864 to 1868 and as governor of Ohio from 1868 to 1872. When he finished the second term as governor, Mr. Hayes moved his family back to Fremont and made his home there for the rest of his life. In 1875, the Republican Party asked him to run for governor again, and he was re-elected. He became known throughout the United States as the three-time governor of the third largest state. In 1876 the Republican

Party **nominated** him (put his name up for voting) to be president of the United States, and he was elected.

The United States faced the same problems under Mr. Hayes that it did when Mr. Grant was president, and he had the same problems in working with Congress. When he was elected, Mr. Hayes said that he would serve only one term, so in 1881 he returned to his home in Fremont. Mr. Hayes loved his family and pictures like the one above made people like him. Today you can visit the Hayes Presidential Center in Fremont and learn more about Rutherford B. Hayes.

James Abram Garfield

James A. Garfield (1831-1881) was elected as the twentieth president of the United

Photograph of James A. Garfield taked during the last year of his life.

238

States in 1880, but he served for only a few months. As a boy, he worked on a canal boat hauling coal to Cleveland. His picture as president is on the opposite page.

James Garfield married Lucretia Rudolph of Geauga County in 1858, and the next year he was elected to the General Assembly of Ohio. While serving as an officer in the Civil War, he was elected to Congress and served well for almost twenty years. In 1880 he attended the Republican National Convention to help John Sherman get the nomination as president. Mr. Sherman was born in Fairfield County, Ohio but lived most of his life in Richland County. The leaders of the Republican Party could not agree on anyone until someone suggested James Garfield. He was then nominated to be president.

James Garfield was elected president in November 1880 and took the oath of office in March 1881. He made a good start at being president, but on July 2, 1881, he was shot by a man who was mentally ill. The picture below is an artist's idea of what happened. Mr. Garfield died two months later and was buried at Lakeview Cemetery in Cleveland. You can visit his former home in Mentor in Lake County.

This is an artist's ideas of the assassination of President James Garfield. Why is this not a photograph?

Benjamin Harrison

Benjamin Harrison (1833-1901) served as the twenty-third president of the United States from 1889 to 1893. His picture as president is below.

An artist made this charcoal and chalk drawing of Benjamin Harrison about the time he became president.

Mr. Harrison was born in 1833 in the home of his grandfather, William Henry Harrison, at North Bend in Hamilton County. After graduating from Miami University in 1852, he studied law. He then moved to Indianapolis, Indiana where he lived the remainder of his life. In 1853 he married Caroline Lavinia Scott.

Benjamin Harrison became deeply involved in politics and church work, but he was always more interested in fairness than political advantage. He served as a United States Senator from Indiana from 1881 to 1887. The leaders of the Republican Party asked him to run for the presidency, and he was elected in 1888. Mr. Harrison promised that he would improve the employment policies of the government, provide benefits for veterans of the Civil War, and enforce the rights of African-Americans to vote. Again, Congress did not help him, so he could not reach his goals. In 1893 Benjamin Harrison returned to his Indiana home and died there in 1901. You can visit his former home in Indianapolis.

William McKinley

William McKinley (1843-1901) was the twenty-fifth president of the United States, serving from 1897 until he was killed at the beginning of his second term in 1901. His picture as president is on the next page.

Mr. McKinley was born in 1843 at Niles in Trumbull County. While a college student, he enlisted in the Union Army early in the Civil War. After the war, he studied law and began to practice in Canton, the

An artist painted this portrait of William McKinley shortly after he became president.

good luck, Mr. McKinley made a habit of wearing one. When he died, the General Assembly honored him by making the scarlet carnation our state flower.

In 1886 Marcus A. Hanna, a very wealthy owner of steel mills and coal companies in Cleveland, urged the Republican Party to nominate Mr. McKinley for the presidency. When they did nominate him, Mr. Hanna arranged to have Mr. McKinley run for the office without leaving his home in Canton.

William McKinley was a hard-working president at the time when the United States was having problems with Spain. In 1898 these problems led to the Spanish-American War. When the war ended, Cuba became an independent nation. The United States gained control of Puerto Rico, Guam, and the Philippine Islands.

Mr. McKinley was easily elected to a second term in 1900. Less than a year later, during a visit to Buffalo, New York, he was shot by a mentally-ill man. He died a few days later, and vice president Theodore Roosevelt became president.

As you can see in the picture on the next page, a large number of people attended the official opening of the beautiful building put up in Canton to honor him. You can also visit a nearby museum to learn more about his life and work.

county seat of Stark County in 1867. He married Ida Saxton in 1871.

Mr. McKinley became active in political affairs, and he served in Congress from 1877 to 1883 and from 1885 to 1891. He was then elected governor of Ohio for four years. The first time he ran for political office, Mr. McKinley met a man wearing a scarlet carnation. When the man told him that scarlet carnations were symbols of

241

The people of Ohio honored William McKinley by building this memorial to him in Canton. The picture was taken on the day of dedication. Who are the people along the lower-right edge of this picture?

William Howard Taft

William Howard Taft (1857-1930) was the twenty-seventh president of the United States and served from 1909 to 1913. You learned something about his birthplace and saw him in the picture on page 192. The picture on this page shows him as president. As you can see, he was a very large man who weighed more than 300 pounds.

Mr. Taft attended Yale University and graduated from the Cincinnati Law

Picture to the right: An artist made this etching of President William Howard Taft in 1911.

School in 1880. He married Helen Herron, and they had two sons and a daughter, each of whom made great contributions to good government in Ohio. Mr. Taft's father and grandfather were also involved in politics, and some of his grandchildren and great-grandchildren were still active in our state in 1990.

At the close of the Spanish-American War, Mr. Taft was named governor of the Philippine Islands. He was a friend of President Theodore Roosevelt. When Mr. Roosevelt decided not to run for re-election in 1908, he helped Mr. Taft win the nomination of the Republican Party. Mr. Taft worked hard to pass laws limiting what big businesses could do. This made the Republican leaders angry. When he ran for re-election in 1912, he was badly defeated. In 1921 he was named Chief Justice of the United States Supreme Court. He served in that position until he died in 1930.

Warren Gamaliel Harding

Warren G. Harding (1865-1923) was the twenty-ninth president of the United States, but he served less than one term from 1921 to 1923. He was born in 1865 near Blooming Grove, a small town where Crawford, Marion, and Richland Counties meet. When he finished school, he worked for a newspaper in Marion. His picture as president is on this page. His former home in Marion is now a museum.

Warren Harding married Florence Kling DeWolfe in 1891. She was a very capable woman who helped to make a success of the newspaper. Mr. Harding was a very

This is a portrait of Warren Harding in the last year as President of the United States.

handsome and friendly man. He became interested in politics and was easily elected to the General Assembly. Later he served as lieutenant governor of Ohio. He was defeated when he ran for governor in 1910 but was elected to Congress in 1915.

The people of Marion built this beautiful memorial to honor their neighbors Warren and Florence DeWolfe Harding. Why do you think there is a very ordinary fence around this memorial?

On election day in 1920, the voters in the United States knew that the next president would be a newspaper man from Ohio. The Democratic candidate for president was James M. Cox, a newspaper man from Dayton, who was then the governor of Ohio. The Republican candidate was Warren G. Harding, a newspaper man from Marion. Mr. Harding was elected.

In the summer of 1923, the President and Mrs. Harding took a trip to Alaska and the Western States. Shortly after they reached San Francisco on the way home, Mr. Harding died of an unknown cause. In 1931 the people of Marion built the beautiful memorial you can see above to mark the graves of Mr. and Mrs. Harding.

Only one other state, Virginia, has been the home of eight presidents of the United States. Since William Henry Harrison was born in Virginia, he is part of the eight from both Ohio and Virginia. It is most unlikely that any other state will ever tie this record.

Let's Review Part 3

New Words

nominate
slogan

New Things to Do

Choose one of the presidents of the United States mentioned in this part and learn more about him. Write a short report telling why you chose to study this man and what you learned that was most surprising to you.

What have we learned?

Free people want as few laws as possible, but large numbers of people cannot live together in peace unless everyone obeys the laws. In 1803, when there were about 60,000 people scattered over the 40,000 square miles of Ohio, the citizens adopted a simple constitution to guide their lives.

By 1851 there were almost 2,000,000 people living in Ohio, and many of the old laws were no longer useful. For this reason, the state adopted its Second Constitution. This is still the basic law of our state, but it has been amended many times over the years.

During the last half of the 19th century, Ohio played a leading role in dealing with social problems that affected our nation. Between 1868 and 1924, eight political leaders of Ohio were elected President of the United States to help our nation deal with these problems. Unfortunately, some of the problems remain with us as we approach the 21st century.

Map Projects

Find the following places on your map of Ohio.

Place	County
Blooming Grove	Crawford
Canton	Stark
Conneaut	Ashtabula
Fremont	Sandusky
Georgetown	Brown
Hillsboro	Highland
Kenyon College	Knox
Marion	Marion
Mentor	Lake
Miami University	Butler
New Vienna	Highland
Niles	Trumbull
Oberlin College	Lorain
The Ohio State Univ.	Franklin
Ohio University	Athens
Point Pleasant	Clermont

Find the following places on your map of the United States.

Place	State
Buffalo	New York
Covington	Kentucky
San Francisco	California
West Point	New York

Find the following places on your map of the world.

Place	Continent/Ocean
Cuba	Caribbean Sea
Guam	Pacific Ocean
Philippine Islands	Southwest Pacific Ocean
Spain	Europe

Books to Read

The following books will help you understand Ohio Government during the 19th Century and the presidents of the United States from Ohio. Your local library may have other books on these subjects.

Encyclopedia of Presidents Series is a series of books with each one presenting a biography of one president.

First Ladies, by Rhoda Blumberg, has a short biography of the wife of each president of the United States.

Leaders of Labor, by Roy Cook, presents the biographies of eleven important leaders in the history of the American trade unions.

A Nation Torn: The Story of How The Civil War Began, by Delia Ray, presents a simple report of events throughout the United States that led to the start of the Civil War.

Out of the Midwest, by Frank Siedel, is a collection of stories about events in Ohio. The story about the "three R's" is included.

The Presidents in American History, by Charles A. Beard, presents a short biography of each president of the United States.

The Tafts, by Cass R. Sandak, is a short biography of William Howard Taft and his family.

Chapter 12

How did life change in the 20th century?

Let's learn...

- **how turmoil in the world affected Ohio.**

- **how working conditions changed.**

- **what happened during the Great Depression.**

- **how we can enjoy free time.**

In the last five chapters, you have learned how Ohio changed during the 19th century. In the next four chapters, you will learn how it changed even more during the 20th century! Turmoil in Europe during the 19th century increased during the first half of the 20th century. This led to two of the worst wars in history. Both wars caused the population of Ohio to increase greatly. After the end of the second war, turmoil in Asia encouraged many citizens of that continent to migrate to our state.

Working conditions were bad at the beginning of the 20th century. They were worse during the Great Depression of the 1930s. During these difficult years, labor unions gained new powers to improve the lives of workers. As the economy grew during the second half of the century, people had more free time to do things they enjoyed. The time line on the next page will help you understand this chapter.

As you study the 20th century, talk to your parents, grandparents, and the oldest people you know. Tell them what you are studying, and ask them what they remember from their early years. They will enjoy talking about "the old days", and you will learn many things that are not in this book.

Part 1

How did turmoil in the world affect Ohio?

During the early years of the 20th century, turmoil in eastern and southern Europe encouraged millions of people to migrate to the United States. Many of the men found work in the large factories of northeastern Ohio and in the coal mines and oil fields of eastern Ohio. By contrast, since 1950 far more people have come from countries of Asia and the Middle East than from Europe.

World War I (1914-1918)

The industries of Ohio and the United States grew during the early years of the 20th century. The economy of the southern states, including *Appalachia*, did not grow. The region called the *South* included the states of Alabama, Georgia, Louisiana, Mississippi, North and South Carolina, and Tennessee. The region called *Appalachia* covered the hilly land of southeastern Ohio, West Virginia, eastern Kentucky and Tennessee, and western Virginia and North Carolina. When World War I broke out in Europe in 1914, many of the industries of Ohio began to make war **materiel** (military equipment of all kinds). This combination of conditions encouraged unemployed people from Europe, Appalachia, and the South to move to Ohio to find work. The stories in the boxes on page 250 tell how unskilled people from these regions tried to improve their lives by moving to Akron and Cleveland. You will learn about the industries of these cities in Chapter 14.

Time Line of Events Discussed in Chapter 12

Year	Events
1980-1920	Immigrants from eastern and southern Europe
1914	World War I began in Europe
1917	United States entered World War I
1918	World War I ended
1919	Eighteenth Amendment to Constitution prohibited making and using alcoholic drinks.
1920	Nineteenth Amendment to Constitution gave women right to vote
1922	Communists gained control of Russia and created the Union of Soviet Socialist Republics
1929-1939	The Great Depression
1939	World War II began in Europe
1941	Japan attacked the United States
1941-1945	United States fought in World War II
1947	India gained freedom from Great Britain
	Pakistan separated from India
1949	Communists gained control of China
	Old Chinese Government took control of Taiwan
	Philippine Islands freed by United States
	Israel established as a new nation
1950	Communists gained control of North Korea and attacked South Korea
1950-1954	United States helped South Korea in Civil War with North Korea
1954	Communists gained control of North Vietnam
1955-1975	United States helped South Vietnam defend itself against North Vietnam
1967-1973	Arabs and Israelis fought each other
1975	Communists gained control of Cambodia and Laos
1980-1989	Iran and Iraq fought each other
1989	Communist governments of USSR and Eastern Europe collapsed

Why Poor People Moved to Akron During World War I

By 1915 Akron was growing fast. The word spread over the countryside, "There's work in Akron.", and men came by the thousands. Thirty thousand workers arrived in 1916; between 1910 and 1920, the population jumped from 69,000 to 209,000.

Workers came pouring over the Ohio border from West Virginia and Kentucky. The shortage of help in the rubber industry made wages go up. And people who got jobs told their friends back home about the opportunities in Akron. Akron was discussed in the...lands of eastern Europe, but they could not pronounce the name. "Through the black belt of America ran the rumor of [high wages] to be picked up...working [in rubber factories]. In the hills of Scotland, the Akron wage news was told, in the hills of [southern Europe], in the hills of Tennessee."

Adopted from: *The Ohio Guide*, WPA Writers' Program, p. 171

How African-American Workers Were Found

War production by northern industry created a demand for labor. Northern factory owners encouraged African-Americans to migrate to the North by sending labor agents into the South to find *Negro* workers. These opportunities for jobs and the increasing racial problems in the South increased the migration to the North. Some Cleveland businessmen paid their labor agents one dollar for every Negro workman found. The agents of some Cleveland companies carried pictures of the homes of wealthy Negroes which were shown to southern sharecroppers as examples of "the sort of places you'd live in up in Cleveland."

Adopted from: W.W. Giffin, *The Negro in Ohio*, 1914-1939, pp. 19-21

When the United States entered the war in 1917, almost 4 million young men joined the army or navy. Later you will learn how women went to work in factories to make war materiel. The war ended in November 1918, and tens of thousands of young men and women of Ohio married and began having children. These new families also increased the population of our state.

World War II (1939-1945)

By 1930 the nations that were defeated in World War I were preparing for another war. Germany and Italy began World War II in September 1939. By December 1941, they had conquered almost all of Europe except Great Britain and parts of Russia. At the same time, Japan seized control of large parts of eastern Asia and islands in the Pacific Ocean. The industries of Ohio and the United States were very busy making war materiel for our friends in Europe. In December 1941, Japan attacked Pearl Harbor in Hawaii, and the United States declared war against Germany, Italy, and Japan. Factories then began to work 24 hours a day for 7 days each week to create war materiel. At the close of the war in 1945, the United States worked with many other countries to create the *United Nations* in the hope of preventing future wars.

From December 1941 until August 1945, almost 16 million men and women entered the armed forces of the United States. At the same time, many factories were operating twenty-four hours a day for seven days a week. As a result, thousands of men and women from Appalachia and the South found jobs in the manufacturing centers of Ohio.

The ten years from 1941 to 1950 brought more changes to the lives of people living in Ohio and the United States than any other single **decade** (ten-year period). Many of the children, who were born after World War I, married before they began military service in World War II. Still more of them married after they were released from military duty. Beginning in 1946, each year the number of new babies jumped greatly. Your parents, or grandparents, may have been part of the "baby boomers", as the children born after World War II were called.

Conflicts in Asia and The Middle East

Asia is the largest continent and the home of more than 3 billion people. It is almost twice as big as North America, and it has more than half the people of the world. The map on the next page shows the nations we will be considering. This map shows that Asia includes the nations around the eastern end of the Mediterranean Sea — the area we often call the *Middle East*. It includes most of the land of Russia, although the largest cities of Russia are in Europe. It also includes China, Japan, and Korea, which are parts of the *Far East*.

During the last half of the 20th century, wars in all parts of Asia encouraged people to migrate to the United States and many of them settled in Ohio. The diagram on page 253 shows when people from various

251

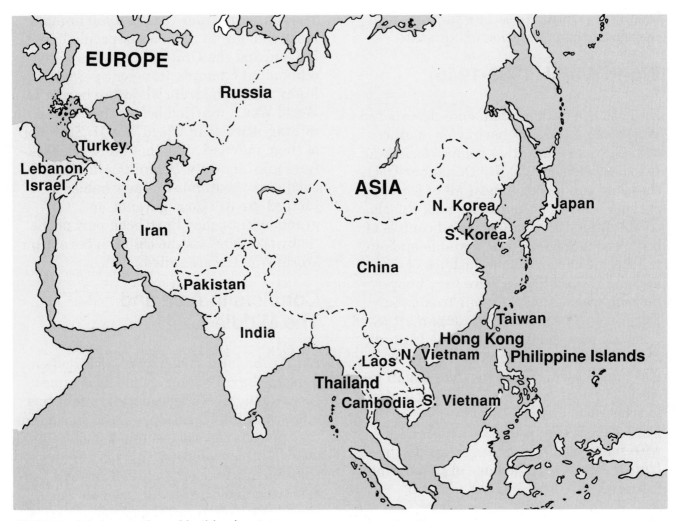

Nations of Asia mentioned in this chapter.

parts of Asia came to live in our state. The census information in Appendix B (page 383) shows how many people from Asia lived in your county in 1990. We will now look at the events that had the greatest effect on our state.

Middle East: When the nation of Israel was established in the Middle East in 1948, conflicts developed throughout the region that have not yet been settled. These conflicts caused thousands of people, especially from Lebanon and Iran, to migrate to the United States and many settled in Ohio.

People from Asia Living in Ohio
1990 Census

People from Asia Living in Ohio in 1990

	Year Arrived					
	1990 Totals	1980- 1989	1970- 1979	1960- 1969	1950- 1959	Pre- 1950
Cambodia & Laos	4,791	4,791				
China & Hong Kong	20,175	16,178	2,225	922	345	505
India	20,848	13,342	5,508	1,711	213	74
Japan	10,485	6,761	1,441	969	1,141	173
Korea	11,237	5,226	4,493	1,267	241	10
Middle East	7,903		4,553	1,270	762	1,318
Philippines	10,268	4,581	3,552	1,626	352	157
Vietnam	4,964	2,318	2,580	61	5	0
Other Asia	11,586	1,838	7,611	1,357	451	329
Total Asians	102,257	55,035	31,963	9,183	3,510	2,566

Many people came to Ohio from Asia after World War II.

India: During the five years following the close of World War II, great changes took place in India. The people of that nation gained freedom from Great Britain in 1947. Almost immediately, some of the people declared their independence from India and formed the nation of Pakistan. Poor economic conditions in both these countries encouraged thousands of their young men to come to the United States to study, and many came to the colleges of Ohio.

Japan: During the 1930s and early 1940s, Japan conquered most of China, Korea, and smaller nations of southeastern Asia. After the United States entered World War II, Japan was badly damaged and finally defeated. In the late 1940s, the United States began to help the people of Japan rebuild their economy. This help was so effective that by 1970 our nation was buying more goods from Japanese industries than we were selling to them. As a result, Japanese industries began to buy American companies and/or build new factories in our country, including several in Ohio. You will learn more about these in Chapter 14.

Communism: In the late 1940s, Communists seized control of China, and a small group of Chinese people fled to the island of Taiwan to establish the *Republic of China*. The United States helped the people of Taiwan when the Communists tried to attack the island.

In 1950 the United States took the lead in the *United Nations* to prevent Communist China from seizing Korea. As a result, thousands of United States soldiers, sailors, and airmen fought in Korea for almost four years. Some of our armed forces were still there in 1994.

During the 1950s, students from the Republic of China (Taiwan) and Korea began to attend colleges in the United States, and hundreds of them came to Ohio. Some of these students returned to their homelands after graduation, but many more remained here and brought their families to live with them.

In 1955 the United States began to help the people of South Vietnam protect themselves against the Communist rulers of North Vietnam. After the United States withdrew from Vietnam in 1975, hundreds of thousands of people fled from South Vietnam. When North Vietnam attacked the neighboring countries of Cambodia and Laos, many of these people fled to other nations. Hundreds of thousands of them came to the United States and many settled in Ohio.

Let's Review Part 1

New Words

decade
materiel

New Things to Do

Talk to your parents and/or grandparents about how your ancestors happened to come to Ohio. Work with your classmates to write a list on the chalk board of each person and where her/his family lived before coming to Ohio. Ask those from the most unusual places to tell the class what they learned about their family migrations.

Part 2

How did working conditions change?

At the beginning of the 20th century, working conditions were very poor when compared to today. Many owners of companies *exploited* their workers by making them work long hours, under unsafe conditions, for low pay. A very small number of people, including John D. Rockefeller of Cleveland, became very wealthy as they gained control of the natural resources of the United States. A small but growing number of merchants, craftsmen, and other educated people formed the "middle class."

National Cash Register Company

A few **employers** (owners of business who hire workers) took great personal interest in their **employees** (workers) and gave them personal help when they had special needs. This practice was called *paternalism* because the employer acted as "father" to the employees. During the early years of the 20th century, the *National Cash Register Company* of Dayton was a leader in this form of management.

In 1884 John Henry Patterson, a descendent of Robert Patterson — one of the founders of Dayton — bought the rights to make a machine popularly called "thief catcher." This machine was designed so that employees could not steal money from merchants. Patterson soon organized the *National Cash Register Company* (NCR) to make these machines. He became very successful at selling these *cash registers*. He also did everything he could to make his workers happy, as you can learn from the box on the next page.

The entire future of the company changed in June of 1904, when Charles F. Kettering was hired as an "electrical expert." Within two years, Mr. Kettering invented devices that made it possible to operate cash registers by electricity. By 1910 NCR was making nine of every ten cash registers used in the United States. You can learn about Charles Kettering in the box on page 257.

In 1972 NCR employed 20,000 people in Dayton making mechanical cash machines, while other companies were making

Labor Relations at National Cash Register Company

In a fatherly way, John Patterson gave his employees fringe benefits that were unheard of in industrial relations. He gave them shower baths, clothes lockers, swimming pools, hot lunches, medical care, and inspiring talks. Women employees were taught how to manage their homes. Children of employees were taught how to save their money, how to chew their food, and how to avoid scattering germs when they sneezed. In return for these benefits, he required absolute loyalty to the company and good workmanship.

Adapted from: Moskowitz, et.al.: *Everybody's Business,* p.443

1990 NCR was the leading manufacturer of automatic bank-teller machines and employed almost 56,000 people throughout the world.

Labor Unions

In the last chapter, you learned that some workers organized trade unions before 1900 to protect themselves from unfair treatment. As companies grew between 1900 and 1920, more and more workers joined unions to protect their interests.

You also learned that several small unions joined together in 1886 to organize the *American Federation of Labor* (AFL). These unions represented skilled craftsmen who worked alone or in small groups. For example, carpenters, painters, and electricians formed their own unions, but they cooperated with each other through the AFL. Very few women were employed in these trades.

Because workers in mass-production industries, such as automobiles, clothing, and steel faced different problems, they organized themselves differently. The *International Ladies Garment Workers Union*, for example, was organized to deal with the problem of "piece work" that you read about in the box on page 191. In 1935 Congress passed the *National Labor Relations Act* to make it easier for mass-production workers to form unions. Several of these unions quickly joined

electronic cash machines. When the company began making electronic machines, it changed its name to *NCR Corporation*. Employment in Dayton dropped to about 5,000, as NCR built new factories in other states and nations. In

Charles Franklin Kettering, An Ohio Inventor

Charles F. Kettering was born in 1876 on a farm in Ashland County. As a boy, he loved to work with machinery. He won a scholarship to the Loudonville High School. He was such a good student in high school that, after graduating, he was hired to teach in two small schools near Loudonville. In 1898 he entered The Ohio State University to study engineering. Eye problems forced him to drop out of college after the first year, and he took a job installing some of the first telephones in Ashland County. He also met Olive Williams of Ashland, whom he later married.

Mr. Kettering returned to The Ohio State University and earned a degree in electrical engineering. In 1904 he accepted a job in the research department of the National Cash Register Company. During the next five years, he created the most widely used cash machines in the world. He then began to invent devices for automobiles, including the first electric starting system. From 1918 to 1956, Charles Kettering was Vice President for Research of the General Motors Corporation. In this position, he helped to create many products that are still widely used.

Mr. and Mrs. Kettering lived the rest of their lives in Montgomery County. The family home, called *Ridgeleigh Terrace*, is near the Kettering Memorial Hospital in the city of Kettering. Their son, Edmund, gave the home and the hospital to the people of that city.

together to create the *Congress for Industrial Organization* (CIO).

During the last half of the 1930s, four of the largest CIO unions had thousands of members in Ohio: the United Automobile Workers, the United Rubber Workers, the United Mine Workers of America, and the United Steelworkers of America. Each of these unions staged *sit-down* **strikes** (stopped work) for better wages and working conditions. This means that the workers went to their jobs one morning, and then refused either to work or to leave

257

During the late 1930's, CIO members staged several "sit-down" strikes in automobile factories. What are these strikers sitting on?

the factories or mines. The picture above shows a sit-down strike in an automobile factory. When the United States entered World War II, Congress outlawed strikes in industries making war materiel.

The various unions of the AFL and CIO sometimes quarreled over which should represent workers in particular jobs. In 1955 the two organizations united to form what is popularly called the *AFL-CIO*. A few strong unions, including the United Mine Workers of America, refused to join the AFL-CIO, and they are still separate groups. The total

membership of all unions in the United States reached 19,700,000 in 1975 but dropped to 17,000,000 by 1989.

Women

As you now know, in 1900 some women were working hard to gain the same legal rights that men enjoyed. As you also know, during World War I, several million young men left their jobs and entered the army and navy. Since the factories making war materiel needed help, women were hired to do many jobs that employers had thought they were "unfit" to do. For example, the

picture above shows a woman operating a machine in a factory.

As women proved that they could work as well as men, they demanded the right to vote. The male voters finally approved two amendments to the United States Constitution that many women had wanted for a long time. In 1919 the Eighteenth Amendment prohibited the manufacture and sale of alcoholic beverages. In 1920 the Nineteenth Amendment gave women the right to vote.

Before World War I, very few lower-income students went to school beyond the eighth grade. At the same time, most girls and boys of upper-income families went to a public high school or a private academy. Far more upper-income boys than girls went to college. Throughout the 1920s and 1930s, more and more young women went to high school and college. Most of those who worked outside their homes were office workers, school teachers, nurses, and librarians.

During the Depression, women had trouble finding jobs because many people said, "Women who work are taking jobs away from men who need them." When the United States entered World War II, women again filled many jobs that had been closed to them. The picture on this page shows how women were urged to work in war industries. "Rosie the Riveter" became a national symbol of patriotism. Women even became members of the Armed Forces of the United States to perform jobs that did not involve fighting.

Between 1945 and 1965, many more jobs opened for women, but very few were admitted to the study of medicine, law, architecture, or engineering until the 1970s. Many women operated small stores, but few were managers of big businesses.

Women worked in many ways to help win World War II. How does the appearance of this woman differ from the woman shown on the previous page.

Let's Review Part 2

New Words

employee
employer
strike (labor)

New Things to Do

1. Look at the cash registers in the stores you visit. Also look at the automatic banking machines you pass. Write down the name of the company that made each of these machines. How many of these machines have NCR or National Cash Register Company on them?

2. Look in the "yellow pages" of your telephone directory under the heading of Labor Organizations. Make a list of the unions that are listed — note that some unions may have more than one "local" in your area. Try to find a member of your family, a friend of your family, or a neighbor, who is a member of a labor union. Talk to this person about unions, and write a short report about the role of labor unions in your community.

3. Ask an older woman you know to tell you how the role of women has changed in her lifetime. Compare what you learn with what your class mates learn about this.

Part 3

What happened during the Great Depression?

When the economy of an area is very good, we say that it is a time of **prosperity** because almost everyone has a job. When the economy is bad, we say that it is a time of **depression** because many people have no work. Between the end of World War II and 1991, there were a few times of **recession**, or mild economic depression, but no serious economic troubles.

During the first nine months of 1929, most citizens of Ohio were happy and prosperous. Many low-income families still lived in the type of housing you can see on page 187, but most had electric lights and indoor toilets. Many middle-income families owned homes and automobiles.

In October 1929, the economy of the United States began to fall. Within two years, the economies of many nations of the world fell more than any time before. Thousands of Ohio businesses closed and hundreds of thousands of workers lost their jobs. Those who continued to work accepted big cuts in pay. Hundreds of banks closed, and people lost money they had saved "for a rainy day." The picture on the next page might have been taken in any city of the United States. The picture on page 263 was taken in Ohio.

In 1932 Franklin D. Roosevelt was elected president of the United States, because he promised to solve the economic problems of our nation. In 1933 Congress created many new programs to create work for people. You can still see the results of four of these programs in our state.

Works Progress Administration (WPA)

The WPA created jobs for large numbers of people who were paid 40 cents an hour. Unskilled workers built city streets using hand tools such as picks, shovels, and wheelbarrows. Skilled workers drew maps of every county of Ohio. College-trained historians wrote books about the history of Ohio and the large cities of our state. If you go to your public library, you will probably find a copy of *Ohio Guide* that was written as a WPA project.

Public Works Administration (PWA)

PWA has the same letters as WPA, and many people were confused about these two programs. PWA programs gave money to states and local units of government to

During the Great Depression, people did many things to earn money. Do you think a photographer just happened to snap this picture? Explain your answer.

During the Great Depression, many Ohio farmers lost their land. What does it mean to sell something "at public auction?"

build public buildings. If your town post office, city hall, or school was built between 1934 and 1942, it might have been a PWA project. Each of the PWA buildings has a marker near the main door that says it was built as a Public Works Administration project.

Civilian Conservation Corps (CCC)

The purpose of the CCC program was to put young, unmarried men to work repairing land that had been damaged by removal of the trees and/or poor ways of farming. For example, look back to the map on page 29 and find the Muskingum River. In 1933 a large part of the soil along this river was badly **eroded** (washed away). The State of Ohio established the *Muskingum Conservancy District*, and men from several CCC camps worked to improve the region. Several CCC projects became state parks including Lake Hope State Park in Vinton County and Shawnee State Park in Scioto County. The CCC workers were given room, food, and clothing. They were also paid about 25 cents an hour.

During the late 1930s, Metropolitan Housing Authorities built many housing projects for low-income people. How do these buildings compare to an apartment house you have seen?

Federal Housing Programs

The Federal housing programs created during the 1930s still affect many cities in the United States. We will look at only one of them now and at others in the next chapter.

Earlier in this chapter, you learned about the thousands of poor people who came to Ohio during World War I. The only housing these people could afford was in the old houses of the big cities. The owners of these places often lived in outlying areas and did not keep the buildings repaired. As these buildings decayed, the old neighborhoods became slums.

In 1933 President Roosevelt made a speech in which he said, "one third of our nation is ill-fed, ill-housed, and ill-clothed." Shortly after this speech, Congress created *Metropolitan Housing Authorities* (MHA) to help cities provide good housing for the poor. Large numbers of houses in the oldest parts of cities were torn down. New groups of modern apartment houses, like the ones above, were built on the cleared land. You can see buildings of this kind in many cities.

In 1938 Cleveland opened one of the earliest MHA projects. The Stokes family was one of the first to move into this development. Carl and Louis Stokes grew up to become political leaders of Cleveland. You can read about them in the box on the next page.

The MHA program is still in operation in all large cities. It continued to build groups

How Public Housing Helped The Stokes Family

"... My mother, Louis and I [Carl B. Stokes] lived ... in a rickety old two-family house. We covered the rat holes with the tops of tin cans. The front steps always needed fixing, one of them always seemed to be missing. The coal stove kept the living room warm; we used heated bricks and an old flatiron wrapped in flannel to keep warm in the bedroom. The three of us shared one bed.

"Poor people are [crowded] into such neighborhoods, where survival too often means that they are forced to prey on each other. When my mother washed the clothes on Saturday night, she hung them in the kitchen to dry. Hanging them outside meant you didn't want them anymore. When Louis and I would take our wagon down to get the [free] dried peas, flour, rice and dried milk that was [given] to [people on] welfare..., we took along a baseball bat to get the food home past the other kids and sometimes even adults."

"We were delivered from the [worst part] of our poverty in 1938, when I was eleven. Cleveland was the first city in the country to construct housing for the poor with federal funds. For some time after the plans for the housing were known and Mother had [asked] for an apartment, we lived in day-to-day [hope] of getting out of our rickety old house. She would tell Louis and me about steam heat, painted walls, beds of our own, but I'm sure these things meant little to us at the time. We had no experience to give these words meaning."

"The day we moved was pure wonder. A sink with hot and cold running water, a place where you could wash clothes with a washing machine, and an actual refrigerator. And we learned what it was to live in dependable warmth. For the first time, we had two bedrooms and two beds. My mother for the first time had a room and a bed of her own."

From: Stokes, *Promises of Power*, pp. 22-25

of large apartment buildings through the 1960s. Today, public housing projects are often built in the form of one or two-family buildings scattered throughout the area.

Let's Review Part 3

New Words

depression (economic)
erode
prosperity
recession (economic)

New Things to Do

1. Look in you telephone directory for your local Metropolitan Housing Authority. This may be listed under the name of the biggest city in your county or under the name of the county. If you have no MHA in your county, go to your public library and look at a directory of a big city.

2. On your map of the county, locate each of the projects in your county.

Part 4

How can we enjoy our free time?

It is easy to answer some questions that people ask you: What is your name? Where do you live? How old are you? How far do you travel to go to school? It may be more difficult to answer other questions: How do you feel? What do you enjoy doing? What do you like to read, see, or hear? Whom do

you like? These questions are related to the **quality** (character) of your life. Your answers to these questions may change from year to year.

Today you have many "advantages" of modern life that girls and boys did not have in 1900, including reliable electric service, radio and television, clothes that are easy to clean, and comfortable transportation. But are you *happier* than they were? Many people enjoy life most when they are doing interesting and worthwhile activities. In this part, we will look at a few of the activities in our state that can make our lives more interesting.

Religion

There are two questions that almost everyone asks sometime in life: "What is the meaning of life?" and "What is the meaning of death?" The great majority of people look for answers to these questions in some form of *religion*. In 1900 the only religious groups that most Americans could name were *Protestant, Catholic,* and *Jewish*. As thousands of people came to Ohio from Asia during the 20th century, they brought other forms of religion with them. In almost every large city of Ohio today, you can attend religious services in Christian churches, Jewish synagogues, Moslem mosques, Buddhist shrines, and Hindu temples. As you can see on the next page, some of the most beautiful buildings in Ohio are centers of worship. On the other hand, many people reject the teachings of organized religions but believe in a *Supreme Being* whom they worship in their own way.

The Moslem center of worship in Perrysburg is the largest mosque in Ohio.

St. Peter in Chains cathedral was built during the 1840s.

Isaac M. Wise Temple is the home of reformed Judaism in the United States.

Recreation

Have you ever thought of *recreation* as re-creation? Human beings re-create themselves in many ways: some enjoy physical activity, some do craft work at home, and others travel to distant lands. For some people, the biggest social event each year is the county fair. *The Ohio State Fair*, held in Columbus every August, advertises that it is the greatest fair in the United States. You can see a picture of the entrance to it on the next page.

In every county, you can find recreation areas operated by a city, the county, or the State of Ohio where you can enjoy very active — or very quiet — play without cost. There are also many activities that cost money. You can take boat rides on Lake Erie or the Ohio River. You can go to athletic events varying in skill from the *Little Leagues* to the highest-paid

The Ohio State Fair is supposed to be the largest in the United States? What happens at a state or county fair?

professional teams. You can go to very large amusement parks at Cedar Point in Erie County, Geauga Lake in Portage County, and Kings Island in Warren County. You can visit zoos in several cities and even go to a *Sea World* in Portage County hundreds of miles from the sea.

The Ohio Historical Society owns at least sixty historic sites where you can learn more about the places and events mentioned in this book. For example, you can visit the Afro-American Museum in Greene County, which is shown in the next column. During summer months, you can visit outdoor plays based on events you learned about in earlier chapters. *Trumpet*

The National Afro-American Museum and Cultural Center is near Central State University in Greene County. Why do you think the word National is in the name?

in The Land is presented in Tuscarawas County near the site of the massacre at

Gnadenhutten. *Tecumseh* is presented in Ross County where that Shawnee leader lived as a boy. *Blue Jacket* is presented in Greene County on the site of the village where he lived.

Creative and Performing Arts

Are you interested in drawing, painting, modeling clay, writing stories, or poetry? These activities are often called *creative arts*. Are you interested in singing, dancing, playing a musical instrument, or acting? These activities are often called *performing arts*. Throughout history, wealthy people have given money, and sometimes housing and food, to people who are especially talented in the creative and performing arts. Some wealthy Ohioans have given money to build concert halls and art museums in our state. Others have given collections of books to libraries or collections of art to museums.

Several pictures in this book are copies of works of Ohio artists, including the one on on the next page. This picture is usually called *The Spirit of '76*, but Archibald M. Willard, the artist, first called it *Yankee Doodle*. You can learn more about Mr. Willard from the box on page 271.

Have you ever attended a *craft fair*? Has someone you know shown craft work at a fair? If your answer is "yes" to either of these questions, you know that *folk art* is very popular today. This kind of art includes ceramics, quilting, wood-working, and other activities that many people do as *hobbies*.

Literature

Many people enjoy reading for relaxation and/or inspiration. Ohio has been the birthplace and/or work place of many widely-known writers, but we can mention only two.

Harriet Beecher Stowe: Harriet Beecher was born in Connecticut to a family that worked to abolish slavery. The family moved to Cincinnati in 1832, and Harriet lived there until 1850. During these eighteen years, she married Calvin Stowe and did all she could to make people aware of the evils of slavery. The Stowe family left Cincinnati and returned to Connecticut, where Harriet wrote books for the next forty years. Based on her experiences in Cincinnati, she wrote *Uncle Tom's Cabin* in 1852. This book became a "best seller" and convinced many people that the slaves should be set free.

Paul Laurence Dunbar: One of the best known American poets of the early 20th century was Paul Laurence Dunbar. His former home in Dayton is now a museum of his life and writings. The picture on page 271 shows him at home. The parents of Paul Dunbar were both born into slavery, but they escaped to Dayton by way of the *Underground Railroad*.

The Spirit of '76 is one of the best-known works of art ever made. Do you think this painting was made from a photograph? Explain your answer.

Paul was born there in 1872. Paul's mother worked and sacrificed to make it possible for him to attend high school, where he was the only African-American student. Paul spent all of his free time reading and writing. He was editor of the school magazine and wrote the graduation song for the class of 1891. The only job Paul could get before or after graduation was operating an elevator.

When he was 19, Paul decided to create a newspaper for the 5,000 African-American citizens of Dayton. Orville Wright, his high school classmate and friend, printed the paper. Orville and his brother Wilbur also helped Paul create a small book of poetry. You will learn more about the Wrights in Chapter 14.

Archibald M. Willard and The Spirit of '76

In 1836 Archibald M. Willard was born at Bedford in Cuyahoga County. His family moved to Wellington in Lorain County when he was 19 years old. Archibald found work there in a factory that made horse-drawn vehicles, where he helped to decorate the vehicles. If you look at the words at the top of the picture on page 211, you will see the kind of art work that was very popular at the time.

The hundredth anniversary of the signing of the *Declaration of Independence* was celebrated in Philadelphia in 1876. Archibald created a large painting, which he called *Yankee Doodle*, and offered it to the fair for display. The four-hundredth anniversary of Columbus finding America was celebrated in Chicago in 1892. Mr. Willard painted another picture of the same size and subject for this fair and named it *The Spirit of '76*. The picture on the opposite page was made from this second painting. In later years he painted several more scenes of the same kind.

Based on: *Archibald M. Willard and The Spirit of '76*, Ohio Historical Society booklet.

This photograph of Paul Laurence Dunbar was taken in his home in Dayton. What is the large metal object on the right side of the picture?

A century ago, William Dean Howells, a native of Belmont County, was one of the greatest writers in America. He was so pleased with Paul Dunbar's book of poetry that he wrote a story about it for an important magazine. This story made Paul famous throughout the English-speaking world.

By the time he was thirty years old, Paul Dunbar had two great problems, alcoholism and **tuberculosis** (a deadly disease of the lungs). He died in 1906 and was buried in Dayton. Friends felt that he had written his own funeral sermon in a poem he called *Compensation.*

> Because I loved so deeply,
>   Because I loved so long,
> God in his great compassion
>   Gave me the gift of song.
>
> Because I have loved so vainly,
>   And sung with such faltering breath,
> The Master in infinite mercy
>   Offers the boon of death.

Let's Review Part 4

New Words

quality
tuberculosis

New Things to Do

1. Keep a diary of how you use your free time during one week. At the end of the week, add up the times you spent in each kind of activity. Write a statement about how you could have made better use of the time.

2. Work together with your class mates to create a list of recreation activities available in your community. Note what it costs to use each one. How many of these opportunities have you used?

What have we learned?

In 1900 Ohio had only 4 million people spread over the 88 counties. The industries of Ohio were growing, but most people worked long hours for low pay. During World War I, there were many jobs available in our state, so people migrated here from eastern Europe and the southern states. The Great Depression of the 1930s was a difficult time in many parts of the world, but we still benefit from some projects that provided jobs for people. World War II created jobs for everyone who wanted to work, and there has been no serious economic depression since.

Since World War II, conflicts in Asia — including the Middle East — have encouraged millions of people of that continent to move to the United States, and many of them have come to Ohio. As a result of these events, almost 11 million people now live in Ohio, and most of us live in urban areas.

Because of the activities of labor unions and new laws, most people work fewer hours each week for better pay. As a result, there are more opportunities for recreation and more ways in which we can enjoy life. In the next chapter, you will learn how our cities have changed because of all these events.

Map Projects

Find the following places on your map of Ohio.

Place	County
Ashland	Ashland
Bedford	Cuyahoga
Lake Hope State Park	Vinton
Muskingum Conservancy Dist.	Muskingum River Valley
Shawnee State Park	Scioto
The Ohio State University	Franklin
Wellington	Lorain

Find the following places on your map of the United States.

Place	State
Appalachia	States to south and east of Ohio

Find the following places on your map of the world.

Nation	Continent
Cambodia	Southeastern Asia
China	Eastern Asia
India	Southern Asia
Iran	Western Asia
Israel	Western Asia ("Middle East")
Japan	Eastern Asia ("Far East")
Korea	Eastern Asia ("Far East")
Laos	Southeastern Asia
Lebanon	Western Asia ("Middle East")
Pakistan	Southern Asia
Taiwan	Island east of Asia
Vietnam	Southeast Asia

Books to Read

The following books will help you understand the ideas discussed in this chapter. Your library may have other books on these subjects.

Books about life before 1950

V Is for Victory, by Sylvia Whitman, explains life in the United States during World War II.

When I Grew Up Long Ago, by Alvin Schwartz, is a collection of ideas that people, who were children around 1900, remembered in their old age.

Books about poor people

The Great Depression, by R. Conrad Stein, presents a short explanation of the effects of the Great Depression of the 1930s. It includes many pictures.

The Homeless, Profiling The Problem, by Margaret O. Hyde, tells how homeless people live in America today.

Poverty in America, by Milton Meltzer, describes the lives of poor people in America today and explains how the government tries to help them.

Books about African-Americans

Extraordinary Black Americans, by Susan Altman, tells how 85 individual African-Americans helped to improve the lives of all of us.

Freedom's Children, by Ellen Levine, explains how thirty-three African-American young people took part in the civil rights movement of the 1960s.

A Long Hard Journey, The Story of The Pullman Porter, by Patricia McKissack, tells the story of the first labor union organized by African-Americans. It also shows how this union helped the civil rights movement of the 1960s.

Books about Asians

An Ancient Heritage: The Arab American, by Brent Ashabranner, is a collection of stories of people who migrated from the Middle East to the United States during the 20th century.

The Chinese American Experience, by Dana Ying Hui Wu, tells how Chinese workers came to the United States over the past 150 years.

The Koreans in America, by Wayne Patterson, describes how and why citizens of Korea moved to the United States during the 20th century.

Lee Ann, The Story of A Vietnamese — American Girl, by Trina Brown, tells the story of a Vietnamese girl who now lives in the United States.

The New Americans, by Brent Ashbranner, explains how people from other nations become citizens of the United States.

Where The River Runs, by Nancy Graff, is the story of a family that escaped from Cambodia to find new life in the United States.

Chapter 13

How did patterns of living change?

Let's learn...

- **how forms of energy changed.**

- **how forms of transportation changed.**

- **how energy and transportation changed cities.**

You have learned how steam energy changed transportation and manufacturing during the last half of the 19th century. By 1900 steam was being used to create a new form of energy — electricity! By 1950 electricity was available almost everywhere in Ohio. This form of energy changed the way we live.

You have also learned that petroleum was important to the economy of our state in 1900. Steam-powered automobiles were the "toys" of inventors in 1900. When inventors began to build gasoline-powered engines, automobiles gradually became the most popular form of transportation ever created. By 1950 diesel railroad engines were replacing steam engines.

In this chapter, you will learn how electric energy and petroleum-powered transportation changed the cities of Ohio during the 20th century. The census information in Appendix B, page 383, and the map on page 180, will help you understand the changes that have occurred.

Part 1

How did forms of energy change?

In Chapter 10, you learned how important coal was to railroads and industries during the 19th century. By 1900 electricity, petroleum, and natural gas were beginning to change life in Ohio. The diagrams on the next page show the sources of energy used in Ohio and the entire United States in 1982. As you can see, coal was still the most important fuel in Ohio, while petroleum was second, and natural gas third. You can also see that petroleum was the most important fuel in the entire United States, while natural gas was second, and coal third. In this part, you will learn how sources of energy changed the way we live.

Energy in Homes

In 1900 most urban and rural families warmed each room of their homes by burning coal or wood in a small fireplace and/or cast-iron stove. By 1940 most urban families burned coal in furnaces to enjoy cleaner and more uniform heat. By 1960 most urban houses had heating systems that burned natural gas for even cleaner heat. At the same time, most houses outside of urban areas had furnaces that burned fuel oil. Many houses built after 1965 had electric heating systems.

By 1900 some people living in cities could buy *manufactured gas* that they could use for cooking and/or lighting their homes. But many families in both urban and rural areas had wood-burning cook stoves. By 1950 all homes in cities were using gas or electricity for cooking, and many farm homes were using *bottled gas* for cooking. In 1900 wealthy people in cities often had both gas and electric lighting systems. By 1950 electricity was available everywhere.

Energy in Factories

Before World War II, almost every factory in Ohio burned coal to create steam. The

Gross Energy Consumption by Fuel, 1982, Ohio and U.S.

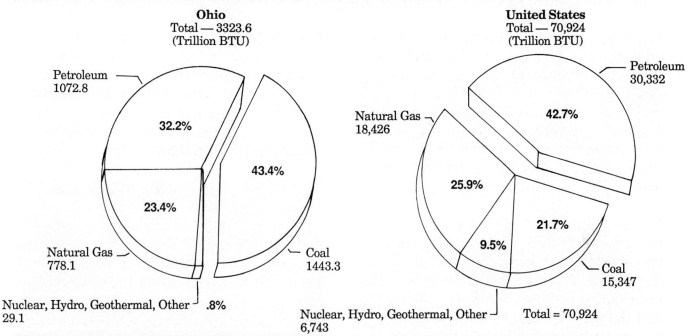

Ohio
Total — 3323.6
(Trillion BTU)

Petroleum
1072.8

32.2%

43.4%

23.4%

Natural Gas
778.1

Coal
1443.3

Nuclear, Hydro, Geothermal, Other   .8%
29.1

United States
Total — 70,924
(Trillion BTU)

Petroleum
30,332

Natural Gas
18,426

42.7%

25.9%

21.7%

9.5%

Coal
15,347

Nuclear, Hydro, Geothermal, Other   Total = 70,924
6,743

The sources of energy used in Ohio are the same as those used in the entire United States, but the proportions are different. Look at a dictionary for the meaning of British Thermal Unit. How many "zeroes" are in a trillion?

---

steam was used to heat the buildings and to operate steam engines that turned shafts to move the "forest of leather belts" you saw on page 212. Some factories generated their own electricity. The picture on page 200 shows the kind of power plant that you could find in any factory. Today you can see such things only in museums. Since 1950 almost every factory uses gas or oil for heating and electricity for operating machinery.

Petroleum Pipe Lines

One of the most important rules in using energy is: use the kind of energy that is most efficient and most economical. When wood was free for the taking, everyone burned wood. As the forests disappeared, railroads made it possible to move coal easily from mines to users. In the earliest days of using petroleum, it was hauled from wells to refineries in barrels. This was a very expensive form of transportation, and it could not be used for natural gas. As industries learned to use gas, entrepreneurs built pipe lines from the wells to the users.

During World War II, the United States built thousands of miles of pipelines to move petroleum from the oil fields of

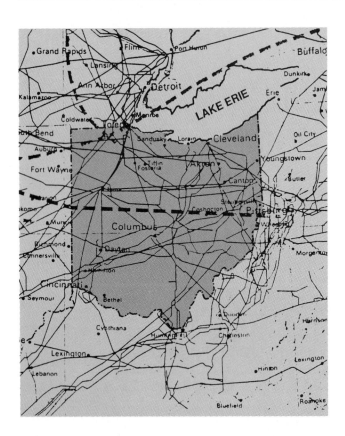

Several thousand miles of pipe lines carry petroleum products below the surface of Ohio. Where is your home on this map?

Louisiana, Texas, and Oklahoma to New England and other places on the East Coast. After 1945, some of these pipe lines were used to move natural gas. During the 1950s and 1960s, many more miles of gas lines were built. The map above shows the pipelines that carry gas and petroleum through our state today.

Electricity

Where does electricity come from? Almost all of the electricity used in Ohio comes from coal! If you live near Lake Erie or the Ohio River, you may have seen buildings similar to the one shown below. Nuclear

The Cardinal Electric Power Plant in Jefferson County was originally a Rural Electrification Administration project. What kind of fuel does this plant use?

Thomas Edison was born in this house in Milan. It is two-stories high in the rear. Why are there two chimneys on this house?

energy can also be used to create electricity, and there are two such power plants along Lake Erie. You will learn about the problems of nuclear energy in Chapter 16.

What do you do when suddenly the lights go out in your house? Have you thought about what your life would be like without electricity? Perhaps you have thought about this when a storm or an accident cut off power to your home. Three men, who were born in Ohio, laid the foundation for the reliable electric service we have today. Thomas Edison, Charles Brush, and Charles F. Kettering each became interested in electricity during the 19th

century and invented many devices to make it safe and dependable.

Thomas Alva Edison: Electricity was something scientists "played with," but there were few real uses before Thomas Edison began to work with it. Edison was born in 1847 at Milan in Erie County. His family moved to Michigan when Tom was seven years old, and he never again lived in Ohio. Above, you can see the house in which he was born as it looks today.

While Mr. Edison did much of his work in New Jersey, his work shops were later moved to Greenfield Village at Dearborn, Michigan, where you can visit them today.

279

Edison invented a way to create electricity and distribute it to users. He is best known for the many electrical devices he invented including light bulbs, motion-picture projectors, and *gramophones* which recorded and played back sounds.

Charles Francis Brush: Charles Brush invented the first practical machine to create *direct-current* electricity. This form of electricity was used to operate all electric streetcar systems. He also invented electric *arc lights* which were the only source of very bright lighting until about 1970. Mr. Brush was one of the founders of the *Cleveland Electric Illuminating Company* that still serves northeastern Ohio today.

Charles F. Kettering: In addition to what you learned about Charles Kettering in Chapter 12, he made it possible for people in rural areas to have electricity. In 1913 he built a small, gasoline-powered, electric system and used it to light the house of his parents in Ashland County. In 1916 he established the *Domestic Engineering Company* in Dayton to build electric generators for public sale. Some farm houses may still have the original wiring from their first Kettering system.

By 1920 almost every city in Ohio had an electric power plant, but only Kettering systems were used in rural areas. During the Great Depression of the 1930s,

Congress created the *Rural Electrification Administration* (REA). This program made it possible for farmers to have electric power. By 1940 almost half the farms of our state had electricity, and by 1950 all farms were electrified.

Communications

One of the first uses of electricity was to improve communications. The first telegraph message was sent through wires in 1837, using the energy of batteries. In 1861 a battery-powered telegraph line was built to California. Battery-powered telephones were invented in 1872. By 1900 both forms of communication were powered by electricity from central power plants. Have you or your parents received a telegram in the past year? Telegrams were an important form of communication in 1950, but they are seldom used today. If you look back to the picture of Lancaster in 1886, page 186, some of the wires that you see on this picture are telegraph wires.

When you think of all the changes in energy and communications that took place during the 20th century, it is difficult to predict what may happen in these fields during the 21st century.

There are five different forms of transportation shown in this picture. The short poles with three cross bars carry telegraph wires. Why are there so few automobiles on this highway?

Let's Review Part 1

New Things to Do

For one full day, make a written record of your use of electricity. Every time you begin to use something electrical, write down the time and purpose of the use. If you walk into a lighted room, note the time and the fact that it was already lighted. Do not forget your electric alarm clock if you use one. Write a statement about what you learned from this experience.

Part 2

How did forms of transportation change?

The picture above is one of the most interesting transportation pictures ever taken. It was taken somewhere in Montgomery County about 1910 to show five forms of transportation. On the far left, you can see the Great Miami River, which was an important transportation route before the Miami and Erie Canal was opened. To the right of the river, you can see an electric **interurban** (between

This Shay locomotive was made in Lima, Ohio about 90 years ago.
What fuel does this engine use?

cities) car that carried people and packages along the route of the Miami and Erie Canal during the early 1900s. On the highway, you can see an automobile. To the right of the highway, you can see the Miami and Erie Canal with a canal boat. On the far right, you can see a steam-powered railroad train. The picture

also shows two sets of wood poles that support wires. The shorter poles, with the three cross-bars, carry telegraph wires.

What would the picture look like if you could find this location today? The river is used for fishing and boating. The interurban line disappeared before 1940.

The highway may be four lanes wide and carry thousands of automobiles and trucks every day. The canal may be under the widened highway. If the railroad track is still in place the trains are pulled by diesel-powered engines. The telegraph lines were removed before 1980. We will now look at how these changes took place.

Railroads

In 1900 railroads were the most important form of transportation for people and freight movements outside of cities. The steam-powered engines created large amounts of smoke and soot, but people accepted these problems as the price of good transportation. Almost one-third of all steam locomotives used in the United States were made at Lima in Allen County.

The picture on the previous page shows a special kind of locomotive made at Lima for the logging industry. This locomotive is still in use in a historical park at Cass, West Virginia. Today you must go to a museum to see steam locomotives — or *Iron Horses*, as they were called. You can do this at the *Ohio Railroad Museum* in Franklin County, at Lincoln Park and the *Allen County Museum* in Lima, and at the *Henry Ford Museum* at Dearborn, Michigan.

From 1850 to 1950, railroads were important to the development of cities. Near the end of Chapter 9, you learned how entrepreneurs built Glendale and other **suburban** (near but outside city limits) railroad communities so that wealthy people could live from five to fifteen miles away from the city and still get to work easily.

Railroads also influenced the location of every factory. Factories needed coal to produce steam, and the only economical way to move large amounts of coal was by railroad. Every factory also needed raw materials, such as iron, wood, paper, or clay, to create products that people wanted to buy. After the products were created, they had to be moved to central places where people could buy them. The best way to move both raw materials and finished products was by railroad.

Diesel-powered locomotives were invented during the 1930s, and by 1960 all railroads in the United States used diesel or electric locomotives. Diesel engines are much more efficient and cleaner than steam engines. But changes in highway transportation since 1950 have changed the importance of railroads in our lives. Today there is no useful rail passenger service in our state.

The Good Roads Movement

By the end of the 19th century, streets of the large cities were paved so that vehicles could move over them in all kinds of weather. These paved streets encouraged the use of a new form of transportation that was inexpensive, clean, and faster than walking. Can you guess what it was? Bicycles! How long did it take you to learn to ride a two-wheeler? Did you go to a bicycle school like the one below?

During the 1880s and 1890s, thousands of bicycle owners joined the *League of American Wheelmen*. By 1900 the League was leading a *Good Roads Movement* to urge political leaders to pave rural roads.

Can you imagine learning to ride a bicycle under conditions like this?

They did this so that bicycle riders could ride into the countryside on Sundays and holidays. Unfortunately, the counties and states had no money to pave roads. After several years of effort, the voters convinced their Congressmen to pass the *Federal Aid Road Act of 1916*. This was the first time that Congress agreed to spend money for public highways since the National Road was built. In 1925 the Federal government established the system of numbered highways that we have today, but many miles of these roads were not yet paved.

As rural highways were improved during the 1920s, entrepreneurs began to offer travelers a new form of transportation — **intercity** (between cities) bus service. This was a very important form of transportation until about 1990.

The greatest change in highway transportation came in 1956 when Congress created the *National System of Interstate and Defense Highways*. You know this as the *Interstate System*. One of the goals of this system was to reduce traffic congestion in cities. As the new roads were built, they made it easier for people to move away from the big cities. During the years since 1960, so many people have moved away from the cities that the greatest congestion today is near the interchanges in suburban areas.

Public Transportation

Public transportation continued to influence the development of urban areas through 1930. Do you remember the horse-drawn streetcar in the picture of page 188? About 1890 electric motors took the place of horses to move these cars, and this development changed our cities greatly. The picture on the next page shows how popular they once were.

Electric streetcars affected development in three ways. In some cases, the streetcar company bought land outside the city limits, built a streetcar line to the area, and created a subdivision of houses. In many other places, entrepreneurs built new subdivisions and then asked the streetcar company to provide service to the area. In a few places, a streetcar company built an amusement park at the end of a car line. This increased business because people would use the streetcars to get to the park.

By 1940 the streetcars used in larger cities were much bigger and more comfortable than the one shown on the next page. By that time, motor buses were replacing streetcars because they could provide more flexible service. You learned about *omnibuses* in Chapter 9: can you guess why public transit vehicles are called *buses*? Buses have had little influence on the development of cities. Today far more buses move students to

In 1900 electric streetcars were the most important form of transportation in cities. What time of day, and what month of the year, was this picture made? Explain you answer.

and from their schools than carry people in regular transit service.

Streetcars disappeared from Ohio during the 1950s except for one line in Cleveland. Today you can ride from the Cleveland Hopkins Airport, near the southwestern corner of that city, through the center of town, to Shaker Heights on the east side of Cleveland. You can see a few electric streetcars in the *Ohio Railroad Museum* and several in the *Henry Ford Museum*.

Motor Vehicles

The greatest changes in transportation and the development of cities came after the invention of vehicles that moved by

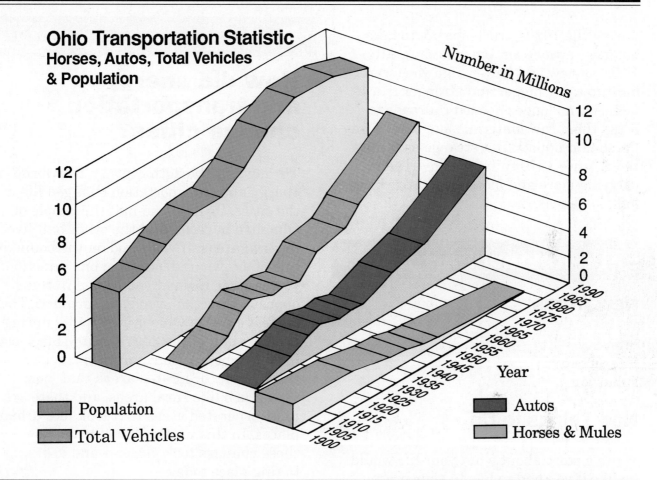

Ohio Transportation Statistic
Horses, Autos, Total Vehicles
& Population

Number in Millions

Year

- Population
- Total Vehicles
- Autos
- Horses & Mules

themselves, which is the meaning of *auto* (self) *mobile* (moving). In 1900 horses and mules were important sources of power for urban transportation. By that year, a few inventors in Ohio were trying to make self-propelled *motor vehicles*. This term includes all automobiles, buses, and trucks. The graph above shows how the population of Ohio, the number of automobiles, and the number of horses and mules changed from 1900 to 1990. In

the next chapter, you will learn about motor vehicles made in Ohio.

Do you have any idea how much your life depends on *trucks*? There may be a few things you use today that have never been carried in trucks but not many! Trucks became important during World War I to move war materiel in Europe, but the highways of the United States were too poor to use them. As highways were paved during the 1920s, trucks began to take business away from the railroads. After 1950, as new and better highways were built to carry bigger and stronger trucks, factories no longer needed railroads to bring them raw materials and carry away finished products. But strange as it may seem, since 1970 railroads have been carrying more and more loaded trucks over long distances.

Let's Review Part 2

New Words

intercity
interurban
suburban

New Things to Do

Write a story about what your life would be like if you had to live in your present house for one month with no electricity and no fuel to operate motor vehicles.

Part 3

How did energy and transportation change cities?

Throughout the 20th century, new forms of energy and transportation changed life in the cities. In 1900 one-half the people of Ohio live in cities, and the other half lived in rural areas. If you stood on the boundary line of a town and looked in one direction, you saw the town; if you looked in the opposite direction, you saw farmland. The biggest cities of Ohio grew rapidly during the first half of the 20th century, but most have lost population since 1950. Today there are incorporated areas that look very much like rural areas, and there are unincorporated areas that look like urban places. In this part, you will learn how these changes took place — and are taking place today.

Life in Rural Areas

As electric service was extended after World War II, life in rural areas changed greatly. Paved roads and better vehicles made it possible for farmers to sell their products and/or shop in larger central places. This led to the decline of many of the small 19th century central places.

As gasoline-powered engines were developed for motor vehicles, they were also used to replace horses and mules for powering farm tools. Since 1960 farm machines, like those shown on this page and the next, have made it possible for a family to operate a farm of several hundred acres. But this "labor saving" equipment is so expensive that many farm families must now work at other jobs to earn money to keep their farms.

The graph on page 291 shows the changes between 1900 and 1982. The total number of farms dropped from 276,719 to 86,934, while the average size of farms increased from 89 acres to 177 acres. During the last half of the 20th century, large areas of rural land were "urbanized," as you will soon learn.

Life in Cities

Improved highways and motor vehicles also made it possible for people in urban areas to live farther from the places where they worked and shopped. During the last half of the 20th century, the big cities of Ohio, and the areas around them, have changed tremendously. The diagram on

Modern farm machines make it possible for one family to farm hundreds of acres of land. What is this machine doing?

Modern farm machines like this are used to pick tomatoes. Why does this operation require more workers than the one shown on page 289?

page 174 showed how an urban area developed during the 19th century. The box on page 292 explains how urban growth continued in the 20th century.

Changes in Housing

When walking was the most important form of transportation, people lived close together in houses like those shown on page 187. When electric streetcars made it possible to travel three miles in thirty minutes, or less, entrepreneurs built new subdivisions along the car lines. When new factories were built out along the railroad lines, new subdivisions were created nearby so that workers could walk

from home to work. Parcels of land in the suburban areas were larger than in the walking city, and houses did not cover all of the land area. As you can see on page 294, houses of this time had front porches that were used as outdoor "living rooms" on summer evenings. Many houses had one "blind" side, with no windows, to gain privacy.

As automobiles became popular during the 1920s, land developers subdivided areas within a city that were not on streetcar lines. In addition, farmers sold large lots to people who wanted to live away from the noise and dirt of the city. Almost every new house had a garage

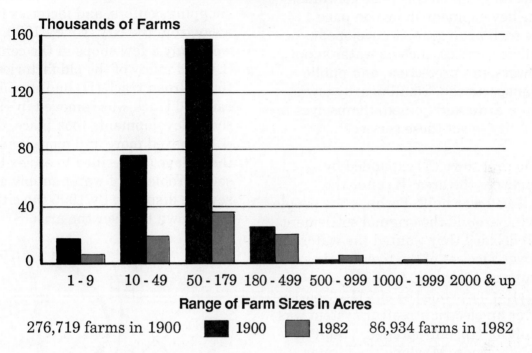

Sizes of Ohio Farms
in 1900 and 1982

Thousands of Farms

276,719 farms in 1900   ■ 1900   ■ 1982   86,934 farms in 1982

because automobiles of that time could not be left out in the cold. When the owners of older houses bought autos, they often added garages to their property. Every year after 1920, fewer people rode streetcars within the cities and railroads between the cities.

Federal Housing Programs

In the last chapter, you learned how Congress created the *Federal Housing Administration* (FHA) program to provide good housing for low-income families.

Several other FHA programs had much greater effect on the cities of Ohio during the last half of the 20th century.

FHA Mortgage Guarantee: During the 1930s, a family could build a very comfortable house for less than $10,000, but few people could afford the required cash payment of $2,000. One FHA program made it possible to buy such a house with a cash payment of $1,000. During the late 1930s, this program encouraged construction of new houses on vacant land within cities. It also

291

An Example of Urban Changes

The diagram on this page continues the development shown on page 174. As each town grew, it developed new public services, such as water supply, sewers, fire protection, and public transportation. Small nearby towns often **annexed** (joined) themselves to the city to get these services.

The first town (E) expanded by *annexing* the area (K) after the railroad was built. Perhaps the people living around the original settlement (C) decided they wanted the water and sewer services of the town so they annexed their land to (E+K), and (E+K+C) became the city (L). Shortly after an electric streetcar system was built for (L), entrepreneurs built new subdivisions (M) along the former turnpike (F). They annexed these areas to (L) in order to get water, sewer, and transit services. During this period the town (G) incorporated as a village for wealthy people who could drive to work in the city. Because of the railroad, several industries built factories (N) near the town (J), and the area incorporated as a village.

During the 1960s, an interstate highway (P) was built parallel to the old turnpike (B). During the 1970s, interstate highway (R) was built parallel to the railroad (H). As each new highway was completed, entrepreneurs built new housing developments, shopping centers, and factories further away from the city (L). By 1980, there were only a few shops in the center of (L), and many of the old factories along the railroad track (H) had closed. The railroad track was removed in 1990. As these developments took place, the city (L) annexed more and more land, and the village (J) decided to annex to (L) to solve problems of water supply and sewage disposal. By 1995 the city of (L) had grown to cover the area (S).

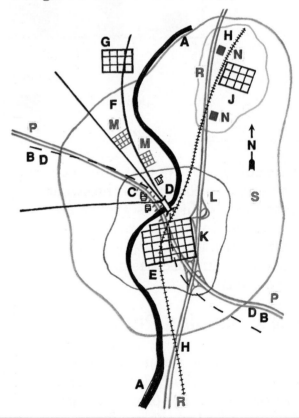

Urban Illustration Key

A. Stream

B. Trail created by natives and animals

C. Three friends buy land, divide it into three parts, and build homes close together

D. Turnpike company improves the trail and builds a bridge

E. An entrepreneur lays out a town along the turnpike

F. Second turnpike company builds a new road northward from bridge

G. Another entrepreneur lays out new town along turnpike

H. Two towns compete to have railroad built on that side of stream

J. Third town built along railroad track

K. First twon expanded

L. Places E+K+C incorporated as a city

M. New subdivisions along road F

G. Town incorporated as a village

N. Factories built along railroad track near town J and area incorporated as a village

P. Interstate highway built along route of old highway B

R. Interstate highway built along railroad. Railroad removed later.

S. Larger area, including village J annexed to L

encouraged new subdivisions outside city limits.

Very few houses were built during World War II. In 1945, Congress created a program that allowed veterans of the Armed Services to buy a $10,000 house with a cash payment of $500. This led to a tremendous demand for new housing. New subdivisions were built wherever builders could find suitable land. You can see a typical house built under an FHA program on page 295.

Housing Act of 1968: By 1968 Congress was concerned that low-income families could not afford to rent or buy decent housing. A new program, called *Section 8* housing, was created to help such people. The first part of this new law encouraged builders to create new houses, or remodel old ones, for low-income families. Such families could buy a $20,000 house with a cash payment of only $200. The second part of the act encouraged construction of apartment houses for low-income families in suburban areas.

Many *Section 8* projects were built in the cities of Ohio, but few have been built in suburban areas. In fact, many suburban places have done everything possible to prevent such housing from being built. The result is that most low-income people continue to live in the old central cities, while upper-income people move to the suburbs. The need for low-income housing is almost as great today as it was thirty years ago.

As entrepreneurs built new housing subdivisions after 1950, they also built new factories, new office buildings, and new shopping centers. They paid little attention to the boundaries of cities and villages. Sometimes they annexed their lands to an existing incorporated place. Sometimes they created new incorporated places. Many times they simply changed land from rural uses to urban uses.

Shopping

Between 1900 and 1940, patterns of shopping also changed. Small stores were opened near the new subdivisions, because many people still walked from their homes to stores that sold food and other daily needs. As these suburban shopping places were built, entrepreneurs built large apartment houses nearby without parking places for automobiles. People living in these outlying areas traveled to the central business district (CBD) by streetcar to buy more expensive goods. By 1960 many of the streetcar-era shopping centers had lost importance. During the 1970s and 1980s, some entrepreneurs remodeled these business districts by building parking areas, but few such areas are as important today as they were in 1950.

These were modern subdivision houses in 1900. Why did these houses have front porches?

The Federal Housing Administration helped thousands of Ohioans to buy houses during the 1950s. How does this house differ from the one shown on the opposite page?

Is there a *Kroger* store in your area? *The Kroger Company* is an excellent example of how shopping patterns changed with improved transportation. In the 1880s, Bernard H. Kroger opened the store you see on page 296. By 1920 *The Kroger Grocery & Baking Company* operated small stores along streetcar lines in almost every neighborhood of Cincinnati. These stores were about the size of the original store. By 1980 there were Kroger "superstores" in many parts of the United States, and every store had a parking lot for hundreds of automobiles.

As automobiles became popular, they required shops for gasoline, oil, tires, and repairs. Can you imagine an automobile service station like the one shown on page 298? This was the first gasoline station in the United States. You can read about it in the box on page 297.

Before World War II, the CBD of every city was the most important area for shopping, business, and entertainment. Almost all streetcar lines entered the CBD. When people began driving automobiles to the CBD, parking became a serious problem. As the interstate highways were built, entrepreneurs created large shopping centers in outlying areas. Do you know why these large centers are called *malls*? The word comes from the old English term *pall-mall* (pronounced *pell-mell*) meaning *alley*.

Bernard H. Kroger opened his first grocery store in the 1880s.
How does this store compare to a Kroger store you have seen?

Businesses in the CBD reacted to this shift in population in one, or more, of three ways. First, they tried to have the city government build parking garages in the CBD to attract motorists downtown. Second, the largest stores opened branches in the new shopping malls. Third, small businesses moved to the outlying malls.

Today many suburban shopping centers attract more customers than the CBD.

Institutions

Before 1950, all hospitals, schools, museums, and places of public entertainment were located so that people

The First Gasoline Station in America

Pataskala is a small town in the southwest corner of Licking County. About the time The Standard Oil Company [that you learned about in Chapter 10] started to make [kerosene] to light the lamps of the world, Harvey Wickliffe began to sell it to his neighbors in Pataskala. He carried the kerosene in a big tank on his horse-drawn wagon.

When a young man in town bought an automobile, Harvey decided to expand his business to include gasoline, so he bought a second tank and marked it Gasoline-Danger.... He immediately lost business because old customers would not let him approach their homes with this dangerous liquid.

One of Harvey's customers, George Hunsaker, operated a General Store, and he put a gasoline tank and pump outside the store to sell fuel to passing motorists. Harvey noticed that people who wanted to buy gasoline had to wait until George took care of customers inside the store.

Harvey said to the store owner, "You know what I think George? I think the grocery business and the gasoline business don't mix. Maybe there ought to be a regular gasoline store with a man waitin' to fill up their tanks the minute they drive up to the pumps."

"Be all right for the automobile guys— but a fella'd starve to death in such a business."

"I'm not so sure," Harvey said thoughtfully. "You mad enough to sell me your gas pump?"

"I'm mad enough if you're crazy enough to buy it."

"All right," Harvey said, "I'll be after it as soon as I find a place to put it."

Harvey found an old building at the corner of Oak and Young Streets in Columbus, and created an automobile service station about three blocks east of the Capitol.

From: Siedel, *Out of The Midwest*, pp. 99-104

The first gasoline station in the United States opened in Columbus in 1912. How does this station compare to a gasoline station near your home?

could get to them by streetcars. Since 1950, parking has been a major problem for these institutions, and some hospitals and universities have opened branches in suburban areas.

As people moved to the suburbs before World War II, many continued to attend churches near the center of the city that could be reached by streetcars. Others went to new churches built within walking distance of their new homes. Today some churches operate buses to transport their members, and every large church has some arrangement for parking.

From 1890 to 1950, motion picture theaters were important places of entertainment, and the finest movie houses were in the CBD. Small movie theaters were built in suburban business districts so that people could walk to them. When television became popular during the 1950s, many movie theaters closed. Some of these buildings were changed to other uses, but many were removed. Today most theaters are at shopping centers that have large parking areas.

Before 1900, accountants, doctors, dentists, engineers, lawyers, and other professional people had their offices in the CBD. By 1910 some professional people had their offices in suburban areas along the streetcar lines. In 1940 many doctors still visited patients at their homes, because the doctors had automobiles but few patients had them. Today few doctors go to patients' homes, but many have offices in two or more places so that patients can get to them more easily.

Places of Employment

Before 1940, almost all business offices were in the CBD, and almost all manufacturing plants were along railroads. When the United States began to supply war materiel to England, France, and Russia in 1939, it built new factories in outlying areas. The buildings were one-story high and away from all streetcar lines. Special buses carried workers who did not have automobiles. After the war, many of these factories changed to making goods for peacetime

use. These buildings became the pattern for the factories you see today.

Two new developments made it possible to build these factories away from railroads. First, natural gas and electricity took the place of coal as the source of energy. Second, bigger and better trucks, operating over bigger and better highways, made it possible for companies to build factories and warehouses wherever local laws permitted. Because of these changes in locations of factories, in every year since 1960 more miles of railroad track have been removed than have been built.

Development of Metropolitan Areas

By 1940 the areas near the largest cities of the United States had become complicated patterns of housing, shopping, institutions, and centers of employment. Because of these new interrelationships, the United States Bureau of the Census created **metropolitan** areas. This word is made up of two Greek words meaning *mother city*. Each census since 1940 has found more people living in the eight largest metropolitan areas of our state.

In 1950 Ohio was the only state to have as many as eight cities with more than 100,000 people. Each of these was the center of a metropolitan area. In 1990 Ohio still had eight large metropolitan areas but only six cities of more than 100,000. The

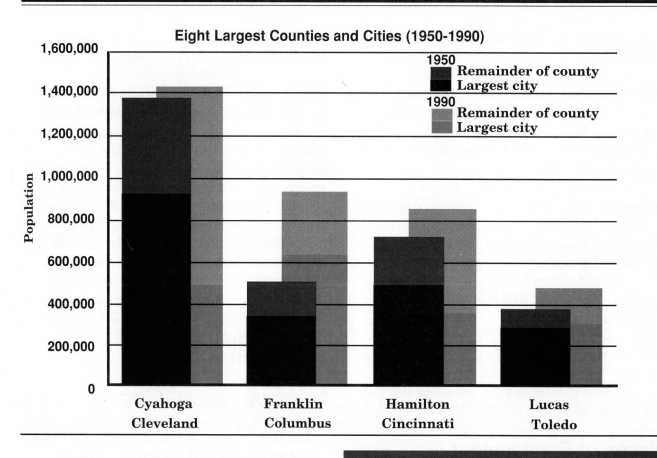

Eight Largest Counties and Cities (1950-1990)

Population

| 1950 |
| **Remainder of county** |
| **Largest city** |
| 1990 |
| **Remainder of county** |
| **Largest city** |

Cyahoga / Cleveland Franklin / Columbus Hamilton / Cincinnati Lucas / Toledo

diagram above shows the relationships between the cities of Akron, Canton, Cincinnati, Cleveland, Columbus, Dayton, Toledo, and Youngstown and their counties in 1950 and 1990. You can see that all of the largest counties grew in population, but Franklin County grew the most. You can also see that six of the largest cities lost population, and only Columbus had large growth. In Chapter 14, you will learn how the population growth of these eight counties spilled over into surrounding counties. In Chapter 15, you will learn why Columbus grew.

Let's Review Part 3

New Words

annex
metropolitan

New Things to Do

1. Visit an old business district in your town or county seat. Make sketches and write a report on what has been done to the area to provide parking spaces for automobiles.

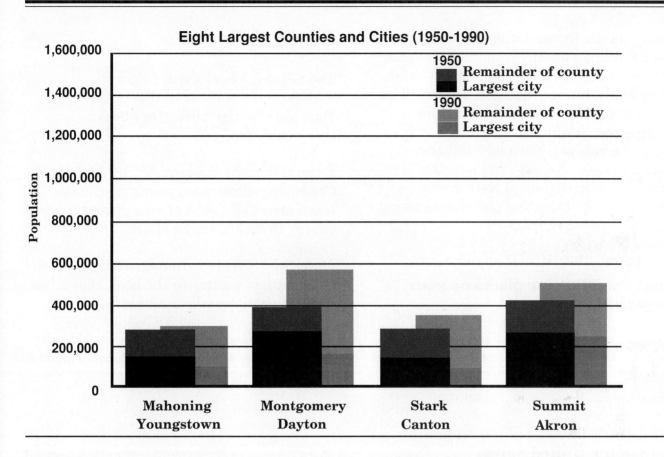

Eight Largest Counties and Cities (1950-1990)

2. Visit a new business district near where you live. Make sketches and write a report on how this area provides for automobiles.

3. Write a short statement about how you "feel" when you visit these two kinds of shopping areas.

What have we learned?

Life in rural areas did not change much between 1840 and 1930. During those years, almost everyone living in a rural area looked forward to trips to the big cities for shopping and recreation.

By 1930 paved highways and automobiles were making such trips more pleasant than they had been earlier. Between 1930 and 1960, improved highways, wide-spread electric service, and new Federal programs relating to housing encouraged more and more people to move away from the noise and dirt of the cities.

Today people in rural areas of our state have the same energy resources and ease of transportation as those living in cities. As a result, many citizens of the big cities now work, shop, and seek recreation outside the city limits. In the following chapters, you will learn how industry affected these changes, and how the problems of government have grown because of the changing patterns of living.

New Places

Find the following places on your map of Ohio.

Place	County
Lima	Allen
Milan	Erie
Pataskala	Licking

Find the following place on your map of the United States.

Town	State
Cass	West Virginia

Books to Read

The following books will help you understand the ideas in this chapter. Your library may have other books on these subjects.

Energy: Science through Art, by Andrew Charman, encourages young people to learn about all forms of energy, and to use energy to create works of art.

Materials: Science through Art, by Andrew Charman, is similar to the book above, but deals with materials of all kinds.

Know Your Hometown History, by Abigail Jungreis, is a guidebook for discovering the history of your hometown.

Chapter 14

How did the economy of Ohio change?

Let's learn...

- about businesses.

- about the important industries of Ohio.

- about the role of Ohio in the "space age."

In Chapter 10, you learned how the industry of Ohio developed during the 19th century. In the last two chapters, you learned how life changed as the population of our state grew during the 20th century. The average person today has a much easier and more comfortable life than the average person in 1900 because the economy of Ohio, and the United States, grew as fast as the population! There are many places in the world today where people live as they did in 1900, because economic growth has not matched population growth.

In this chapter, you will learn how to start a new business, and how thousands of individual businesses relate to the ten most important industries of our nation. The diagrams on the next page show information about the industries of Ohio: we will use these many times in this chapter. You will also learn how people of Ohio have worked to improve our knowledge of outer space.

Part 1

What is a business?

We have used the word *business* several times in the last two chapters without defining it. A **business** is an operation established by an entrepreneur to earn money. Just as every city in Ohio began as a small settlement, so every business began from the ideas and work of one person or a small group of people. A business can be operated by a single person working alone. It can be operated by two or more people working together as partners. While most businesses remain small, a few grow to become

large corporations that employ thousands of workers.

Businesses and *companies* are closely related. Every *company* is a business, but not every business is a company. For example, doctors and lawyers operate businesses, but they are not considered to be companies. Corporations and companies are also closely related. Every corporation is a company, but not every company is incorporated. We will be using these terms throughout this chapter.

Some young people decide at an early age that they do want to "go into business." If you are interested, there are two organizations that can help you: *Junior Achievement* and the *4-H* program. Junior Achievement has offices throughout Ohio and the United States. The *4-H* program was established in Springfield, Ohio in 1902 to help young people understand the business operations of agriculture. It now has branches in most counties of the United States.

Starting A New Business

Have you seen a new store or other business open in your neighborhood, and then close after a few months? This happens many times every year all over our state. It may seem easy to start a new business, but people who are successful follow each of the following steps.

Workers in Ohio Industries

1986

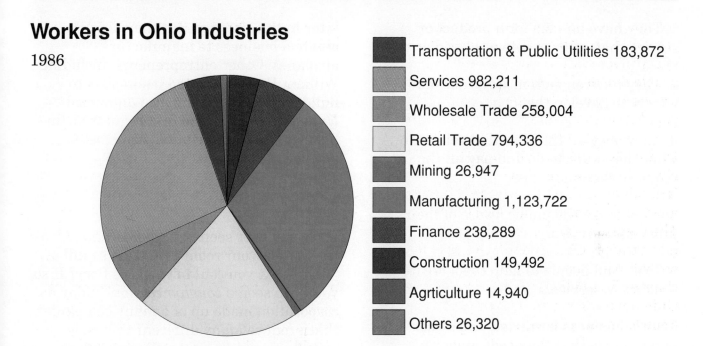

Transportation & Public Utilities 183,872

Services 982,211

Wholesale Trade 258,004

Retail Trade 794,336

Mining 26,947

Manufacturing 1,123,722

Finance 238,289

Construction 149,492

Agrticulture 14,940

Others 26,320

Companies in Ohio Industry

1986

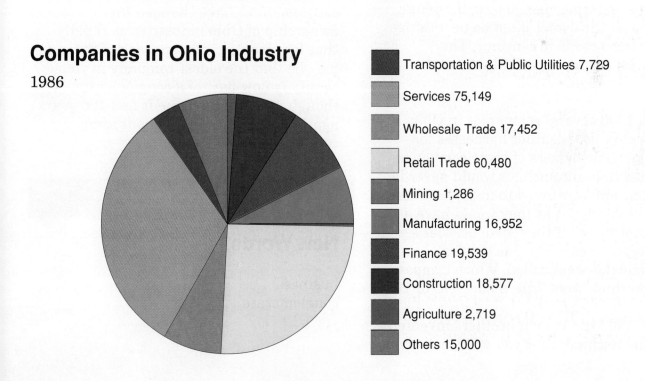

Transportation & Public Utilities 7,729

Services 75,149

Wholesale Trade 17,452

Retail Trade 60,480

Mining 1,286

Manufacturing 16,952

Finance 19,539

Construction 18,577

Agriculture 2,719

Others 15,000

1. They have an idea for a product or service that other people need and/or want.

2. They have enough money, time, and energy to develop the idea.

3. They obey all the laws that relate to what they want to do and pay all the required fees and taxes.

4. They make the public aware of their product or service.

5. They find people to help them create the product or service.

After a business is started, the owner must realize that the needs and/or desires of people change over the years; therefore, the owner must do new things if the business is to continue. The following examples will illustrate this need to change.

(1) In 1900 several companies in Ohio made very good leather harnesses for horses. Some owners of these companies decided that automobiles would never be popular and continued to make harnesses. Others decided that they would have a brighter future if they made leather seats for *horseless carriages*, as the first automobiles were called. Which companies do you think were still in business in 1925?

(2) In 1903 the Wright brothers invented a "flying machine" that you will learn about later in this chapter. But they did not create a business to manufacture airplanes. Other entrepreneurs, including William Boeing, created businesses to build airplanes. Boeing also organized *United Airlines* as the first regular airline business. Who contributed the most to our lives today?

Conglomerates

Have you ever seen a *conglomeration*? Has the floor of your room ever been so full of "stuff" that you couldn't see the floor? If so, you have seen a *conglomeration*! Today a corporation made up of a many companies, that produce many different things, is called a **conglomerate**. Since 1970 *conglomerates* have changed the ownership of Ohio industries so rapidly that few people can keep track of them. It may be that the oldest company in your county is now part of a conglomerate, even though it has same name it had 100 years ago. You will learn more about some conglomerates in Part 2.

Let's Review Part 1

New Words

business
conglomerate

New Things to Do

Work with your classmates, in teams of three, to lay plans to create a new business to raise money to purchase something that your class or school needs. Each team should prepare a complete set of plans for a product or service that the class can create and sell. You can call the *Junior Achievement* or the *4-H* organization in your county for helpful literature. Each group should then present its suggestions to the class, and the class should decide which is best.

Part 2

What are the industries of Ohio today?

The economy of Ohio is very complicated because it includes many kinds of activities that you will learn about in this chapter. All of the businesses of our state are parts of one or more of the ten industries shown in the graphs on page 305. The upper graph shows the number of Ohio people who work in each industry. The lower graph shows the number of Ohio companies in each industry. You will now learn about these industries in alphabetical order.

Agriculture

The label *Agriculture* on the charts on page 305 includes companies and workers engaged in farming, forestry, and fishing. Farming is the most important industry in northeastern Ohio. Forestry is important in southeastern Ohio, because private companies are permitted to cut trees in the state and national forests of that region. While thousands of people enjoy catching fish as a sport, few companies raise fish to sell as food.

If you look back to the diagram on page 291, you can see that there were 86,934 farms in Ohio in 1982. The diagram on page 305 shows that there was a total of 2,712 *companies* in agriculture, forestry, and fishing in 1986. What happened to all these farms in such a short time? You learned the answer to this in Part 1. The number of farms did not go down between 1982 and 1986. The 2,712 *companies* involved in agriculture were created since 1950 by buying many small farms to form the largest farms shown on page 291. Today there are a few large corporations that own and operate thousands of acres of farmland throughout the United States. These companies operate farms as food *factories*.

Some farms raise only a single crop, while others raise several kinds. Today the most important field crops are corn, soybeans, hay, and wheat. Ohio also produces large

Migrant workers live in small houses like the ones shown. Why would the workers have baskets like the two shown here?

quantities of tomatoes, celery, sugar beets, grapes, and other fruits and vegetables. Cows are raised for both milk and meat, pigs for meat, and sheep for wool. For many years, every farm raised a few chickens for eggs and meat. Today most of the chickens and eggs you eat come from what can be called *chicken factories* because the birds are raised on racks inside special buildings.

Migrant Workers

Have you heard of **migrant workers**? Migrant workers move their homes from place to place as they look for work. They are very important in the operation of some farms, because some crops — especially fruits and vegetables — require large numbers of workers for planting and/ or harvesting. For many years, the federal government has allowed thousands of families from Mexico to migrate back and forth between Texas and Michigan to help plant and/or pick crops. In Ohio, most of them have worked in the northwestern quarter of our state. Every member of a family, except the smallest children, work long hours in the fields. Land owners pay them minimum wages and provide simple housing like that shown above.

Fewer migrant workers are used today than during the 1950s, because new machines, like the ones on pages 289 and 290, do many jobs the migrants once did. The people operating the machine on page 290 are migrant workers.

Construction

Businesses related to the construction industry build and/or repair all kinds of **structures**, including houses, stores, churches, factories, airports, harbors, railroads, highways, pipe lines, sewers, electric power lines, dams, and power plants. Many of these businesses have a single worker, who is the owner — for example, the plumber who makes repairs in your house. Very few construction companies have more than 100 workers.

For example, *Watiker & Sons, Inc.* of Zanesville employs about 75 workers to create millions of dollars worth of highways and buildings each year. Albert D. Watiker, Jr. organized this company in 1973. In 1993 it was one of the 50 largest companies — of all kinds — in the United States to be owned and operated by African-Americans.

Some construction companies specialize in repairing structures. The natural forces of erosion and weathering, which you learned about in Chapter 2, affect structures in the same way they affect mountains. In addition, heavy trucks and traffic accidents cause damage to highways and bridges. For example, the picture below shows an 80-year-old bridge being replaced without rerouting traffic.

The construction industry creates our transportation system. What seems to be happening here?

This fire engine was made in Ohio and used in Alaska. How did this engine get to the scene of a fire?

Finance, Insurance, and Real Estate

When Ohio became a state, the industry relating to finance, insurance, and real estate was very small. As you learned in earlier chapters, many people who lived on farms had very little money. When they bought things in a nearby town, they often **bartered** (traded) butter, eggs, chickens, or other crops for goods and/or services they needed. As manufacturing and trade increased, money became the most important way to measure the value of goods and services. Banks and other **finance** companies were organized so that people could keep their money in a safe place, and/or borrow money when necessary.

In 1950 fewer than 90,000 people of Ohio worked in banks, savings and loan associations, insurance companies, and real estate companies. As you can see from page 305, almost three times as many worked in these activities in 1986. If you look back at the graph on page 300, you may wonder why Columbus and Franklin County grew so much between 1950 and 1990. A part of the reason is that several large insurance companies moved into the city during these years.

Manufacturing

As you can see on page 305, more Ohioans work in manufacturing than any other industry. In fact, the word *industry* is sometimes used to mean *manufacturing*. For example, for many years, Ohio, Indiana, Illinois, Michigan, and Wisconsin were called *The Industrial Heartland of America*. You could go to many parts of the world and find products manufactured in these states. The fire engine shown above was made in Cincinnati in 1907 and used in Alaska for many years. Today it is in a museum in Seward, Alaska.

310

Manufacturing Jobs in 1966 and 1988

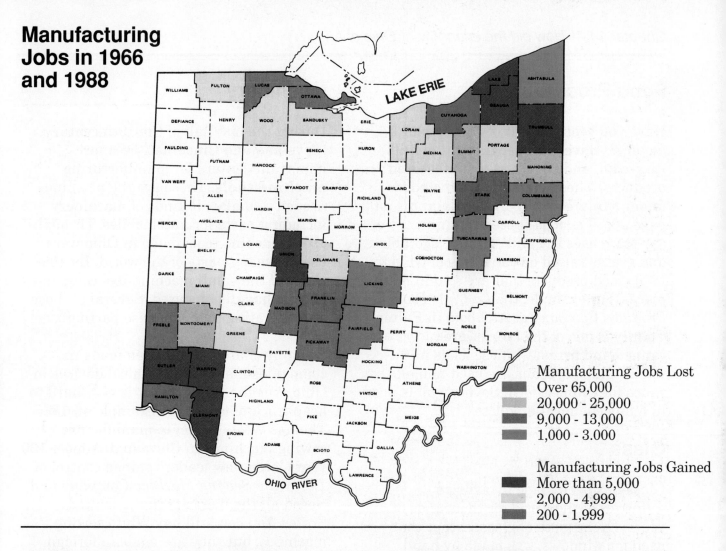

Manufacturing Jobs Lost
- Over 65,000
- 20,000 - 25,000
- 9,000 - 13,000
- 1,000 - 3,000

Manufacturing Jobs Gained
- More than 5,000
- 2,000 - 4,999
- 200 - 1,999

By 1970, manufacturing was **declining** (going down) in these states for several reasons. Steel mills and automobile factories in Germany and Japan were able to sell their products in the United States for lower prices than Ohio companies charged. Tires and many other products could be made at lower costs in other states than in Ohio. As you learned in Chapter 12, NCR decided to make new electronic devices in other places to replace mechanical devices made in Ohio. By 1980 some people were calling the old Northwest Territory *The Rust Belt*.

In the last chapter, you learned how housing, shopping, and industry moved outward from the eight largest cities after 1950. The map above shows how manufacturing jobs also moved from the largest counties to nearby counties. We will now look at a few examples of manufacturing activities that are important to the economy of our state today.

311

Food Processing

Have you ever thought of a bakery as a factory? Have you ever thought of milk, ice cream, and yogurt as manufactured products? These products are included under *manufacturing* in the diagrams on page 305. The food-processing industry of our state uses the milk, fruits, vegetables, and grains raised on the farms of Ohio to make food products that are sold in many places. For example, the *La Choy Food Products Company* at Archbold in Fulton County is one of the largest producers of canned and frozen Chinese foods in the world. Ohio soybeans are used to make soy sauce for Chinese food. Soybean oil is used in many chemical products.

Glass

Glass has been made in civilized countries of the world for thousands of years. Every piece of glass, except that used for windows, was made by hand until 1900. In that year, Michael J. Owens of Toledo invented a machine to make glass bottles quickly. He then organized the *Owens Bottle Machine Company* in Toledo in 1907. For most of the 20th century, Toledo was known as an important center of glass-making in the United States. In recent years, the Owens Bottle Machine Company has grown to become a conglomerate. Its home office is still in Toledo, but it makes no glass bottles in Ohio.

Machinery

During the last half of the 19th century, Cleveland and Cincinnati became important centers for manufacturing **machine tools**. These are the machines needed to make all kinds of machinery, including parts for automobiles. Through 1970, machine tools made in Ohio were used in many parts of the world. By 1990 many of the small machine-tool companies of Ohio had disappeared. Several of those still operating had Japanese partners.

So many changes have been made in companies making mechanical devices in Ohio over the years that it is very hard to keep track of them. For example, in 1866 Thomas White began to manufacture sewing machines in Cleveland. Almost 100 years later, new leaders gained control of *The White Sewing Machine Company* and closed all the factories in the United States. You can still buy White sewing machines, but they are made in foreign countries. These new leaders began to buy other manufacturing companies. The diagram on the next page will help you understand how Thomas White's company changed over the years to become a conglomerate called *White Consolidated Industries* (WCI). In 1993 WCI was bought by a Swedish conglomerate that makes Electrolux products!

What happened to Thomas White's Sewing Machine Company?

Year	Event	Products
1866	Thomas H. White established The White Sewing Machine Co.	Sewing machines
	Company also made	Bicycles, Roller Skates
1880's	Company bought Cleveland Screw Co.	Machine Tools
1957	New owners gained control Changed name to White Consolidated Industries (WCI)	
1966	Bought textile machine maker	Textiles
1967	Bought Gibson appliance maker and Franklin applicance maker	Appliances
1968	Bought Kelvinator applicance maker	
1971	Bought Bendix refrigerator maker	
1973	Bought Athens Stove Works	
1976	Bought Westinghouse applicance maker Formed White-Westinghouse Company	
1993	WCI bought by Electrolux SA, a Swedish conglomerate that operates would-wide under Electrolux, WCI operates 16 manufacturing plants in the United States.	

Some people call the appliance that keeps food cold a "fridge." In Dayton, early in the 1920s, General Motors Corporation made the first "mechanical ice box" and called it *Frigidaire*. For many years, the popular name for all electric refrigerators was "frigidaire", but now many people say "fridge." In 1979 General Motors sold the refrigerator business to WCI.

Winton automobiles, made in Cleveland, were the first cars to travel across the United States in both directions. This one made the trip from east to west. On which side of the car did the driver sit?

Motor Vehicles

In 1890 there were no motor vehicles. Ever since 1950, almost one-seventh of all jobs in the United States have been related to making, repairing, and operating automobiles, trucks, and buses. Ohio businesses have played leading roles from the earliest days of this industry.

By 1890 several inventors were making small steam engines that burned petroleum products. Some of these engines were used to move *horseless carriages*, as early automobiles were called. In 1900 Thomas White, whom you learned about earlier, helped his son Rollin create *The White Company* to manufacture steam-powered automobiles. The Whites built a large factory in Cleveland and made about 1,500 "steamers" each year until 1910.

The White Company began to make trucks in 1912. *White* trucks are still made today, but in Virginia by Volvo, a large Swedish company.

Alexander Winton also began to build horseless carriages in Cleveland. He created a simple form of the **internal combustion** engines used in automobiles today. In 1898 he sold 25 machines for $1,000 each. The next year, he sold 1,000 machines for $2,000 each. In 1903 a Vermont doctor and his driver used a Winton car to make the first automobile trip across the United States. They traveled from San Francisco to New York City in 64 days over unpaved roads! A short time later, the Winton car you see above was used to travel from New York City to San Francisco. The last Winton automobile was made in 1924.

Motor Vehicles Made in Ohio — 1991

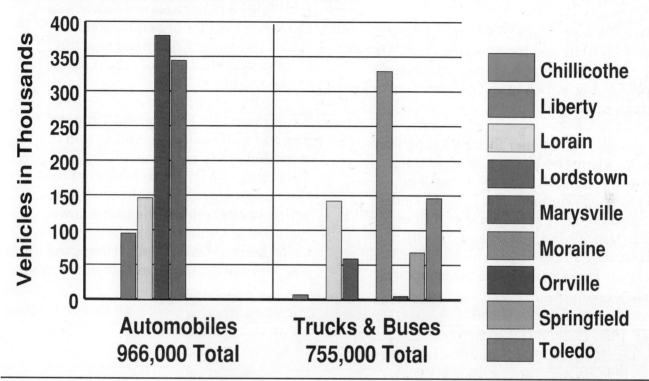

**Automobiles
966,000 Total**

**Trucks & Buses
755,000 Total**

Chillicothe
Liberty
Lorain
Lordstown
Marysville
Moraine
Orrville
Springfield
Toledo

Many other kinds of automobiles were made in Ohio, but today you can see them only in museums and in advertisements in old magazines. *The Crawford Auto-Aviation Collection* of the *Western Reserve Historical Society* in Cleveland has a large number of old cars.

The diagram above shows the numbers of automobiles and trucks made in Ohio during 1991. In that year, Ohio produced one out of every six autos made in the United States. In that same year, Ohio produced one out of every five trucks made in the United States. Today it is sometimes difficult to separate *automobiles* from *trucks*. On the one hand, the *Navistar International Transportation Company* factory, in Springfield, makes more heavy trucks than any other factory in the world. On the other hand, the "trucks" made in Lorain, Lordstown, Moraine, and Toledo are pick-up trucks and vans, including minivans which many people use as autos. The most popular vehicle built in Toledo is the *Jeep*. If you talk to anyone who served in the armed forces of the United States at any time since 1940, he/she can almost certainly tell you of an adventure with a *Jeep*.

Paper and Printing

In 1986 more than 30,000 people were employed in making paper in Ohio. Almost 70,000 were employed in printing and publishing, which is an industry that uses large amounts of paper.

Several of the paper factories that were built along the Miami and Erie Canal during the 19th century are still in operation. For example, in 1846 Daniel Mead bought part of a paper mill in Dayton. By 1882 he owned the entire company and changed the name to *Mead Paper*. Eight years later, his company bought a paper mill near Chillicothe. In 1990 the factory shown below was the largest center of employment in Ross County. In 1988 Mead was the largest manufacturer of school supplies in the world.

Where was this book made? On page iii you will find that the printing and binding were done by The C. J. Krehbiel Company. This company has been printing books in Cincinnati since 1871. Almost 100 years ago, it printed one of the best-known histories of Ohio: *Howe's Historical Collections of Ohio*. Henry Howe, the author, was no relation to the author of this book.

Large modern factories, like this Mead paper mill in Chillicothe, cover several acres of land. Parking for employees may require more land than the factory. A large part of the "smoke" from the tall stack is water vapor. How does this factory differ from the one shown on page 209?

SOHIO signs were replaced by BP signs in 1991. What do the symbols SOHIO and BP stand for?

Petroleum

We have used the word petroleum in two ways, both as a natural resource and as a product. As it comes from the ground, petroleum has few uses. After it has been *refined* — which is a form of manufacturing — it has many uses.

You have learned that John D. Rockefeller formed the *Standard Oil Company* in Cleveland about 1900. Within a few years, the company was so large that it completely controlled the petroleum industry of the United States. In 1911 Congress forced Rockefeller to break up his business into several smaller companies. As you travel about, watch for gasoline stations with the names *Amoco, Chevron, Mobil, Texaco,* and *Exxon.* Each of these was once a part of Rockefeller's company. Do you remember gasoline stations called *SOHIO? The Standard Oil Company of Ohio (SOHIO)* was Mr. Rockefeller's company. By 1987 *The British Petroleum Company (plc)* of England owned *SOHIO,* and later it changed the name of all the service stations to *BP.* The pictures above show the "before and after" signs. The offices and refinery of *The Standard Oil Company (Ohio)* were in Cleveland. *BP America, Inc.* now has its offices in that city.

What happened to the rubber compoanies of Ohio?

Began	County	Original Company Name	Company Name in 1994
1870	Summit	The B. F. Goodrich Co.	Michelin Tire Co. (France)
1898	Summit	Goodyear Tire & Rubber Co.	Goodyear Tire & Rubber Co. (USA)
1902	Summit	The Firestone Tire & Rubber Co.	Bridgestone Corp. (Japan)
1915	Summit	General Tire & Rubber Co.	GENCORP Inc. (no longer makes tires)
1920	Wayne	Wooster Rubber Co.	Rubbermaid, Inc. (USA)
1930	Hancock	Master Tire & Rubber Co.	Cooper Tire & Rubber Co. (USA)

In 1887 fourteen small petroleum companies in northwestern Ohio united to form the *Ohio Oil Company*, with headquarters in Findlay, Ohio. By 1946 Ohio Oil was using the brand name *Marathon*, and in 1962 the company name was changed to *Marathon Oil Company*. In 1982 the *United States Steel Corporation* bought the Marathon company but kept the main office in Findlay. Later, United States Steel changed its name to *USX Corp.*

Rubber and Plastics

During the 19th century, rubber was used for many things. It became even more important during the 1880s for bicycle and carriage tires. In Chapter 12, you learned about workers migrating to Akron to work in rubber factories during the World War I. By the end of that war, Akron was known as "The Rubber Capital of The World."

In 1870 Benjamin Franklin Goodrich organized *The B. F. Goodrich Company* in Akron, Ohio to make rubber tires. In 1898 F. A. Seiberling also decided to make rubber tires in Akron. He named his company *Goodyear Tire & Rubber Company* to honor Charles Goodyear, the man who discovered how to make natural rubber more useful. In 1900 Harvey S. Firestone organized *The Firestone Tire & Rubber Company* in West Virginia to sell rubber carriage tires. In 1902 he too began to manufacture tires in Akron. In 1915 the *General Tire and Rubber Company* was

What happened to the steel companies of Ohio?

County	Name of Company in 1920	Name of Company in 1990
Butler	The American Rolling Mill Co.	ARMCO Steel, Inc.
Cuyahoga	Jones & Laughlin Steel Corp.	LTV Steel
Cuyahoga	Republic Steel Corp.	LTV Steel
Lorain	United States Steel Co.	USX Corp.
Mahoning	Jones & Laughlin Steel Corp.	LTV Steel
Mahoning	Youngstown Sheet & Tube Co.	LTV Steel

also established in Akron. By 1920 almost one-half of all the rubber products in the world were made in Akron.

What is the situation now? The diagram on the previous page shows how the names of most of these companies changed during the 1980s. Several still have their main offices in Akron, but no tires and few rubber products are made there today.

Ohio is also the home of two other important rubber companies. The *Cooper Tire and Rubber Company* was established at Findlay in Hancock County before 1930 to make tires and other products from rubber. Its main office is still in Findlay, and it has two manufacturing plants in Ohio. *Rubbermaid, Inc.* was established in 1920 to make a variety of household products from rubber and plastics in Wooster, the county seat of Wayne County. Today Rubbermaid products are sold in many parts of the world.

In Chapter 10, you learned about the importance of leather during the 19th century. Many of the items that were once made of leather or rubber are now made of **plastic** (from a Greek word meaning "to mold"). In 1920 *celluloid, Bakelite,* and *Formica* were the only forms of plastics. Celluloid was used for motion picture film, but its most popular use was to make removable collars and cuffs for men's shirts. The shirts were worn for several days, and the celluloid parts were washed each night. Bakelite was used as an insulating material for electrical equipment. Formica was created in Cincinnati in 1913. For many years, it was used in place of mica as electrical insulation. (In Chapter 2 you learned how the Hopewell people used mica.) Since 1935, Formica has been used to make long-wearing and easy-to-clean table and counter tops. Today large quantities of raw materials for plastics are made in chemical

319

The liquid steel you see here in the ARMCO Steel Company at Middletown may be part of a refrigerator or automobile your family owns. What would you guess to be the temperature of the liquid steel?

factories along the Ohio River in Washington County.

Steel

In Chapter 10, you learned about the Hanging Rock Iron Region of Ohio. You also learned how Cleveland became a center of the iron industry by 1900. By that year, most iron was being changed into *steel*, which is a much stronger material. In 1920 Ohio was the home of five of the largest steel companies in America. The table on the previous page

shows how the names of the companies changed during the 1980s. By 1990, LTV Steel had closed the large steel mills in Cuyahoga and Mahoning Counties, and each of the three companies had Japanese partners. In addition to these big companies, there are several small mills that make steel out of scrap iron, which is a long-used form of "recycling."

In spite of all these changes, in 1990 Ohio was the second largest steel-producing state following Indiana. In the picture above you can see steel-making at the

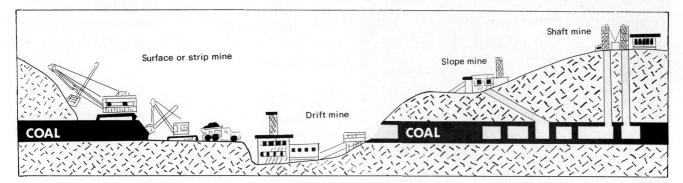

Coal is mined in a variety of ways, but most of it is removed by surface or strip mining. Where would the boys in the picture on page 201 be on this diagram?

ARMCO steel mill in Middletown. You can compare the size of the bucket of liquid steel in this picture to the entire size of the Buckeye Furnace on page 31.

Mining

The diagrams on page 305 show that almost 27,000 Ohio workers were employed in mining in 1985. This industry also includes *quarrying*. You learned about 19th century quarrying in chapter 10, and the industry has scarcely changed except for the machinery used. The most important products of Ohio mines today are **gypsum** (a very soft rock used to make plaster), salt, and coal. The gysum mined in Ottawa County is made into plaster, a material that is used in the construction of almost every building. Almost one-third of the salt used in the United States comes from Ashtabula, Cuyahoga, Lake, and Wayne Counties, but only a small number of workers are needed for this work.

Coal Mining

In Chapter 10, you learned about coal mining in the 19th century. The diagram above shows all possible ways to remove coal from the earth. As larger and larger pieces of earth-moving equipment were built during the 1940s, surface mining methods were used instead of shaft mining. Today huge machines, like the one shown on the next page, remove thousands of cubic yards (cubic meters) of earth and rock to uncover layers of coal in southeastern Ohio. In one scoop, they can move a volume of material equal to the size of an average classroom. Machines like this are made by *Dresser Industries, Inc.* in Marion County and used all over the world.

The American Electric Power Service Corporation put this machine in operation near Zanesville in 1989. Machines like this are made by Dresser Industries, Inc. in Marion County. What combination of length, width, and depth of the bucket of this machine would equal the size of your classroom?

Until about 1980, the coal companies merely tore up the landscape as shown

on the next page, took the coal, and moved to another location. Before a coal company can open a strip mine today, it must show how it will return the area to usable condition.

As coal mining changed from underground to surface methods, the number of workers dropped greatly. For example, more than 3,000 coal mining jobs disappeared from Harrison County between 1970 and 1990. You can look back to page 29 to see where Ohio coal was mined in 1987.

Trade

Trade is an important industry in all parts of the world. If you add together the people working in retail and wholesale trade, shown on the diagram on page 305, the number is almost equal to those working in manufacturing. If you add together the number of companies, the sum is larger than the number in any other industry.

Wholesale trade companies buy large quantities of goods and sell them in smaller quantities. For example, the *La Choy Food Products Company* in Archbold creates thousands of cans of Chinese food and packs them in boxes. It then sells hundreds of boxes to each of dozens of wholesale grocery companies throughout the United States. Each wholesale company keeps the boxes in a warehouse, and sells a few boxes at a time to dozens of restaurants and grocery stores.

Every time you buy something, you are making a retail trade. Candy stores, for example, buy large amounts of different kinds of candy from wholesalers. Then they sell single pieces of candy to you and your friends.

In 1988 four of the largest retail trade companies in the United States had their headquarters in Ohio. The fourth largest retailer was *The Kroger Company* of Cincinnati. Kroger sells many kinds of foods, drugs, flowers, and other items in "superstores" throughout the eastern United States. The eighth largest retailer was *Federated Department Stores, Inc.*, whose headquarters are in Cincinnati. Federated operates some of the best-known department stores in America, including the Lazarus stores in Ohio. The

thirty-eighth largest retailer was *Revco D. S. Inc.* of Twinsburg in Summit County. Revco began in the 1950s as a single drug store in Detroit, Michigan. In 1988 there were 1,200 Revco drug stores throughout the United States. In 1994 Revco bought the Hook-SupeRx Drug Company, which had more than 1,000 stores in the United States. The forty-first largest retailer was *The United States Shoe Company, Inc.* of Cincinnati. U.S. Shoe manufactures shoes in several small towns of Ohio. It owns several widely known brands of clothing and shoe stores throughout the United States. In the winter of 1989, the management of U.S. Shoe suddenly announced that the company was for sale, but no one had purchased it as of July 1994.

Before laws were adopted to control strip mining, Companies took coal and left the landscape looking like this scene in southeastern Ohio. Why were the trees in the center not removed?

Service

Have you ever asked someone to do something for you that you did not want to do yourself? Have they answered, "Do you think I'm your servant?" We often say that the pioneers who settled Ohio had to take care of themselves. Actually they helped, or *served*, each other in many ways. Groups of people got together to "raise" houses or barns, as you saw on page 168. They helped each other clear land, harvest and/or thresh grain, and shared each others' joys and sorrows.

Today our society is so complicated that we cannot be independent. Workers in the service industry help us do things we cannot, or do not want to do for ourselves. The diagrams of page 305 show how important the service industry is to our economy.

Medical doctors, dentists, and nurses provide health-care services. Child-care centers make it possible for many mothers to work outside their homes. Barbers and beauty operators provide personal-care services. Auto mechanics, appliance repair people, and telephone operators provide technical services. Professional athletes and television stars offer entertainment services. Ministers, priests, rabbis, and church secretaries provide spiritual services. Hotels, motels, and amusement parks provide other forms of services. In 1950 there were fewer than a half-million jobs in service industries of Ohio. As you can see on page 305, there were almost twice as many in 1986.

Education and Research

Is education an industry? Are you a product? All kinds of schools are included under Services in the diagram on page 305. In the 19th century, many businesses needed many employees who could do hard physical work. In the 21st century, many businesses will need employees with higher-order mental skills. Because of this situation, the educational services of Ohio are of great concern to the business leaders of our state. If the schools do not "produce" enough young people with the necessary skills, other industries will suffer.

Research is the service industry that discovers new ideas. Every company that hopes to stay in operation for a long time has some employees who develop ways to improve the company. The *Battelle Memorial Institute* in Columbus is the largest private research company in the world. It studies problems related to many branches of science throughout the United States and in several other nations.

Ohio was a great industrial state in 1900. A few of its businesses may still operate as they did in that year. Most of the businesses have changed so much that people of 1900 would not recognize them. Education and research are constantly creating new ways to create products. What will the industries of Ohio be like in the year 2100?

Let's Review Part 2

New Words

barter
decline
finance
gypsum
internal combustion
machine tool
migrant worker
plastic
research
structure

New Things to Do

1. Ask your parents to read this part of the book, and decide which kind of industry they work in. Write the name of each of the ten industries on the chalk board in your classroom. Have each classmate put her/his name under the industry in which his/her parent(s) work. Does the arrangement of names have any relationship to the main industries of your county?

2. Make a list of all the things you use in one day that are made of plastic. (Don't forget the tops of tables and other furniture.) Opposite each item, write down what kind of material that object might have been made of in 1900.

Part 3

What role has Ohio played in the space age?

What do you know about spaceships? You certainly know more about space travel than your great-grandparents did at your age! The only things they knew, they learned from a radio program called, *Buck Rogers in the 21st Century*! Citizens of Ohio have been leaders in travel through the air for 100 years.

During the Civil War (1861-1865), there were two forms of "travel" by air. First, hot-air balloons were used to lift soldiers above the ground to spy on the enemy. Second, specially-trained pigeons were used to carry what might be called "airmail" messages. Almost forty years passed before the Wright Brothers of Ohio discovered the secrets of powered flight.

The Wright Brothers and Their Sister

In 1869 Milton and Susan Wright moved their family to Dayton so that Mr. Wright could work for the *Church of The United Brethren in Christ*. Wilbur was their youngest child at the time. In 1871 the family moved into a new house at 7 Hawthorn Street, close to the home of the Dunbar family you learned about in Chapter 12. Within the next four years, two more children, Orville and Katharine, were born.

When Mr. Wright was assigned to travel throughout the area west of the Mississippi River, the family moved to Iowa. In 1884 they returned to 7 Hawthorn Street in Dayton. Katharine was only fifteen years old when her mother died in 1888. Mr. Wright assigned Katharine to be the acting mother of the family.

When Wilbur and Orville graduated from high school, they did not know what work they wanted to do. Orville liked to build mechanical devices, and one day he made a simple printing press. This led the brothers to go into the printing business. As you learned in Chapter 12, they printed Paul Dunbar's newspaper and a small book of poems that he wrote.

In 1892 the Wright brothers rented a store close to their home and started to sell and repair bicycles. Orville designed and built a machine to make bicycles. During these years, their father traveled widely for the church, and Katharine studied at Oberlin College, which you learned about in Chapter 11.

In 1896 Wilbur and Orville read a newspaper article that said a bicycle builder would probably invent a heavier-than-air flying machine. This led the Wright Brothers to become **aeronautical** (the science of flight) engineers. They began to spend all of their free time studying and experimenting with gliders, which are heavier-than-air but have no motor. They also experimented with gasoline engines. After Katharine graduated from Oberlin, she taught Latin in the Dayton schools and managed the family home at 7 Hawthorn Street. The

Katharine Wright played an important role in the success of her brothers Wilbur and Orville.

Wilbur (left) and Orville (right) dressed in this way in their shop and when they flew. Here they are prepared to fly a bolt of silk cloth from Dayton to Columbus. What do you think is in the tank marked "B 16?"

picture on the previous page shows her at about this time.

In 1900 the Wright brothers needed a special place to test a glider they had built. The United States Weather Service told them that the best weather conditions could be found on the sand dunes at Kitty Hawk, North Carolina. They took the glider apart in Dayton and carried it in boxes by railroad, boat, and horse-drawn wagon to Kitty Hawk. There they put it back together and learned many things about flying before they returned to Dayton.

The brothers returned to Kitty Hawk in the autumn of 1901, 1902 and 1903, and each time they used a more complicated flying machine. On December 13, 1903, they succeeded in using a gasoline-powered engine to fly a distance of 120 feet in 12 seconds. Later that day, they flew 852 feet in 59 seconds.

Within a few days, Wilbur and Orville Wright were famous around the world, but their problems were just beginning! Other people had also been working with flying machines. Some of them said the Wrights stole their ideas. Others tried to steal the Wrights' ideas. Every newspaper and magazine wanted to print stories about them, and several nations wanted to honor them. Katharine Wright stopped teaching so that she could help her brothers with their public relations and business affairs. The brothers only wanted to continue improving their airplane. In the picture above, you can see the Wright Brothers

During World War I, 3,000 airplanes like this were manufactured in Dayton. What do you think the wings were made of?

prepared to fly a bolt of silk cloth from Dayton to Columbus on November 7, 1910.

Wilbur died of typhoid fever in May 1912, just a few days after the family bought land in Oakwood, to the south of Dayton, to build a new home. You can see this house today, but it is used for private purposes. Katharine died in 1929 and Orville in 1948.

Today you can visit the scene of the Wright Brothers' flight in North Carolina. You can see their first airplane in the Smithsonian Institute in Washington, D.C.. You can visit their Hawthorne Street house, but it is now in Greenfield Village at Dearborn, Michigan. And you can visit their bicycle shop on Williams Avenue in Dayton. You can see their second airplane,

and a copy of their shop, in the *Carillon Historical Museum* at Dayton, Ohio. You can actually fly in a reproduction of their 1911 model "B" plane at the Dayton General Airport on S.R. 741.

Airplanes

In 1916 two friends from *The National Cash Register Company*, Charles Kettering and Edward Deeds, formed a company with Orville Wright. They organized *The Dayton Wright Airplane Company* and built a factory in Moraine in Montgomery County. Soon after the United States entered World War I on April 3, 1917, this new company received an order to build 400 training planes by the end of 1917. You can see a picture of one of these planes above. You can see the plane itself, and the

General Electric aircraft engines made in Hamilton County provide power for almost half the large airplanes of the world. If the worker is six feet tall, what are the dimensions of this engine?

largest collection of military airplanes in the United States, at the *Air Force Museum* in Greene County.

During World War II, hundreds of military planes were made in Columbus, and engines were built in Hamilton County. The first civilian jet plane service in the world began in May 1952, and this event opened a new era of transportation. Today *General Electric Aircraft Engines* (GE) builds jet engines like the one shown above where simpler aircraft engines were built during World War II.

In 1943 the Federal Government established a laboratory to study aircraft engines at the Cleveland Airport. In 1958 the *National Aeronautics and Space Administration* (NASA) was formed and named this laboratory the *Lewis Research Center*. Today it works on developing engines for space travel and operates a museum of the history of humans in space.

Space Exploration

In April 1957, the Union of Soviet Socialist Republics surprised the world by announcing that it had shot a capsule called *Sputnik* into space. Sputnik circled the earth in less than two hours and landed safely. Almost five years later, in February 1962, John H. Glenn, Jr., a

329

John H. Glenn, Jr. of Muskingum County was the first American to circle the earth three times in outer space.

native of New Concord in Muskingum County, became the first citizen of the United States to circle the earth three times in a space capsule. You can see his picture above. In July 1969, Neil A. Armstrong, a native of Wapakoneta, the county seat of Auglaize County, became the first human being to walk on the moon. Today you can visit the *Neil Armstrong Air and Space Museum* at Wapakoneta and learn many things about space exploration. You can see his picture on the next page.

After retiring from the space program, John Glenn became a businessman and made his home in Grandview Heights in Franklin County. In 1981 the citizens of Ohio elected him to the United States Senate and re-elected him in 1987 and 1993. After leaving the space program, Neil Armstrong moved to a farm in

Neil A. Armstrong of Auglaize County was the first person to walk on the moon.

Warren County. He served on the faculty of the University of Cincinnati for ten years and continues to serve our state and nation in several ways.

In 1977 Judith Resnik of Akron was enrolled for training in the first group of astronauts that included women. She became the second woman astronaut in outer space, and the picture on the next

331

Judith Resnik of Summit County was on her first trip in space when this picture was taken. She died when the Challenger exploded in 1986.

page shows her on this flight. In 1984, just six seconds before her second space flight was to "blast off," something happened to the engines so that the flight was cancelled. Her third spacecraft, the *Challenger*, was launched in January 1986. A few seconds later, it exploded and killed Judith and her six associates.

In 1900 people could travel between almost every pair of cities in Ohio in a railroad

train pulled by an engine made in our state, but they could not fly. Today people can fly from the largest cities in Ohio to places all over the world within one day in planes powered by engines made in Ohio, but they cannot travel by train in our state. Have we really made progress?

Let's Review Part 3

New Words

aeronautical

New Things to Do

Look at all the items that are related to airplanes and air travel in the "yellow pages" of your telephone directory. Write a short report on the help you might get if you wanted to buy a small airplane and operate it from an airport in you county.

What have we learned?

At some time in their life, many people think of going into business for themselves. If they follow the five steps outlined in Part 1, they may be successful. The economy of Ohio grew during the 20th century because some entrepreneurs created new businesses, while others improved existing ones.

Manufacturing has been one of the greatest industries in Ohio for 150 years. Products made in our state can be found throughout the world. As conditions have changed, some companies that once employed thousands of workers have left our state. But many new companies that make products of the "plastics age" and "space age" have been opened. In addition, as the number of jobs in manufacturing has declined, jobs in the fields of finance and service have increased.

In 1899 the Superintendent of the United States Patent Office gave up his job because 800,000 ideas had been patented. He felt that so many wonderful things had been invented, that there could be few new ideas. He could not have dreamed that more than 4,600,000 patents would be issued by 1990. Do you think the head of the U.S. Patent Office today will resign for the same reason?

Map Projects

Find the following places on your map of Ohio.

Place	County
Grandview Heights	Franklin
Lorain	Lorain
Lordstown	Trumbull
Moraine	Montgomery
New Concord	Muskingum
Oakwood	Montgomery
Twinsburg	Summit
Wapakoneta	Auglaize
Warren	Trumbull
Wooster	Wayne

Find the following place on your map of the United States.

Place   **State**
Kitty Hawk .... North Carolina

Books to Read

The following books will give you more information about subjects discussed in this chapter.

Astronauts and Cosmonauts, by Patricia Humphlett, is full of information about the space program and the men and women who led the way into space travel up to 1984.

Great Lives, by Milton Lomask, contains short stories about twenty-seven people who invented or discovered things that improve our lives.

John Glenn — Astronaut and Senator, by Michael D. Cole, is a short biography of the Ohioan who was the first American to travel in space.

The Robots Are Here, by Alvin and Virginia B. Silverstein, explains how robots are made, and how they imitate the actions of humans.

See Inside An Airport, by Jonathan Rutland, has many pictures of the jobs that must be done so that people can travel in airplanes.

The Wright Brothers, by Charles Graves, explains how the Wright Brothers invented the airplane. There are many line drawings.

The Wright Brothers: How They Invented The Airplane, by Russell Freedman, tells the story of the Wright Brothers and their "flying machine." It includes many pictures taken by the Wrights.

Chapter 15

How is Ohio governed today?

Let's learn...

- how our state government is organized.

- how we pay for government.

- how elections are held.

- how laws are created.

- how local governments are organized.

In Chapter 11, you learned that during the 19th century the three most important purposes of government were: to protect citizens from turmoil, to keep records of all important events, and to collect money to pay for these services. You also learned that laws must be changed to meet new conditions. During the 20th century, the citizens of Ohio decided that their government should also provide many new services relating to the health, safety, and well-being of the people. They agreed to pay higher taxes for this fourth group of services. In this chapter, we will explore how state and local government affect our lives today.

Part 1

How is the government of Ohio organized?

In Chapter 11, you learned how the government of the United States, and each of the fifty states, is divided into legislative, executive, and judicial branches, as shown on page 222. In Ohio, and in most other states, the legislative branch is called the General Assembly. The executive branch is headed by the Governor, and the judicial branch is headed by the Supreme Court. The General Assembly meets in the capitol, which you can see on the next page, and the Governor has his office in the same building. The Supreme Court meets in the tall building to the left of the capitol. If you look back to page 188 you can see the capitol as it was about 1870. The biggest

difference between these two pictures cannot be seen. Today the lawn around the capitol covers a large parking garage!

The diagram on page 338 shows more details about the three branches of our state government, including the length of time each elected person serves. Almost all of the departments under the governor were created by amendments to the Second Constitution during the 20th century. These departments have their offices in several buildings in Columbus, including the ones shown on page 339. We will discuss the organization of our government in the order the offices are shown on this diagram.

Executive Branch

Article III of the Second Constitution said: "The Executive Department shall consist of a governor, lieutenant governor, secretary of state, auditor, treasurer, and an attorney general, who shall be chosen by the electors of the state...." Today each of these officers is elected for a four-year term. The governor is permitted to serve only two terms in a row, but the other officials may be re-elected any number of times. The governor and lieutenant governor are elected together as members of the same political party. Each of the other officers may be a member of a different party. You will learn about political parties later in this chapter. The box on page 339 shows how each elected

Our Capitol was built between 1831 and 1869. The tall Rhodes State Office Building on the left was built during the 1980s. There is a parking garage under the lawn. What is the small building closest to the camera?

official and each department relates to the four purposes of government mentioned in the introduction to this chapter.

Governor: The governor of Ohio takes part in making laws by either *signing* (approving) or **vetoing** (disapproving) acts of the General Assembly. The governor is responsible for enforcing the laws of the state with help from other elected officials. The lieutenant governor serves in place of the governor when necessary. The twenty-three department heads shown in the box on page 338 are appointed by the governor.

Other Elected Officers: The *attorney general* is the lawyer for the executive branch of the state government. When questions arise about the meaning of a law, people can go to the attorney general for an opinion of what it means.

The *secretary of state* is responsible for keeping accurate records of all the laws of Ohio. This officer is also in charge of all matters relating to state and local elections.

The *auditor* makes certain that money is available to pay for all projects approved by the General Assembly. The auditor reviews the financial records of every county, township, village, and city to make certain that they are correct. The auditor also keeps records of land owned by the state.

Organization Chart of Ohio State Government

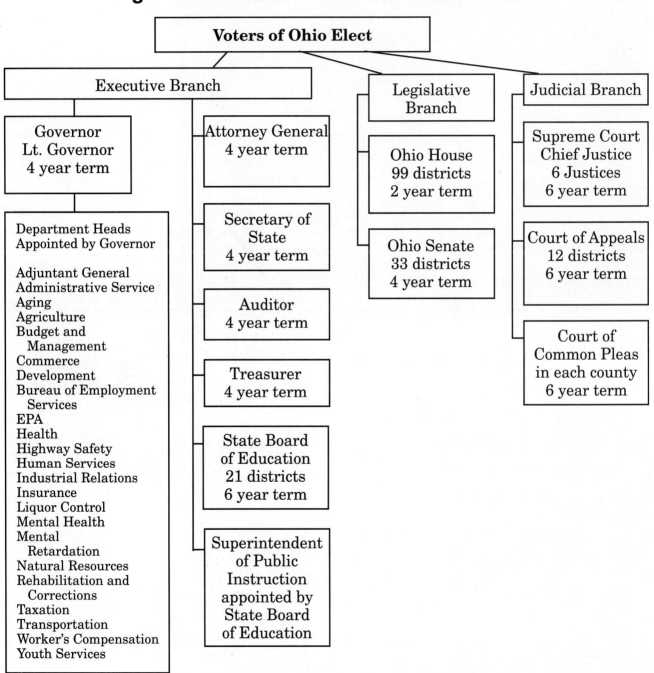

Voters of Ohio Elect

Executive Branch

Governor
Lt. Governor
4 year term

Department Heads
Appointed by Governor

Adjuntant General
Administrative Service
Aging
Agriculture
Budget and
   Management
Commerce
Development
Bureau of Employment
   Services
EPA
Health
Highway Safety
Human Services
Industrial Relations
Insurance
Liquor Control
Mental Health
Mental
   Retardation
Natural Resources
Rehabilitation and
   Corrections
Taxation
Transportation
Worker's Compensation
Youth Services

Attorney General
4 year term

Secretary of
State
4 year term

Auditor
4 year term

Treasurer
4 year term

State Board
of Education
21 districts
6 year term

Superintendent
of Public
Instruction
appointed by
State Board
of Education

**Legislative
Branch**

Ohio House
99 districts
2 year term

Ohio Senate
33 districts
4 year term

Judicial Branch

Supreme Court
Chief Justice
6 Justices
6 year term

Court of Appeals
12 districts
6 year term

Court of
Common Pleas
in each county
6 year term

The State Office Building on South Front Street was built during the 1930s. What is the name of the river in this picture?

Roles of Government in the late 20th Century

Prevent Turmoil
Governor and Lieutenant Governor
Judicial Branch
Attorney General
Adjutant General
Highway Safety
Liquor Control
Rehabilitation and Corrections

Keep Records
Auditor
Secretary of State
Budget and Management

Raise Money
Treasurer
Taxation

Well-Being of Citizens
State Board of Education
Aging
Agriculture
Commerce
Development
Employment Services
Environmental Protection
Health
Human Services
Industrial Relations
Insurance
Mental Health
Mental Retardation
Natural Resources
Transportation
Worker's Compensation
Youth Services

The *treasurer* receives many of the taxes and fees paid to the state, and pays all bills for departments of the state. Everyone who works for the state receives pay checks signed by the treasurer. The treasurer also takes care of all state funds not needed for current expenses.

State Board of Education: The State Board of Education is made up of people elected from all over Ohio. This board helps the General Assembly understand the problems and needs of more than 700 public school districts in Ohio. The members meet monthly in Columbus to direct the Superintendent of Public Instruction who carries out the instructions of the board.

Legislative Branch

The General Assembly is made up of two *houses*, the *House of Representatives* and the *Senate* (from a Latin word meaning "old man"). All representatives are elected every two years for two-year terms. One-half of the senators are elected every two years for four-year terms, so that there are some experienced people in the Senate at all times.

Judicial Branch

The *Supreme Court* deals only with questions relating to the Ohio Constitution. It decides whether particular laws are written and/or enforced as required by the Constitution. The seven judges are elected to the Supreme Court for terms of six years. All judges in Ohio are elected with the help of political parties.

State Courts: As you can see in the box on page 338, there are two kinds of courts under the Ohio Supreme Court: courts of common pleas and courts of appeal. Each county has a court of common pleas with judges elected by the people of the county. These courts make decisions about all violations of *statutory laws*. They also try to settle quarrels between citizens — sometimes by using the ideas of *common law*.

The eighty-eight counties are divided into nine judicial districts, and each district has a court of appeals. Each district court tries to settle complaints about decisions of the courts of common pleas within its district. All complaints about decisions of the courts of appeals are taken to the Ohio Supreme Court. In a few situations, the United States Supreme Court will hear complaints about decisions of the supreme courts of the fifty states.

Let's Review Part 1

New Words

veto

New Things to Do

Use the business pages of your local telephone directory to find all of the branches of our state government listed under the heading *Ohio, State of*. Make up a work sheet with the headings like those in bold face type on page 339. List each of the state offices in your county under one of the four headings.

Part 2

How do we pay for government?

Have you ever heard the old saying, "The only things that are certain in life are death and taxes." *Taxes* are the price we pay for public services that we may, or may not, need. For example, if our house catches fire, a tornado or flood damages our neighborhood, or a foreign nation attacks us, we want government help immediately without discussing how much the help will cost. Whenever citizens want new services, they must either pay more taxes or give up some existing services.

Kinds of Taxes

Citizens of Ohio pay many kinds of taxes to the United States, to the State of Ohio, to their county, and to their township and/or municipality. The table on the next page gives important information about many of these taxes, but we can discuss only a few of them. Most of the taxes we pay to the state go into the *General Fund*. Almost all of the money needed to pay for public services comes from the same fund. Later you will learn how highway taxes go into a special fund to pay for highway improvements.

The graphs on pages 343 are related to the **fiscal year** 1993. The State of Ohio and the United States operate on two different kinds of *years*. Each of them carries out most of its activities on the basis of years that run from January 1 through December 31. Each of them accounts for of its income and expenses on the basis of a *fiscal year*. The fiscal year of Ohio runs from July 1 through June 30. The *fiscal year* of the United States runs from October 1 through September 30.

The upper graph on page 343 shows the importance of the sources of money collected by the state during fiscal year 1993. As you can see, almost three-quarters of all **revenue** (income) was from the sales and income taxes. Ohio has a sales tax of 5% on almost everything you buy, except food and medicine ordered by a doctor. This means that you pay 5 cents to the state for each $1.00 of the value of the purchase. When you go to an ice cream store or a fast-food restaurant, does the cashier ever ask you whether your purchase is "to go" or "eat in"? If it is "to

Taxes Paid by Citizens of Ohio

Kind of Tax	Tax Rate	Money Used For
Real Estate		
Land & buildings	• Varies from place to place city, village, other	• Small amount to state Large amount to schools • Varying amount to county,
Personal Property		
Estate tax at time of death	• Low for small estates • Higher for larger estates	• State general fund
Inventory of business	• Low	• State general fund
Sales Tax		
State	• 5% of sales — not on carry-out food or medicine or medicine	• State general fund
Optional county tax	• Up to 1.5%	• County purposes
Optional transit tax	• Up to 1.5%	• Local public transport
Income Tax		
State	• Maximum of 7.5% for high income	• State general fund
Optional school district	• Maximum of 1.75%	• School purposes
Optional municipal earnings tax	• Maximum of 2.5%	• City or village purposes
Other Taxes		
Tobacco	• $.024 per pack	• State general fund
Alcohol	• Depends on % alcohol	• State general fund
Public utilities	• On gas, electric, and water bills	• State general fund
Highway User Tax		
Gasoline & diesel fuel	• $0.22/gallon	• Highway construction & maintenance
Axle-mile on trucks		
Registration fee (license)	• $45 for auto • $1,000+ for truck	• Highway safety
Driver license fees	• $10 for 5 years	• Highway safety
Lottery		
Advertised as a "game"	• As much as each person wants to spend	• Education

General Fund Revenues

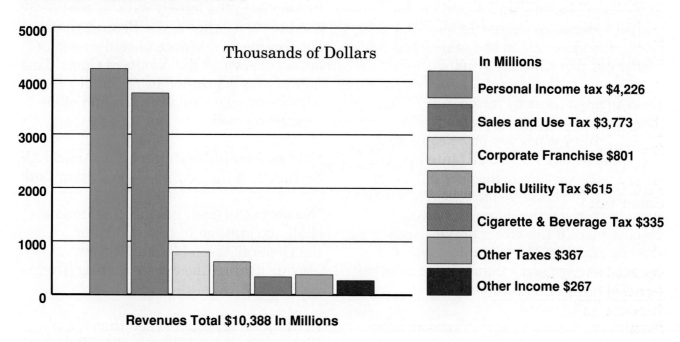

Thousands of Dollars

In Millions

Personal Income tax $4,226

Sales and Use Tax $3,773

Corporate Franchise $801

Public Utility Tax $615

Cigarette & Beverage Tax $335

Other Taxes $367

Other Income $267

Revenues Total $10,388 In Millions

General Fund Expenditures

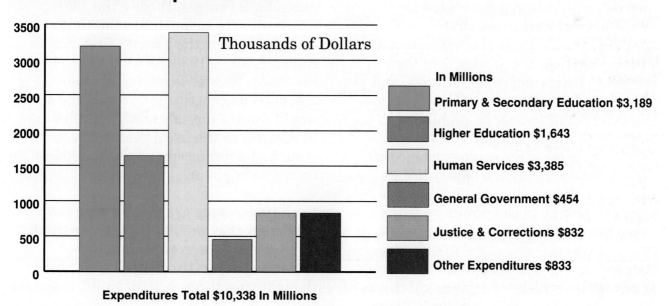

Thousands of Dollars

In Millions

Primary & Secondary Education $3,189

Higher Education $1,643

Human Services $3,385

General Government $454

Justice & Corrections $832

Other Expenditures $833

Expenditures Total $10,338 In Millions

343

go," you do not have to pay the sales tax. State law permits counties and public transit systems to charge up to 1.5% additional sales tax on the same items on which you pay state sales tax.

Ohio adopted a tax on incomes in 1971. The amount you pay is related to the national income tax you pay. People with low incomes pay very small state tax, but people with very large incomes pay up to 7.5% rate. In recent years, school districts have been given the power to collect income taxes if the voters of the school district approve. Many municipalities collect *earnings taxes* that have no relation to national or state income taxes.

The lower graph on page 343 shows how the state spent most of its money in fiscal year 1993. As you can see, about three-quarters of all the expenses were for education and human services.

Lottery: Article XV, Section 5, of the Second Constitution said: "lotteries, and the sale of lottery tickets, for any purpose whatever, shall forever be prohibited in this state." Voters amended this law in 1974 so that the state could earn income from a lottery. Today the lottery brings more than $500 million dollars into the treasury, and all of the profits go to the State Board of Education.

As you may have noticed, the state lottery is advertised widely as a *game*, but it was

created for two important reasons. First, income from the lottery reduces the need to raise other taxes. Second, many low-income people once played a form of lottery known as the *Numbers Game*. This "game" was controlled by criminal gangs who operated outside the law and often created turmoil.

Sale of Alcoholic Beverages: Article XV, Section 9, of the Second Constitution said:

"No license to [sell] intoxicating liquors shall...be granted in this state; but the General Assembly may, by law, provide against the evils resulting [from such sale]."

In Chapter 12, you learned that the Eighteenth Amendment to the United States Constitution banned the use of alcoholic beverages. During the 1920s, this law led to so much turmoil that it was repealed by the Twenty-first Amendment in 1933. As soon as alcoholic beverages became legal again, Ohio amended its constitution so that the state would control the sale of high-alcohol beverages. In the fiscal year 1989, our state had a net income of about $50 million from this business.

Each time people are faced with a new challenge, they are likely to say or think, "Why doesn't the government do something about this?" Each time this thought goes through their mind, it should be followed with the thought, "What am I willing to pay in taxes to get this help?" In a society like ours, the *government* is *us*, and it has only the powers and money that the voters give it.

Let's Review Part 2

New Words

fiscal year
revenue

New Things to Do

1. Each time you buy something in Ohio, other than carry-out food and medicine, you must pay a sales tax. For the next week, collect the sales slips for each purchase you make, and keep a record of how much you pay for each item and the tax on the sale. Since the Ohio sales tax is five cents on each dollar, calculate how much additional sales tax you pay to your county and/or special tax district.

2. Talk to your parents about the taxes they pay to Ohio and to your local units of government. Do they feel that these taxes are "fair" in view of the services they receive?

Part 3

How are people elected to political office?

In the United States, we have a representative form of government. This means that citizens elect representatives to the legislative branch of government to make laws for them. They also elect the officers in charge of the executive branch to enforce the laws. Citizens also elect judges for state, county, and local courts.

The Constitution of the United States includes requirements that people must meet to serve in Congress and as President. The Constitution of Ohio includes requirements for all elected positions in our state government. Hundreds of thousands of citizens meet these requirements, but very few choose to serve in these elected positions. In this part, you will learn about the role of *politics* in selecting officials for our state and national government. The politics of this process is far more complicated than the legal process.

The Role of Political Parties

Have you ever heard someone say, "There are two sides to every question." In fact, there may be many *possible* answers but no one *best* answer. For example, does your school have a problem that affects your opportunity to learn? What would happen if you asked your teacher to let your class discuss this problem? Would every student have a different idea? After an open discussion of the situation, how could the class decide what to do? The only way the class could reach a decision would be by practicing *politics*; that is, by using the art of people working together in groups.

As people work together on problems of government, their ideas can be divided into two types. Some people want to change conditions, while others want to keep them unchanged. Among those who want change, some want the least possible change needed to solve the problem, while others want to change the entire system.

In some nations of the world, a variety of political parties represent many divisions of opinion. Since 1860, the two largest political groups in the United States have been the *Democratic Party* and the *Republican Party*. From time to time, new national political parties are formed that hold very strong ideas on certain subjects, but they seldom last more than a few years. On the other hand, small political parties have been active in some cities and states for many years. Each party tries to help candidates who agree with the ideas of the party, AND who have the talents needed to be elected by the voters.

Very few people are elected to offices in government without the help of a political party. Members of such a party give money, time, and effort to help the candidates do the work needed to be elected. In return, members of the party expect the elected official to take actions that will support their point of view.

Running for Political Office

Have you heard anyone say, "The great thing about this country is that anyone can become president of the United States!" This simple statement does not include the years of hard work that most **candidates** (people hoping to be elected) for president have completed before they run for this high position. The only other route to election as president has been followed by a few military leaders, such as Ulysses S. Grant, who have become famous in time of war.

The success of our form of government depends on able people being willing to use the process of *politics* to be elected to positions in municipal, county, and state governments. Most people who are elected to state offices began their political activity by helping someone else be elected to office. After several years of such work, they ran for an office in their local government. They may have run two, or more, times before being elected. After proving their ability in these ways, a political party may agree to help them run

How A Person Becomes Governor of Ohio

Hundreds of individuals hold political offices all over the state.

A few of these office holders decide they would like to be the next governor. These individuals travel around the state to make themselves known to leaders of one of the political parties.

The leaders of each political party decide which individual will have the best chance to be elected and will help the party most.

Republican Party Chooses a Candidate	Democratic Party Chooses a Candidate	Other Party Chooses a Candidate
One or more other Republicans decide to run outside the party	One or more other Democrats decide to run outside the party	One or more other individuals decide to run outside the party

Primary Election held on first Tuesday after first Monday in May

People who say they are Republicans vote for one of the above. Person receiving the highest number of votes is Republican candidate.	People who say they are Democrats vote for one of the above. Person receiving the highest number of votes is Democratic candidate.	People who say they are members of party vote for one of the above. Person receiving the highest number of votes is other party candidate.

Other people who want to be governor can try to get thousands of voters to sign petitions to have their names put on the ballot.

After the primary election, all candidates travel throughout the state and spend large sums of money on advertising to convince voters to select them as Governor.

General Election held on first Tuesday after first Monday in November

Names of candidates on ballot do not show names of sponsoring parties.
Order of names of candidates are changed from ballot to ballot.

Ballot for Governor
Names of first candidate
Name of second candidate
Name (s) of other candidate (s)

Every voter marks one name. Name receiving largest number of votes is declared to be the next Governor.

for a position in our state or national government. The outline on the previous page shows the many steps required by most candidates to be elected as governor in Ohio.

At every election, you can expect candidates from all parties to make one of the following statements. Candidates, who have been elected before and are running again, will say that voters should "Keep experience!" Candidates who are not in office will say, "It's time for a change!"

Voting

If you want the benefits of living in a free society, you must accept the responsibilities of helping to choose good leaders for elected offices. In the United States, we choose our leaders by *voting*. As you have learned, the United States Constitution originally said that only white males, twenty-one years of age or older, could vote. You have also learned that amendments to the constitution gave African-American males, and later all women, the right to vote.

For many years, the United States has required eighteen-year-old men to serve in the armed forces in times of war. During the 1960s and early 1970s, young men were required to serve in Vietnam. As a group, they said, "If we are old enough to fight for our nation, we are old enough to vote." In 1971 the Twenty-sixth

Amendment to the United States Constitution gave eighteen-year old citizens the right to vote. In 1977 an amendment to the Ohio Constitution gave eighteen-year-olds the right to vote in state elections.

If you want to vote, you must first **register** (sign up) with the *Board of Elections* of the county in which you live. In order to register, you must prove that you are at least eighteen years of age, a citizen of the United States, and live at a certain place within the county. The board of elections will then tell you the place at which you will be allowed to vote. The diagram on the next page outlines the process of registering and voting. The picture on page 350 shows a woman at her voting place.

Elections

Every step of the process of elections is controlled by state and national laws. We will now look at three kinds of elections.

Primary Elections

Primary elections are held in Ohio on the first Tuesday after the first Monday in May of each year. This means that election day cannot be on the first day of May. Primary elections are held to choose the people from the political parties who will run for each office in November. Many other **issues** (questions) may also

How to Vote in Ohio

1. Reach 18 years of age. Or after reaching 18 years, move to another county. Or move into Ohio as an adult.

2. Go to County Board of Elections or other official place to register.

3. Give name, address, and date of birth.

4. Receive instructions from County Board of Elections about where to vote.

5. On election day (primary, general, or special) go to assigned voting place.

6. Tell *election judges* your name and address. Show proof if necessary. Sign *poll book*. Receive *ballot*.

7. Go into private voting booth and mark ballot.

8. Give marked ballot to election judges and leave voting place.

9. If you do not vote in any election for a period of four years, you must go back to the Board of Elections to register again.

be voted on at a primary election. Perhaps your school district will have a tax levy on the next primary **ballot** (list of candidates and issues).

General Elections

General elections are held in Ohio, and many other states, on the first Tuesday after the first Monday in November. Members of Congress and the President of the United States are elected in even-numbered years. All state and county officers are also elected in even-numbered years. Cities, villages, and townships may elect their leaders in either odd or even-numbered years as they choose. In addition to voting for candidates for various offices, there may be many other issues on the ballot. For example, if your school tax levy did not pass at the primary election, it may be on the ballot again in November.

Special Elections

Special elections can be called at any time by any unit of government to meet an emergency. For example, if your school levy was defeated in May and November, the board of education may ask for a special election to try again. In Ohio, more special elections are called for school issues than for any other purpose. The picture on page 351 shows a new rural school in a county that has grown rapidly in recent years. Some of these districts ask for tax

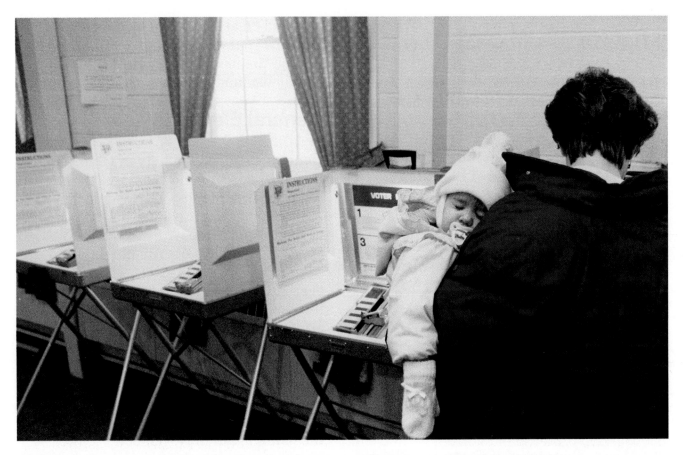

Voting places are used only a few times each year, so all arrangements are temporary. Why do you think the child is in this voting place?

increases three or four times each year, because they need the money, but voters in the district do not want to pay higher taxes.

Apportionment

In a free society, the largest possible number of people have the right to vote, and all votes have equal value. While it is easy to decide who may vote, it is more difficult to make all votes have equal influence. For example, since the members of the executive and judicial branches of Ohio government serve the entire state, these officials are elected *at large*. This means that all voters throughout the state have equal influence.

Schools are crowded in rural areas that are growing in population. Do you ride a yellow school bus?

On the other hand, members of the General Assembly are elected to represent the *districts* in which they live. The Ohio Constitution says that the House of Representatives will have ninety-nine members. The map on the next page is used to elect these representatives from 1992 to 2002. In the seven counties with the most people, the districts are so small they cannot be shown on this map.

The constitution says that the Senate will have thirty-three members. The map on page 353 shows the thirty-three districts used to elect these senators from 1992 to 2002. If you try to fit these two maps together, you will find that each Senate district is made up of three House districts.

Since each of these law-makers represents a *district*, the districts must include the same numbers of people. For example, would it be fair if the law-maker from one district represented 90,000 people, and the law-maker from another district represented 110,000 people? This means that district boundaries must be changed as people move about within the state. The process of dividing the state into districts, so all votes have equal value, is called

Ohio House Districts

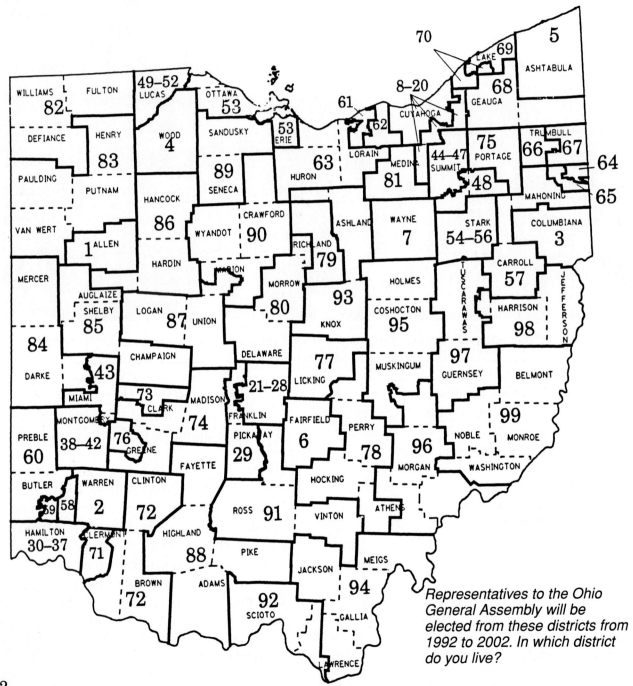

Representatives to the Ohio General Assembly will be elected from these districts from 1992 to 2002. In which district do you live?

Ohio Senate Districts

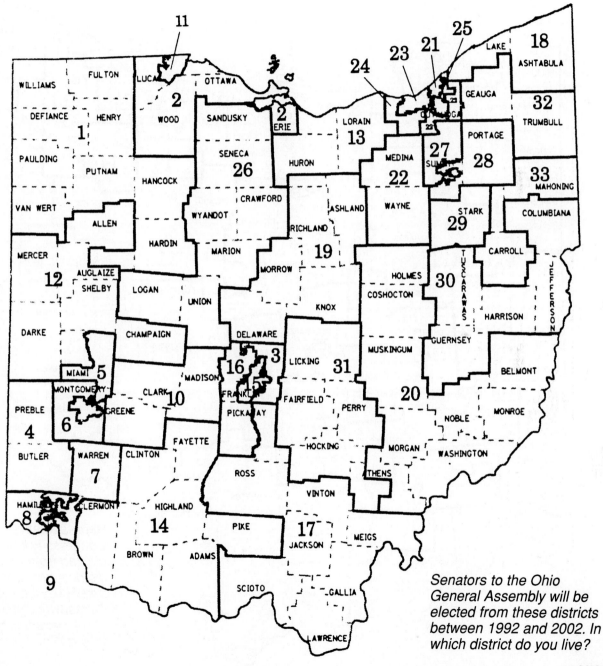

Senators to the Ohio General Assembly will be elected from these districts between 1992 and 2002. In which district do you live?

Ohio Congressional Districts

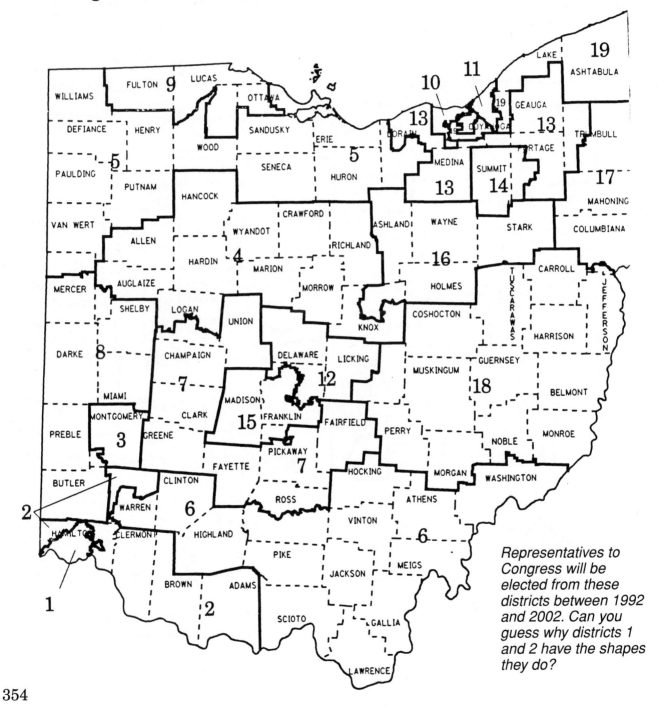

Representatives to Congress will be elected from these districts between 1992 and 2002. Can you guess why districts 1 and 2 have the shapes they do?

apportionment. It is carried out in every state once every ten years after each census of population is completed.

The process of *apportionment* is also used in the election of representatives to the United States Congress. From 1982 to 1992, Ohio elected twenty-one representatives to Congress. Our population increased from 1980 to 1990, but other parts of the United States grew more rapidly. As a result, we now have twenty representatives. The map on the previous page shows the congressional districts of our state from 1992 to 2002. Every state elects two *senators* so that every state has equal influence in the Senate.

Perhaps you now think that we have a complicated process for choosing the people who govern us. People of other nations, who live under rulers they do not choose, look to our system as a symbol of freedom. People who want to live freely must accept responsibility for choosing good leaders.

Let's Review Part 3

New Words

apportionment
ballot
candidate
issue (voting)
register (voting)

New Things to Do

Ask your teacher to explain the last school tax issue that your school district asked voters to approve, including whether or not the issue was approved. Next, ask your parents about how they felt about the issue and how they voted on it. Now have a class discussion about what you and your classmates learned from this activity.

Part 4

How are laws created?

As you learned in earlier chapters, laws are created to solve particular problems at certain times. You also learned that laws can become **obsolete** (no longer useful). In 1951 the Ohio General Assembly repealed 2,361 obsolete laws. At the same time, it rearranged all the remaining laws and called them the *Ohio Revised Code*. But many laws passed since 1951 could be repealed because they are no longer useful.

On the next page, you will find a diagram to help you understand how new laws are created. The first step is for a member of the general assembly to create a **bill** (proposed law) in one of five ways:
1. The member may develop a personal idea.
2. The governor may recommend a new law.
3. The supreme court may require that a law be changed.
4. A special-interest group may use the process called *lobbying*.
5. Individual citizens may use the processes called *initiative and referendum*.

Lobbying

Have you ever been part of a *special-interest group*? If you and your friends beg your parents and/or teachers for permission to do something, you are acting as a small *special-interest group* for your cause. Have you ever bought snacks in the *lobby* of a movie theater? Almost every hotel, motel, and movie theater has a lobby where people can meet. Strange as it may seem, *special-interest groups* and *lobbies* are often related to each other in the world of politics.

In a free society, any person can believe that the government should change the way it acts. He/she can also get other voters to help because the more people who ask for change, the more likely it is to happen. Some special-interest groups are very large, such the medical organizations, business groups, farm organizations, labor unions, and social-welfare groups. These groups often hire agents, called **lobbyists**, to tell the legislators about laws the groups support or oppose. These lobbyists talk to the law makers in the lobbies of the capitol, state office buildings, and nearby hotels. At election time, the special-interest groups help those candidates for the General Assembly who promise to vote for the interests of the group.

Initiative and Referendum

Do you ever surprise your parents or teachers by doing something nice without their asking you to do it? If so, you are showing **initiative**. Have your parents or teachers ever told you and your brothers, sisters, or classmates, to do something you didn't want to do, and you said: "Wait a minute! Let's take a vote on that!" If so, you have called for a **referendum**.

The *initiative* and the *referendum* are two of the most powerful tools the citizens of a free nation have. But the people of Ohio could not use these tools until the constitution was amended in 1912. The process of *initiative* can be used when a group of citizens wants the General Assembly to adopt a new law, but the assembly does not follow the wishes of the group. Members of

Simplified Diagram of How a Bill Becomes a Law in Ohio

House of Representatives   **Senate**

| A proposal is presented by a representative, and is given a 1st reading. | A proposal is presented by a senator, and is given a 1st reading. |

| Proposal is given 2nd reading and sent to a committee. | Proposal is given 2nd reading and sent to a committee. |

| The committee holds public hearings on the proposal, and makes changes as necessary. | The committee holds public hearings on the proposal, and makes changes as necessary. |

| The proposal, as changed by the committee, is given a 3rd reading and voted on by the house. | The proposal, as changed by the committee, is given 3rd reading and voted on by the senate. |

| If defeated, proposal dies. | If approved, proposal goes to other house, and process is repeated. | If defeated, proposal dies. |

If second house makes changes in wording, a committee is formed of members of both houses to work out compromise, which goes back to both houses for new vote.

If both houses agree on same wording, proposal goes to the governor for review.

If governor vetos, proposal goes back to both houses for new vote. If both houses vote for the proposal...

If governor does nothing with proposal for 10 days...

If governor signs approval...

... proposal becomes a law.

the group then get thousands of registered voters to sign **petitions** (legal forms) calling for a public vote on the issue. The process of *referendum* can be used when the assembly passes a law that members of a group do not like. Members of the group then go through the same kind of *petition* process as for an *initiative*. If the petitions have the correct number of legal names, the issue will be voted on at a primary or general election.

As you can see, the processes of creating laws is complicated. Almost all laws are created by the General Assembly after lobbying activities by special-interest groups — some of which favor and some of which oppose each new law. If the General Assembly refuses to pass a law, a special-interest group may use the process of *initiative* so that all voters can show their interest in the question. If the General Assembly passes a law that a special-interest group does not like, the group can call for a public *referendum* on the law.

Let's Review Part 4

New Words

bill (law)
initiative
lobbyist
obsolete
petition
referendum

New Things to Do

Return to the school problem you discussed at the end of Part 3.

1. Divide the class into three or four groups and have each group discuss what the class might do to encourage the principal to take action about the problem.

2. Have a representative of each group present that groups' ideas to the class.

3. Have a class vote on which suggestion seems best.

Part 5

How are local areas governed?

There are two points of view about laws. First, you can do only those things that the law says you can or must do. Second, you can do anything so long as the law does not forbid it. In general, county and township governments can do only what state laws require. Most incorporated towns can do anything except what is forbidden.

County Government

Each county is a part of the state. Each county office is controlled by state laws, and county officials can do only what state laws permit. This form of government was satisfactory before World War II. It cannot deal with many problems in the metropolitan areas we have today. Problems of fire, crime, drainage, and transportation cross the boundaries of incorporated places, but county government controls only unincorporated places.

The diagram on the next page shows the nine county offices and the county court. People are elected to these positions for terms of four years each and may be re-elected any number of times. The diagram also shows the most important things each official does. The people

elected to these positions may represent different political parties or different points of view. They may not always work in harmony with each other.

County commissioners are responsible for all county activities except those assigned by law to the other elected officials. Perhaps the greatest power the commissioners have is to review the spending of the other county officials. While women and African-Americans have been elected to many political offices in Ohio since 1970, white men continue to control county commissions. In 1990, 87 counties were supervised by 230 men, of whom only one was African-American and 31 were women. Montgomery and Portage were the only counties to have two women commissioners.

Alternate Form of County Government: In 1933 and in 1957, the constitution of Ohio was amended so that counties could adopt other forms of government. Up to 1990, the citizens of Summit County have been the only ones to take the initiative to change their county government. During the late 1980s, they adopted a *county council* form of government with seven members of the council, all of whom were men in 1990.

Townships

As you have learned, townships were created as units of local government when

Organization of County Governments

Three County Commissioners

• Approve the budget for each of the other divisions of the county
• May operate one, or more, of the following: Sewer District, Water District, Park District, Regional Planning, Building Inspection, Transit District, Animal Shelter, Cemetery, Land-Use Zoning, Hospital, and Help for the Poor

County Auditor

• Keeps track of how every department of county spends it's money
• Sets value of every parcel of land in county, and assesses real estate taxes

County Engineer

• Builds and repairs all roads owned by the county, supervises all bridges in county
• Makes — and keeps up-to-date — maps of all parcels of land for Auditor
• Must be a registered professional engineer and land surveyor

County Recorder

• Keeps a copy of every legal paper relating to the ownership of every parcel of land in the county
• Keeps a copy of every other legal paper that anyone wants to put on public record

County Treasurer

• Collects all taxes paid to the county
• Pays all employees of the county, and all bills of all branches of county

Coroner

• Determines the cause of death in any case that is doubtful or suspicious
• Must be a licensed physician

Prosecuting Attorney

• Serves as lawyer for every branch of county government
• Represents the public in all cases where a state law has been broken
• Must be a licensed lawyer

Sheriff

• Enforces state laws in unincorporated parts of county
• Operates the county jail

Clerk of Courts

• Keeps all records and documents relating to county court activities

Common Pleas Court

• Every county has at least one judge. The larger the county, the more judges it has.
• Hears all cases involving possible violation of state laws
• May have a special court to handle juvenile cases
• May have a special court to handle probate cases
• Judges must be licensed lawyers.

it was difficult to travel. Today, as in the past, each township is governed by three *trustees* and a *clerk*, each of whom is elected to a four-year term. Township trustees are responsible for all roads not on the state or county highway systems and may operate a cemetery within the township. Perhaps the most important role trustees play is to represent the interests of township residents in the overall problems of the county.

Townships receive small amounts of money from the county commissioners. The citizens of some townships vote to pay special taxes to hire police officers and/or to support fire fighters. This form of government may still be satisfactory in rural areas, but it may not be satisfactory in the metropolitan areas. For example, in 1990 more than 220,000 citizens of Franklin County and 270,000 citizens of Hamilton County lived in highly urbanized areas under the township form of government.

The City of Springboro and Clear Creek Township in Warren County are good examples of what has been happening in metropolitan areas. These units of government are at the northern limit of the Cincinnati metropolitan area, and immediately south of the Dayton metropolitan area. In 1950 Springboro was little more than a cross-roads settlement that included the township hall shown on the next page. Today Springboro is a city

that covers about one-sixth of the area of Clear Creek Township. The population of the township needs the larger township offices shown on the next page. The box below shows how the populations of these places changed in forty years.

Populations of Springboro and Clear Creek Township

1950 and 1990

Place	1950	1990
Springboro	516	6,590
Clear Creek Township	2,254	6,757

Special Districts

All of the boundary lines of states, counties, townships, and municipalities were created by human beings to solve particular political problems. But as you can see from maps in Chapter 2, the drainage systems and natural resources of our state are not related to political boundaries.

Special districts (units of government) are often formed to solve problems that cross political boundaries. Each district is operated by a group of people called a *board, authority,* or *commission.* These people may be appointed or elected to carry out the purpose of the special district. Every district can raise money to pay for its operations.

Before and after views of Clear Creek Township offices in Warren County.

Some of the earliest special districts in our state were formed to drain various parts of the *Black Swamp* that once covered northwestern Ohio. Everyone knew what should be done, but the counties did not have the legal authority, money, or skill to take action. The land owners finally lobbied members of the General Assembly to pass a "ditch law" that permitted them to organize *drainage districts*. During the 1930s, the *Civilian Conservation Corps* worked to improve conditions in the *Muskingum River Conservancy District*.

We will now look at three other kinds of districts that are important today — the *Miami Conservancy District*, school districts, and sewer districts.

Miami Conservancy District: In 1913 the people living in the drainage area of the Great Miami River (see map on page 24 suffered from a tremendous flood. The picture on the next page shows how downtown Dayton was affected. John Patterson, whom you also learned about in Chapter 12, took the lead in organizing relief work for flood sufferers. The National Cash Register Company provided shelter and food for hundreds of people.

A short time after the flood, Mr. Patterson led the people of the Miami Valley in asking the General Assembly to form a *flood-control district*. This law made it possible for all the people living in the Great Miami Valley to build structures to protect themselves against future floods. The *Great Miami Conservancy District* has been a model for flood control projects in other parts of the United States.

School Districts: Every school in Ohio, whether public, private, or church-related, is in a *school district*. Each district must cooperate with the state board of education you learned about earlier in this chapter.

What are the boundaries of the district in which your school is located? If you are in a *local school district* (part of a county system), does your district include any towns? If you are in a city school district, does it include any areas outside the city limits? Is there more than one incorporated place within the district? As you can see, school districts can be very complicated units of government.

Members of your local board of education are elected to four-year terms and have complete responsibility for the public schools of your district. For example, the board hires all superintendents, principals, teachers, and other employees of the system. It also adopts all textbooks and makes all purchases. It supervises state programs for private and church-related schools within the district. The most difficult problem for most boards of education is to raise money to operate the schools. For all this work, the members of your board of education are paid only for their expenses while attending meetings.

Dayton, Ohio, suffered severe damage in the great flood of 1913. What is in the water near the light post to the left of center?

Sewer Districts: Sewer systems must be built so that waste waters flow downward to treatment plants. Many people, who moved from cities to rural areas during the 1930s and 1940s, used *septic tanks* to dispose of sewage. After 1950, the Federal Housing Administration required that subdivisions in outlying areas have local sewage treatment facilities. During the 1970s, the Environmental Protection Administration said that all existing and new buildings must be connected to sewer systems. Almost all main sewers follow the paths of streams, and streams ignore political boundaries. As a result, the only way to solve sewer problems is to create special districts.

Villages and Cities

You have learned many things about the villages and cities of Ohio, but very little about their government. Villages and cities are called *municipal corporations* in the *Ohio Revised Code*.

If the citizens of an unincorporated area decide to form a village or city, they must choose one of three forms of government: the *commission plan*, the *council-manager plan*, or the *federal plan*. Each of these plans includes officials who serve as treasurer, auditor, clerk, and lawyer, but they may have different names for these positions. Under the commission and council-manager forms, these officials are usually appointed by the elected council or by the manager. Under the federal plan, they may be elected.

Commission Plan: Under the commission plan, five people, who are called commissioners, are elected by all the voters in the municipality, and the commissioners appoint the assistants they need. The commissioners elect a chairperson to conduct their meetings, but all five have equal authority and responsibility. Dayton is the largest city in Ohio with the commission form of government, but it was also the first large city in the United States to hire a city manager.

Council-Manager Plan: Under the council-manager plan, a town council is elected by the voters. A mayor is chosen to conduct the meetings of council and to represent the municipality in ceremonies. The council appoints a manager to be in charge of the day-to-day operations of the government. The manager then chooses assistants to help him/her. The council may replace the manager at any time. In 1924 the Charter Committee persuaded the citizens of Cincinnati to adopt the council-manager form of government. For many years, Cincinnati was the largest city in the United States to have a city manager. Today larger cities in other states have this form of government.

Federal Plan: The federal plan is similar to the form of state government in Ohio. The voters elect a mayor as the chief executive officer and a council as a legislative body. The mayor appoints assistants to help her/him. The council may have as few as five members, but not more than fifteen, depending on the population of the municipality. Cleveland and Columbus, the two largest cities in Ohio, use this form of government.

Municipal Courts

Every village and city may have its own court system. In small towns, this is called the Mayor's Court. State laws permit incorporated places in metropolitan areas to combine their courts into Municipal Courts. In such places, the judges are elected from the entire county. These courts deal with violations of laws relating to traffic control and minor crimes, and with personal conflicts.

While our form of government may seem complicated, the basic idea is that local problems should be solved "close to home." Problems that affect a larger area should be solved by the county or a special district. Problems that affect more than one county or district should be solved at the state level.

Let's Review Part 5

New Words

special district (legal)

New Things to Do

1. Use the "business" section of your telephone directory to carry out one of the following projects. There may be a map in the back of the directory or the "yellow pages".

> A. If you live in a village or city, look in the directory under the name of the municipality. Write down the names and addresses of the most important offices listed in the directory. Locate these places on a map of the municipality.

> B. If you live in an unincorporated area, look under the name of your township and your county. Write down the names and addresses of the offices mentioned in Part 5, and locate the offices on a map.

2. Talk to your parents about the government of the place where you live. Ask them whether the local government and/or the schools played a part in their decision to choose the place where you live.

What have we learned?

Two of the most important features of a free society are: (1) that citizens understand how their government operates, and (2) that they take part in it by voting. When only a few people live in an area, the form of government can be very simple. The greater the number of people living in an area, the more complicated government becomes.

In many ways, the government of Ohio is similar to that of the United States and the other states. The operations of Ohio counties are similar to each other even though the counties differ greatly in population. As the populations of metropolitan areas grow and spread over larger areas, new levels of government must be created in the form of special districts.

The grand idea of government of the people, by the people, and for the people will not continue if citizens do not pay attention to what their political leaders are doing. Democracy requires that citizens take part in the processes of government. The surest way for citizens to lose their freedom is to say that government does not concern them.

Chapter 16

What are the challenges of the 21st century?

Let's learn to...

- **protect freedom for ourselves and people of the future.**

- **use our natural resources wisely.**

- **live together in peace.**

Two things are certain about the future. First, there will be changes. Second, no one can say exactly what the changes will be. Throughout this book, you have been learning about the changes that took place during past centuries in the area we call *Ohio*. Today almost everyone is better off than her/his ancestors were a hundred years ago. But changes are taking place so rapidly today that we must try to guide events so that our descendents may have even better lives a hundred years from now. In this chapter, we will look at some of the problems that seem to be most important for the future.

How can we preserve freedom?

In 1776 a small group of men, representing thirteen British colonies, met in Philadelphia to discuss freeing themselves from British rule. On July 4 of that year, they signed a *Declaration of Independence* that said, in part, "We hold these Truths to be self-evident, that all Men are created equal, that they are endowed by their Creator with certain unalienable Rights, that among these are Life, Liberty, and the Pursuit of Happiness..." *Liberty* is another word for *freedom*.

Ever since 1776, the liberty gained by the thirteen colonies has been a light of hope to the world. Even today, the people of some nations are studying the ideas of 1776 in the hope of gaining freedom for themselves. But in order to enjoy freedom, we must accept *responsibility* for our actions.

During the past two centuries, freedom has contributed to the wealth our nation enjoys today. For example, people were free to move from place to place to seek new opportunities and employment. Entrepreneurs were free to exploit natural resources to create more and better products. Since 1950, tens of thousands of people have been free to exploit the benefits of electric energy, petroleum products, and motor vehicles by moving ever farther into the countryside around our largest cities. Unfortunately, while some people were claiming this freedom for themselves, they were denying it to others. We will now look at a few of these continuing problems.

Freedom for Native Americans

You have learned how the people of the United States felt that they were free to make and break treaties with the Native Americans during the 18th and 19th centuries. You also learned that there were very few natives living in Ohio after 1840. Today Native Americans live on 284 reservations in 26 states, including five in Michigan and six in New York. Since 1950, native tribes in several of these places have won law suits against the United States because of treaties broken many years ago. Today the Shawnees are back in the news in Ohio, as you can read in the box on the next page!

Before 1980 no one knew how many Native Americans lived in our state. In 1970 the Bureau of the Census began to use a new system to gather information. It mailed a census form to every house, and the people

Shawnees Reclaim Land, Home in Ohio.

Separated by war, government intervention, broken treaties and time, they became one of the nation's most splintered groups, but now the Shawnees have an Ohio home.

The Shawnee Nation United Remnant Band recently purchased 20 acres south of Urbana, a west-central Ohio city, in Champaign County.

It's not much of a home for a people who once called much of western and southern Ohio home, but still a home. "This is ours," said Hawk Pope, 48, of Dayton, chief of the Shawnee tribal band. "It was (a) rather hurtful thing to drive by miles and miles of land that used to belong to your people.... This puts an end to that." ...

Although the land purchased by the band has no historic significance, it does lie between a former Shawnee village and one of the last known campsites of Tecumseh, a Shawnee chief and famed Indian freedom fighter, Pope said.

From: The Cox New Service: May 18, 1989

living in the house filled out the form. In 1980 and 1990, under the heading of Race, people were asked to identify their race by marking one of the following choices:
___ White   ___ Eskimo or Aleut
___ Black   ___ Asian or Pacific Islander
___ American Indian

In 1980, 12,239 residents of Ohio marked that they were American Indians, that is, Native Americans. In 1990, 20,358 marked that they were natives.
Appendix B on page 383 shows the number of people in each county who said that they were Native Americans in 1990. Are you a Native American, or is there one in your class?

Freedom for African-Americans

The slavery that existed in the southern states for almost 250 years (1619 to 1865) was another example of denial of freedom. When African-Americans gained freedom in 1865, many of them moved to Ohio and other northern states. Still more of them came to Ohio to find work during the two World Wars. While they gained political freedom in 1865, for many more years they were denied the rights of choosing where they could live and where they could seek recreation. Today they have far more freedom of choice in these activities than they did in 1960. Do African-Americans in your community enjoy all the freedoms of other citizens?

Freedom for Women

You have learned how women tried to obtain the rights of citizenship when the Constitution of the United States was being written. You have also learned that they did not gain the right to vote until 1920. Their next challenge was to be accepted as candidates for public office. During the 1950s, a few women were elected to serve on municipal councils in Ohio. Since then, several women have served as mayors in the towns of Ohio and as judges of local courts, and a few have been elected to state offices. Of the twenty-one Ohioans elected to the United States House of Representatives for the 1987-88 term, two were women.

In earlier years, when few women worked outside their homes, it was often said that, "Men work from dawn to dusk, but women's work is never done!" Today many women work outside their homes at jobs that were closed to them in 1950. But far more women now face the combined problems of holding full-time jobs AND caring for children. How does this problem affect your family?

Freedom to Use Drugs

In earlier chapters, you learned about problems created by use of alcohol. Today you may be more aware of problems created by nicotine and *hard* drugs than of problems created by alcohol. All of these drugs create turmoil in several ways, as the following examples show. For many years, drunken drivers have killed more than one-half of all people who die in automobile accidents. Most of the people, who require years of medical treatment for lung cancer and/or emphysema, smoked tobacco for many years. Since 1965, many serious crimes have been committed by people trying to get money to buy "hard drugs." Users say that they have the right to pursue *happiness* in any way they choose. While under the influence of drugs, do they have the right to create turmoil for other people?

How can natural resources be used wisely?

As you learned in earlier chapters, the Ohio Country was a treasure house of natural resources. The United States, as a whole, had even more resources. Entrepreneurs were free to exploit these resources to gain personal wealth, and they gave little thought to the future. We will now look at several events of the 20th century that warn us that we must use our resources more wisely in the future.

The Importance of Trees

As the population of Ohio and the United States grew during the 19th century, most of the trees were destroyed to create farms and/or to provide lumber for the growing cities. By 1930 there were no large forests left in Ohio. Today we know that trees and all green plants play an important role in our lives. Humans and most animals must inhale oxygen to live. At the same time, we exhale carbon dioxide as a waste product. When we burn coal or petroleum to release energy, we are also changing oxygen into carbon dioxide.

In the great "plan" of Nature, green plants take in carbon dioxide as food and release oxygen as a waste product. This process is called **photosynthesis**, from Greek words meaning "put together by light." Trees are especially important in this process, because they have such large areas of green leaves during most of the year.

While creating tremendous amounts of carbon dioxide, we are cutting down large numbers of trees in the tropical rain forests. As a result, the natural balance between oxygen and carbon dioxide in the air is being disturbed. How can we change our ways of living to resolve this conflict?

Reducing Waste of Materials

The political cartoon on the next page shows one of the most important problems we face today. You have learned how people had to live with few resources during the period from 1930 through 1945. During the Great Depression, some people earned money by going through neighborhoods collecting scrap iron, old newspapers, magazines, and rags. During World War II, so many resources were needed for the war effort that a national slogan was, "Use it up! Wear it out! Do without!"

By the end of World War II, everyone was tired of being careful with resources; therefore, the idea of recycling almost disappeared. In later years, the cost of labor increased faster than the cost of materials. As a result, manufacturers often used more materials and less labor to create products. As "supermarkets" and "fast food" restaurants grew, they used more materials for packaging in order to reduce the labor needed to sell their products. Today it is not unusual for the packaging material you throw away to be larger than the item you want. And many of the plastics used in packaging cannot yet be recycled. So what happens to all the "junk" we throw away?

Liquid Wastes: When towns began to build sewer systems in the late 19th century, human wastes were left to flow

Jim Borgman, the prize-winning political cartoonist for The Cincinnati Enquirer, *created this cartoon in 1990. What is this cartoonist trying to tell us?*

into nearby streams or lakes. As factories developed liquid wastes from petroleum products or other chemicals, these wastes were poured into the sewers. Communities along the Ohio River and Lake Erie continued to use this system of disposal until the 1960s. Columbus, and other communities that were not on large rivers or lakes, built sewage plants to treat human waste. Today the United States government requires that all liquid wastes be treated so that the final water is almost fit to drink.

Solid Wastes: For many years, garbage, or food waste, was *dumped* into pits and left to decompose in areas where no one lived. As cities grew after World War II, land developers created new subdivisions near these dumps. People bought the new homes without studying the neighborhood, and then complained about the smells and rats associated with the old waste pits.

Some cities built **incinerators** (furnaces) to burn solid wastes. While these were useful in reducing the volume of waste, they created *air pollution*. By 1970 many cities decided that they could not afford the cost of cleaning the smoke produced by incinerators, so they began to use *sanitary land fills*. These were really *dumps* in which the trash was covered with earth each day. The picture on the next page shows the highest "hill" in Hamilton County, which is a huge pile of solid wastes!

As urban areas continue to expand today, some people fight against building new incinerators, while others fight against new land fills. During the 1980s, a new slogan developed out of these protests — **NIMBY**, which means "Not in my back yard!" Since 1990, Ohio has had a program for recycling paper, glass, and certain plastics and metals. This system saves natural resources and reduces the volume of waste that must be disposed of. Does your family sort out solid wastes for recycling?

Reducing Waste of Energy

You have learned many things about producing, using, and wasting energy. For example, in 1900 Ohio was one of the important sources of petroleum and natural gas in the world. In 1990 Ohio was still the eighth largest producer of these raw materials in the United States. But for many years, the people of the United States have been *using* far more petroleum than we *produce*. Since 1960, at least one-half of the petroleum we use has come from other nations — especially from the Middle East.

In 1973 many of the countries, from which we were buying petroleum, decided to raise the price and to lower the amount they sold. The price of gasoline tripled, and everyone began to try to reduce the waste of energy. The United States started a program to create other forms of liquid fuel. Of the three largest projects, two were important to Ohio. The first of these was to make liquid fuel from coal, and the second was to make it from grain. More recently, diesel fuel has been made from soybeans.

"Mount Rumpke" is made up of trash collected in Hamilton County for almost fifty years. What happens to the solid waste that you create?

Columbus burns its solid waste to produce electricity. What do you think they do with the scrap metal from the trash?

Hundreds of millions of dollars were spent in these projects. Each project produced liquid fuels that would cost more than petroleum, so we continue to use petroleum from other nations.

One idea to save fuel and reduce the volume of solid waste involved the burning of trash in a process called *cogeneration*. When you travel on I-71 just south of Columbus, you can see the building shown above. This is the *Columbus Municipal Electric Plant* that burns solid wastes to create steam to generate electric power. After more than ten years in use, this plant still has so many problems that other cities have not adopted the idea.

Nuclear Power

In 1945 the United States used a form of atomic energy to destroy two cities in Japan by exploding bombs made from the atoms of uranium. The scientists who made these bombs said that atomic energy could be used to generate electricity. They also said that this form of energy would be "clean" because it would not create air pollution. By 1950 some people were thinking that the most important source of energy for the future would be that stored in the atoms of uranium.

In the early 1950s, the *United States Atomic Energy Commission* (AEC) built two large factories in Ohio to separate uranium from its ore. One factory was near the center of Pike County, which is a rural area. The other was near Fernald, a settlement in the northwestern part of Hamilton County. The process of separating uranium from its ore requires large amounts of electrical energy. Therefore, two new coal-burning power plants were built along the Ohio River to supply this energy.

During the 1970s and 1980s, more and more people moved into the northwestern part of Hamilton County and the southwestern part of Butler County. By 1988 people living near the

uranium plant at Fernald were complaining that the air and water of the area were polluted with chemicals from the factory. In 1989 these citizens won a $100 million law suit against the operators of the AEC plant. Today the federal government is spending hundreds of millions of dollars to remove the dangerous wastes from this area.

During the 1970s, the *Toledo Edison Company* built the atomic power plant shown below on the shore of Lake Erie in Ottawa County. The cost of building and operating this plant was so high that the company could not afford it. As a result, it had to unite with the Cleveland Electric

The people of northwestern Ohio get some of their electricity from the Davis Besse nuclear power plant in Ottawa County. What do you think is coming out of the cooling tower on the left?

Illuminating Company to form the Centerior Energy Corporation. For about twenty years, some people in eastern Ohio got electricity from an atomic power plant at Shippingport, Pennsylvania, but this plant is now closed.

Have you heard of Chernobyl, a city in Ukraine? In 1986 an atomic power plant exploded there and killed many citizens of what was then the Union of Soviet Socialist Republics. This accident frightened people all over the world, and very few atomic power plants have been built since. Is nuclear energy a good source of electric power?

The Role of Motor Vehicles

Long before you read this book, you knew that motor vehicles were important to your life. They are useful and convenient forms of transportation, but they create tremendous waste of energy and raw materials. As they burn petroleum products, they create large volumes of carbon dioxide and other gases that are poisonous. When exposed to sunlight, these gases produce **smog**, a word that was created from "smoke" and "fog."

The motor vehicle industry was proud that it made more than 9-1/2 million automobiles and trucks in 1991. If you look ahead to 2001, you can say that they also produced 9-1/2 million sources of solid waste! The picture below shows a typical auto junk yard that you can see in many places. Scrap-metal dealers buy old cars, cut them apart, and separate the metal items from the plastic and rubber items. The metal can be recycled, but what can

This is an automobile junk yard is on the south line of Preble County. Is there an auto junk yard near your community?

No one knows what to do with old automobile tires. What suggestions do you have?

be done with the plastic and tires? Several experiments have been tried using tire rubber for other purposes, but millions of old tires are scattered over the countryside. The picture above shows one of the tire dumps in southwest Ohio that has thousands of old tires. Have you seen an auto junk yard? What happens to the old cars?

Urban Growth

You have learned how metropolitan areas have grown since 1940. Today cheap gasoline and electricity make it possible to live comfortably almost anywhere. People in the suburbs think nothing of driving ten miles to work or shop. As a result, the traffic congestion that once existed in the central city now occurs in many places outside the city.

Each time the people move outward, three forms of waste occur. First, the people abandon useful, older houses in the central city, and use tons of raw materials to create new houses. Second, they demand that new transportation routes and public utilities be built to serve them. Third, they use more energy to move the longer distances. How can we deal with this problem?

How can we live in peace?

Perhaps the greatest desire of the greatest number of people in the world today is to live in peace. You have learned how millions of people came to the United States from many parts of the world because of turmoil in their home lands.

377

While the United States has fought in several wars in other lands, no invaders have approached our shores since the War of 1812. The last fighting on our soil was during the Civil War more than a century ago.

But *peace* is more than absence of war: it is also *freedom from fear*. Today many people are afraid that they will be attacked or robbed if they leave their homes. Many of their fears are related to crimes caused by the use of drugs, as mentioned above. Candidates for political office like to say that they will "get tough with crime," but no crime-control laws have been truly useful to this date.

Social Security

One of the greatest fears that many people have relates to loss of income. How can they live if they cannot earn money? Many of the federal programs adopted during the Great Depression of the 1930s created jobs. Other programs tried to provide *social security* for people who could no longer work because of age or injury. These programs are still in operation.

Since 1935, every worker pays money into the *Federal Social Security Program* that provides income for retired workers and for disabled persons. The State of Ohio operates a *Workmen's Compensation Program* to provide income for workers

who lose their jobs or are injured while at work. The *National Labor Relations Board* protects workers against illegal actions by employers. Some employers provide health care insurance for their workers.

The Value of Money

While some government programs provide greater financial security, other government actions have reduced the value of our money. *Money*, in the form of printed paper and coins, has value only if you can exchange it for goods and services. People save money during their working years in the hope that they will be able to buy things later when they no longer work. Government policies that reduce the value of money create fear. The following numbers will help you understand this.

1. In 1900 a family of four could live in some comfort on an income of $1,000 per year.
2. In 1950 only 5 out of every 100 workers earned more than $10,000 per year.
3. In 1994 a family of four was living below the poverty level if it had an income of $12,000 per year.

Perhaps this will be clearer if you compare the cost of an ice cream cone in 1940 to what you pay today. In 1940 you could get a three-dip cone — with three different flavors if you wanted them — for five cents. What does it cost you to buy an ice cream cone today? Our dollars *look* the same today, but do they have the same value?

Americans are proud of their freedom to pursue "happiness." But not all of them remember that freedom carries the responsibility of doing no harm to others. Great things have happened in Ohio over the past 200 years. Greater things can happen if we all work together to protect our individual and combined freedoms.

What have we learned in this book?

After several months of study, you should know something about the State of Ohio. What do you think Ohio will be like when your children study its history? Of course, no one can give an exact answer to this question, but YOU can play an important part in the future of our state. You can be a good citizen by continuing to learn about, and take part in, the *positive* events in your neighborhood, county, and state. You can discuss these events with your parents, relatives, and friends. The best way to learn these events is by reading newspapers and news magazines. At election time, you can study the candidates for office, and the issues to be decided, so that you can become an intelligent voter.

And every day in simple ways you can do things to improve the quality of life for everyone. You can take part in activities that require more of your energy and imagination and less gasoline and electricity. You can learn to take care of your body so that you do no harm to yourself or others. You can help to recycle materials to reduce the energy needed to create more new materials. You can live in harmony with others to reduce the amount of turmoil in our nation.

The more you learn about your community, state, and nation, the more challenges you will discover. The American system is not perfect, but it is the best political system that human beings have ever lived under. What role will you play in keeping it that way?

Let's Review

New Words

incinerator
NIMBY
photosynthesis
smog

New Things to Do

1. Some scientists dig into old dumps to learn what people once threw away as trash. Play scientist in you home, and make a list of the different kinds of things your family throws away in one week. Identify the items that might be recycled.

2. Go to your public library, and ask to see newspapers from 1940, 1950, 1960, 1970, 1980, and 1990. These may be on microfilm. Choose five things that you use regularly, such as shoes, soft drinks, and bananas. Make a table of the prices of each of these items as you find them in the newspapers. How is this information related to the value of a dollar?

Book to Read

The following books will help you understand the problems discussed in this chapter. Your local library may have other books on the subjects covered in this chapter.

Air Pollution, by Gary Lopez, explains the effects of human activities on the atmosphere and urges changes to reduce these effects.

Alcoholism and The Family, by Gilda Berger, is a thorough discussion of the problems created by alcohol.

Children's Guide to Endangered Species, by Roger Few, is a beautifully-illustrated story about 150 forms of animal life that may soon disappear from the earth.

Gardens from Garbage, by Judith F. Handelsman, explains how to use kitchen wastes to create a vegetable garden.

Fueling The Future, by Janet Pack, explains various forms of energy with many interesting illustrations.

Global Warning: Assessing The Greenhouse Threat, by Laurence Pringle, explains, in simple terms, the importance of preventing damage to the atmosphere.

Kids Guide to Planet Care, by The Sierra Club, describes the problems that humans have created on earth, and suggests ways that young people can improve the situation.

Our Endangered Planet: Rivers and Lakes, by Mary King Hoff, is a nicely illustrated discussion of world-wide problems of water pollution.

Our Global Greenhouse, by April Koral, explains how industry and transportation have affected life for the past 300 years, and suggests ways to reduce these effects.

Recycling, Learning The Four R's, by Martin J. Gutnik, outlines four things that each person can do to protect life on our planet.

Appendix A

Information About Ohio Counties

County	County Seat	Year	Area	Source of Name
Adams	West Union	1797	586	President John Adams
Allen	Lima	1820	405	Uncertain origin
Ashland	Ashland	1846	424	Henry Clay's home in Kentucky
Ashtabula	Jefferson	1808	703	Indian for "Fish River"
Athens	Athens	1805	508	Athens, Greece, center of learning
Auglaize	Wapakoneta	1848	398	Indian for "fallen timbers"
Belmont	St. Clairsville	1801	537	Fr. "belle monte" (beautiful mountain)
Brown	Georgetown	1818	493	General Jacob Brown of War of 1812
Butler	Hamilton	1803	470	General Richard Butler of Indian wars
Carroll	Carrollton	1833	393	Charles Carroll of Declartion of Indep.
Champaign	Urbana	1805	429	French for "plain"
Clark	Springfield	1818	398	Genl. George Rogers Clark of Revolution
Clermont	Batavia	1800	456	French for "clear mountain"
Clinton	Wilmington	1810	410	Vice Pres. George Clinton
Columbiana	Lisbon	1803	534	From "Columbus" and "Anna"
Coshocton	Coshocton	1810	566	Indian for "Black Bear Town"
Crawford	Bucyrus	1820	403	Col. William Crawford of Indian wars
Cuyahoga	Cleveland	1810	459	Indian for "winding stream"
Darke	Greenville	1809	600	General William Darke of Revolution
Defiance	Defiance	1845	414	Location of Fort Defiance
Delaware	Delaware	1808	443	Indian tribal name
Erie	Sandusky	1838	264	Indian tribal name meaning "cats"
Fairfield	Lancaster	1800	506	Beauty of "fair fields" of area
Fayette	Washington CH	1810	405	General LaFayette of Revolution
Franklin	Columbus	1803	543	Benjamin Franklin, U.S. Statesman
Fulton	Wauseon	1850	407	Robert Fulton, inventor of steam boat
Gallia	Gallipolis	1803	471	"Gaul", ancient name of France
Geauga	Chardon	1805	408	Indian for "raccoon"
Greene	Xenia	1803	416	General Nathanael Greene of Revolution
Guernsey	Cambridge	1810	522	Isle of Guernsey, home of settlers
Hamilton	Cincinnati	1790	412	Alexander Hamilton, Sec. of Treasury
Hancock	Findlay	1820	532	John Hancock, of Declaration of Indep.
Hardin	Kenton	1820	471	General John Hardin of Indian wars
Harrison	Cadiz	1813	400	General William Henry Harrison
Henry	Napoleon	1820	415	U.S. Statesman Patrick Henry
Highland	Hillsboro	1805	553	High land of the area
Hocking	Logan	1818	423	"hock-hocking" Indian for "bottle river"
Holmes	Millersburg	1824	424	Major Holmes of War of 1812
Huron	Norwalk	1809	494	Indian tribal name
Jackson	Jackson	1816	420	General Andrew Jackson of War of 1812
Jefferson	Steubenville	1797	410	Vice President Thomas Jefferson
Knox	Mt. Vernon	1808	529	General Henry Knox of Revolution
Lake	Painesville	1840	231	Located on Lake Erie
Lawrence	Ironton	1815	457	Naval Capt. James Lawrence, War of 1812
Licking	Newark	1808	686	Licking River flows through area
Logan	Bellefontaine	1818	495	Benjamin Logan, a local hero
Lorain	Elyria	1829	495	French province of Lorraine
Lucas	Toledo	1835	341	General Robert Lucas of Ohio border war
Madison	London	1810	467	President James Madison
Mahoning	Youngstown	1846	417	"mahoni", Indian word for "at the lick"
Marion	Marion	1820	403	General Francis Marion of Revolution
Medina	Medina	1812	422	Arabian city of Medina
Meigs	Pomeroy	1819	432	Return J. Meigs, Governor of Ohio
Mercer	Celina	1820	457	General Hugh Mercer of Revolution

Miami	Troy	1807	410	Indian for "mother"
Monroe	Woodsfield	1813	457	President James Monroe
Montgomery	Dayton	1803	458	Genl. Richard Montgomery of Revolution
Morgan	McConnelsville	1817	420	General Daniel Morgan of Revolution
Morrow	Mt. Gilead	1848	406	Jeremiah Morrow, Governor of Ohio
Muskingum	Zanesville	1804	654	Indian for "town at the river's side"
Noble	Caldwell	1851	399	James Noble, an early settler in area
Ottawa	Port Clinton	1840	253	Indian tribal name
Paulding	Paulding	1820	419	John Paulding, captor of spy John Andre
Perry	New Lexington	1818	412	Commodore Perry of War of 1812
Pickaway	Circleville	1810	503	Indian for "a man formed out of ashes"
Pike	Waverly	1915	443	Genl. Z.M. Pike discovered Pike's Peak
Portage	Ravenna	1807	493	Indian "Portage Path" across area
Preble	Eaton	1808	426	Naval Capt. Edward Preble of Revolution
Putnam	Ottawa	1820	484	General Isiah Putnam of Revolution
Richland	Mansfield	1808	497	Rich soil of the area
Ross	Chillicothe	1798	692	James Ross of Pennsylvania
Sandusky	Fremont	1820	409	Indian for "cold water"
Scioto	Portsmouth	1803	613	"scionto", Indian word for "deer"
Seneca	Tiffin	1820	553	Indian tribal name
Shelby	Sidney	1819	409	Isaac Shelby, 1st Gov. of Kentucky
Stark	Canton	1808	409	General John Stark of Revolution
Summit	Akron	1840	412	Highest land on Ohio Canal
Trumbull	Warren	1800	612	Jonathan Trumbull, Gov. of Connecticut
Tuscarawas	New Philadelphia	1803	570	Indian for "open mouth"
Union	Marysville	1820	437	Union of parts of 4 counties
Van Wert	Van Wert	1820	410	Isaac VanWert, captor of spy John Andre
Vinton	McArthur	1850	414	Samuel F. Vinton, Ohio Statesman
Warren	Lebanon	1803	403	General Joseph Warren of Revolution
Washington	Marietta	1788	640	President George Washington
Wayne	Wooster	1808	557	General "Mad Anthony" Wayne
Williams	Bryan	1820	422	David Williams captor of spy John Andre
Wood	Bowling Green	1820	619	Col. Wood built Ft. Meigs, War of 1812
Wyandot	Upper Sandusky	1845	406	Indian tribal name

Population Data For Ohio Counties

	1990 Total Pop.	1990 Urban Pop.	1990 Afr.- Amer.	1990 Native Amer	1990 Asian	1950 Total Pop.	1950 Urban Pop.	1900 Total Pop.	1900 Urban Pop.	1850 Total Pop.
Adams	25,371	3,096	47	67	30	20,499	0	26,328	2,003	18,883
Allen	109,755	73,652	12,313	202	572	88,183	53,664	47,976	25,886	12,109
Ashland	47,507	22,923	460	49	271	33,040	16,810	21,184	5,668	23,813
Ashtabula	99,821	52,663	3,138	196	350	78,695	42,076	51,448	22,424	28,767
Athens	59,549	28,472	1,678	167	1,374	45,839	16,505	38,730	10,642	18,215
Auglaize	44,585	24,939	66	50	177	30,637	12,005	31,192	9,274	11,338
Belmont	71,074	34,743	1,308	81	129	87,740	45,786	60,875	25,356	34,600
Brown	34,966	3,627	406	28	30	22,221	0	28,237	3,777	27,332
Butler	291,479	241,476	13,134	379	2,659	147,203	103,909	56,870	35,139	30,789
Carroll	26,521	5,128	135	65	29	19,039	4,244	16,811	0	17,685
Champaign	36,019	11,353	992	68	113	26,793	9,335	26,642	8,425	19,782
Clark	147,548	105,918	13,031	294	653	111,661	82,284	58,939	38,253	22,178
Clermont	150,187	79,745	1,291	218	453	42,182	0	31,610	1,916	30,455
Clinton	35,415	18,067	716	59	138	25,572	7,387	24,202	1,788	18,838
Columbiana	108,276	43,578	1,409	174	219	98,920	59,247	68,590	40,508	33,621
Coshocton	35,427	12,193	415	68	112	31,141	11,675	29,337	0	25,674
Crawford	47,870	30,280	253	67	116	38,738	24,893	33,915	17,124	18,177
Cuyahoga	1,412,140	1,409,786	350,185	2,533	18,085	1,389,532	1,363,764	439,120	405,955	48,099
Darke	53,619	12,863	184	96	114	41,799	8,859	42,532	5,501	20,276
Defiance	39,350	20,432	493	80	121	25,925	13,894	26,387	10,099	6,966
Delaware	66,929	30,168	1,424	104	385	30,278	11,804	26,401	7,940	21,817
Erie	76,779	49,865	6,312	150	265	52,565	31,890	37,650	21,372	18,568
Fairfield	103,461	50,332	1,153	193	378	52,130	24,180	34,259	8,991	30,264
Fayette	27,466	12,983	662	50	102	22,554	10,560	21,725	5,751	12,726
Franklin	961,437	931,415	152,840	2,056	19,437	503,410	441,819	164,460	125,560	42,909
Fulton	38,498	15,989	93	62	137	25,580	3,494	22,801	2,148	7,781
Gallia	30,954	4,831	871	79	136	24,910	7,871	27,918	5,432	17,063
Geauga	81,129	12,803	1,056	83	312	26,646	0	14,744	0	17,827
Greene	136,731	111,192	9,611	398	2,133	58,892	33,030	31,613	8,696	21,946
Guernsey	39,024	11,748	616	70	141	38,452	14,739	34,425	8,241	30,438
Hamilton	866,228	838,745	181,145	1,204	9,198	723,952	669,807	409,479	349,573	156,844
Hancock	65,536	38,955	591	91	401	44,280	26,132	41,993	25,343	16,751
Hardin	31,111	13,769	236	66	115	28,573	12,115	31,187	15,051	8,251
Harrison	16,085	3,439	393	22	15	19,054	3,020	20,486	1,755	20,157
Henry	29,108	8,884	147	53	95	22,423	5,335	27,282	5,267	3,434
Highland	35,728	11,407	692	73	71	28,188	9,988	30,982	8,514	25,781
Hocking	25,533	6,725	234	55	25	19,520	5,972	24,398	3,480	14,119
Holmes	32,849	3,122	52	24	43	18,760	0	19,511	1,998	20,452
Huron	56,240	27,493	597	85	153	39,353	18,456	32,330	13,523	26,203
Jackson	30,230	12,193	218	53	39	27,767	12,195	34,248	14,342	12,719
Jefferson	80,298	44,982	4,488	167	266	96,495	47,589	44,357	20,829	29,133
Knox	47,473	14,550	381	93	195	35,287	12,185	27,768	6,633	28,872
Lake	215,499	193,659	3,528	250	1,447	75,979	43,049	21,680	8,850	14,654
Lawrence	61,834	33,791	1,559	57	75	49,115	20,431	39,534	11,868	15,246
Licking	128,300	69,594	2,217	247	475	70,645	36,928	47,070	18,157	38,846

Population Data for Ohio Counties

	1990	1990	1990	1990	1990	1950	1950	1900	1900	1850
	Total Pop.	Urban Pop.	Afr.-Amer.	NativeAmer	Asian	Total Pop.	Urban Pop.	Total Pop.	Urban Pop.	Total Pop.
Logan	42,310	12,142	804	58	240	31,329	10,232	30,420	6,649	19,162
Lorain	271,126	234,124	21,230	738	1,479	148,162	102,665	54,857	30,995	26,086
Lucas	462,361	438,096	68,456	1,164	4,981	395,551	353,218	153,559	133,678	12,363
Madison	37,068	12,312	2,764	96	157	22,300	5,222	20,590	3,511	10,015
Mahoning	264,806	264,806	39,681	444	985	257,629	213,327	70,134	44,885	23,735
Marion	64,274	34,075	2,707	148	285	49,959	33,817	28,678	11,862	12,618
Medina	122,354	70,027	850	172	684	40,417	13,063	21,958	3,996	24,441
Meigs	22,987	2,725	177	44	20	23,227	7,102	28,620	7,438	17,971
Mercer	39,443	13,985	14	85	100	28,311	5,703	28,021	2,815	7,712
Miami	93,182	54,078	1,779	158	606	61,309	31,412	43,105	21,547	24,999
Monroe	15,497	2,832	19	26	12	15,362	0	27,031	1,801	28,351
Montgomery	573,809	544,943	101,817	1,065	5,886	398,441	335,936	130,146	90,976	38,218
Morgan	14,194	0	570	64	12	12,836	0	17,905	1,825	28,585
Morrow	27,749	2,846	64	49	38	17,168	0	17,879	1,528	20,280
Muskingum	82,068	26,778	3,468	214	152	74,535	40,517	53,185	25,138	45,049
Noble	11,336	0	7	15	9	11,750	0	19,466	0	0
Ottawa	40,029	9,888	265	51	94	29,469	5,541	22,213	4,081	3,308
Paulding	20,488	2,605	236	54	20	15,047	0	27,528	2,080	1,766
Perry	31,557	7,718	57	46	21	28,999	7,193	31,841	4,003	20,775
Pickaway	48,255	11,666	3,036	127	95	29,352	8,723	27,016	6,991	21,006
Pike	24,249	4,477	327	72	41	14,607	0	18,172	1,854	10,953
Portage	142,585	79,562	3,906	292	1,191	63,954	28,394	29,246	8,544	24,419
Preble	40,113	7,396	147	53	65	27,081	4,242	23,713	3,155	21,736
Putnam	33,819	3,999	26	44	25	25,248	2,962	32,525	5,983	7,221
Richland	126,137	86,094	9,981	223	578	91,305	58,553	44,289	22,325	30,879
Ross	69,330	21,923	4,467	155	266	54,424	20,133	40,940	12,976	32,074
Sandusky	61,963	33,322	1,553	94	142	46,114	23,589	34,311	12,745	14,305
Scioto	80,327	34,057	2,458	409	126	82,910	44,165	40,981	17,870	18,428
Seneca	59,733	29,452	1,172	90	234	52,978	31,016	41,163	24,719	27,104
Shelby	44,915	18,710	615	49	393	28,488	11,491	24,625	5,688	13,958
Stark	367,585	286,662	25,052	950	1,529	283,194	201,772	94,747	51,585	39,878
Summit	514,990	485,563	61,185	1,065	4,989	410,032	352,196	71,715	50,268	27,485
Trumbull	227,813	164,299	15,221	341	973	158,915	98,611	46,501	18,567	30,490
Tuscarawas	84,090	39,925	623	138	187	70,320	38,360	53,751	22,639	31,761
Union	31,969	9,660	1,168	57	132	20,687	4,256	22,342	4,688	12,204
Van Wert	30,464	14,083	193	31	78	26,971	13,166	30,394	8,650	4,792
Vinton	11,098	0	4	16	3	10,759	0	15,330	0	9,353
Warren	113,909	72,127	2,415	231	627	38,505	10,006	25,584	5,591	25,560
Washington	62,254	24,602	774	111	185	44,407	16,006	48,245	13,348	29,540
Wayne	101,461	38,745	1,557	130	535	58,716	22,968	37,870	7,964	32,981
Williams	36,956	12,647	23	46	127	26,202	10,232	24,953	5,000	8,018
Wood	113,269	71,680	1,168	197	1,028	59,605	25,902	51,555	13,955	9,157
Wyandott	22,254	9,590	20	20	65	19,785	7,657	21,125	5,171	11,194
Ohio Total	10,847,115	8,081,789	1,154,826	20,358	91,179	7,946,527	5,578,274	4,157,455	2,098,136	1,980,328

Glossary

Chap/Part	Word	Meaning
4 1	**17th century**	years from 1601 through 1700
4 2	**18th century**	years from 1701 through 1800
1	**19th century**	years from 1801 through 1900
1	**20th century**	years from 1901 through 2000
8 2	**abolish**	to put an end to
9 1	**accessible**	easily reached
2 3	**acid rain**	rain mixed with chemicals from smoke
14 3	**aeronautical**	having to do with flying
11 1	**amendment**	change of or addition to a law
8 1	**ancestor**	parent, grandparent, great grandparent...
13 3	**annex**	to add land to the area of a city or village
1	**appendix**	(book) additional information at end of book
15 3	**apportionment**	the process of making all votes have equal weight
8 1	**apprentice**	person in training to learn certain skills
3 1	**archaeologist**	a person who studies the remains of things from earlier times
3 2	**artifact**	anything made by a human being
15 3	**ballot**	official printed form used for voting at elections
14 2	**barter**	to give goods and/or services in exchange for other goods and/or services
3 1	**BCE**	system of identifying years "before the common era"
2 1	**bedrock**	rock formation closest to the surface of the earth
15 4	**bill**	(law) a written statement of a proposed law
3 3	**boulder**	a rounded piece of hard rock more than three inches in size
5 1	**boundary**	the edge of a piece of land
10 1	**brine**	salty water
1	**buckeye**	a nut that looks like an eye of a deer
14 1	**business**	an activity carried on to earn money
2 1	**calcium**	a chemical found in bones, teeth, and certain rocks
7 3	**canal**	a waterway made by human beings to carry water from one place to another, or to move boats from one body of water to another
15 3	**candidate**	a person trying to be elected to an office in government
3 1	**CE**	a way to identify years in the "common era"
6 2	**census**	a count of people or things of certain kinds
7 1	**central place**	a place that people go to do certain things
10 2	**ceramic**	material created by baking clay or sand to a very high temperature
5 1	**chaos**	uncontrolled confusion and/or trouble
3 1	**charcoal**	a form of the chemical carbon made by heating, but not burning, wood
8 3	**cistern**	a special hole in the ground used to store water
11 2	**citizenship**	the right to vote and enjoy other benefits of the government under which a person lives
9 1	**city**	an incorporated place having 5,000, or more people
11 1	**common law**	rules of conduct that are enforced when no statutory law covers a situation
8 4	**communal**	people living together in a group in such a way that the group controls all the resources
6 1	**compromise**	an agreement between two or more people to solve a problem that has several possible solutions

Chap/Part	Word	Meaning
2 3	**concrete**	a construction material made of stone, sand, and a binding material
14 1	**conglomerate**	a mixture of several kinds of businesses that create different products and/or services
5 1	**Congress**	the law-making body of the government of the United States
2 3	**conservation**	the process of making the best possible use of natural resources
5 1	**constitution**	the framework of law that guides the activities of an organization
9 1	**corporation**	a legal body created by the state to carry out certain activities
1	**county seat**	the center of government of a county
5 3	**cultivate**	to treat with special care so that a plant or human relationship will develop in a healthy way
12 1	**decade**	any period of ten years
14 1	**decline**	go down
12 3	**depression**	(economic) an economic situation in which many people are out of work and it is difficult to get money
7 1	**destination**	end point of a trip
2 1	**dissolve**	to melt a solid material in a special liquid
2 2	**divide**	(drainage) the line of highest ground between two valleys
7 1	**economics**	the study of the supply of and desire for goods and services
10 1	**efficiency**	obtaining the greatest benefits from the least expense of time, energy, and/or money
3 3	**effigy**	image or likeness
12 2	**employee**	person paid to work for someone else on a regular schedule
12 2	**employer**	person who pays other people to work on a regular basis
9 1	**entrepreneur**	a person who uses personal time, energy, and talents to create goods and/or services that others want to buy

Chap/Part	Word	Meaning
12 3	**erode**	to wear away, especially by action of moving water or air
2 1	**erosion**	the process of wearing away by the actions of moving water and/or air
8 1	**excerpt**	a small part of a longer written statement
11 1	**executive**	a person responsible for getting other people to work together to complete a job
11 3	**exploit**	to make use of goods and/or services for a profit
4 1	**explorer**	a person who looks for unseen things
8 1	**famine**	extreme shortage of food
2 3	**fertile**	good soil for producing good plants
14 2	**finance**	the process of paying for goods and/or services received
15 2	**fiscal year**	a period of twelve months used for accounting for the funds of an organization
10 1	**flax**	a plant from which linen cloth and/or linseed oil can be made
3 1	**flint**	a very hard mineral that has very sharp edges when broken
2 1	**fossil**	the rock-like form of a creature that lived long ago
10 2	**foundation**	the base on which a building or other structure is built
7 2	**freight**	goods of all kinds that must be moved from one place to another
6 1	**frontier**	outer limits
4 2	**gauntlet**	two lines of people facing each other with sticks to beat upon a person who runs between them
5 1	**General Assembly**	the law-making body in the government of Ohio
2 1	**geologist**	a person who studies the structure of the earth
2 2	**glacier**	a large mass of ice that forms on the surface of the earth over a long period of time, moves slowly "down hill" or toward a warm area, and then melts slowly

Chap/Part	Word	Meaning
5 1	**governor**	the highest officer in the operation of our state
14 2	**gypsum**	a soft white mineral used to make plaster for covering walls
2 1	**igneous**	rocks created by the slow cooling of material from inside the earth
7 3	**immigrant**	a person who moves from one land into another land
16	**incinerator**	a building in which waste products are disposed of by burning
8 1	**indentured**	to be under an agreement to perform work in payment for financial help
5 1	**independence**	freedom
10 1	**industry**	production of goods and/or services
15 4	**initiative**	(law) the process of calling for a public vote on a issue that the legislative body cannot agree upon
4 1	**inscription**	writing
13 2	**intercity**	between cities
14 2	**internal combustion**	the burning of fuel inside an engine to produce useful work
13 2	**interurban**	between city-like areas
9 2	**inventor**	person who discovers new ideas and/or creates new products
15 3	**issue**	question of public policy
11 1	**judicial**	relating to courts of law and solving legal problems justly
10 2	**kiln**	a special oven for heating materials to a very high temperature
11 3	**labor union**	workers united to protect their interests with employers
5 1	**latitude**	the measurement of how far a point on earth is to the north or south of the equator
9 1	**legal**	permitted by law
6 3	**legend**	a story passed down by word-of mouth from parents to children about events that happened before there was writing
11 1	**legislative**	related to creating laws
2 1	**limestone**	the type of rock created from the shells of small animals and plants that lived in a warm ocean
10 2	**livestock**	farm animals such as cows, pigs, sheep, and goats
15 4	**lobbyist**	a person who earns money by telling law makers about the interests of the people who pay for this service
7 3	**lock**	(canal) a structure that makes it possible for a boat to move up or down between two levels of water
7 4	**locomotive**	an engine used to move trains over a railroad
5 1	**longitude**	the position of the point on the earth to the east or west of a north-south line through Greenwich, England
2 3	**lumber**	useable pieces of wood cut from the trunk of a tree
14 2	**machine tool**	a machine used to make parts to build other machines
10 2	**manufacture**	to make something — usually by machinery
9 1	**market**	a place for buying and/or selling goods
4 3	**massacre**	the killing of people who are not able to defend themselves
3 1	**mastodon**	a very large animal, similar to modern elephants, that lived before or during the Ice Age
12 1	**materiel**	all kinds of manufactured items, not including foods
8 3	**merchant**	a person who operates a business of buying and selling goods
5 1	**meridian**	a true north-south line on the surface of the earth that passes through the north and south poles
13 3	**metropolitan**	the entire area that is strongly affected by a large city

Chap/Part	Word	Meaning
3 3	**mica**	a mineral that splits easily into flat, shiny surfaces
14 2	**migrant worker**	a person who moves from place to place during the year to do unskilled work
8 1	**migration**	the movement of groups of people from place to place to establish new homes
4 3	**militia**	citizens who join together to defend themselves against an enemy
2 2	**moraine**	a large, long hill of sand and gravel created by a melting glacier
9 1	**municipal**	having to do with a city or village
2 3	**natural resource**	a material of nature that can be used by human beings
16	**NIMBY**	letters that stand for the saying "not in my back yard"
11 4	**nominate**	place a name on a voting list for possible election to a public office
3 3	**obsidian**	a black, glass-like mineral created by eruption of a volcano
15 4	**obsolet**e	no longer useful
9 2	**omnibus**	a form of public transportation that does not use electric motors
5 1	**ordinance**	a law passed by a legislative body
10 2	**ore**	rock that contains a valuable mineral
2 3	**organic matter**	any material that contains the chemical carbon
7 1	**origin**	place of beginning
5 1	**parcel**	(land) a small area of land that has legal boundaries
11 1	**passport**	the legal paper that allows a person to leave a country of citizenship and return to it
7 2	**pavement**	the hard surface on a highway that will carry vehicles in all conditions of weather
8 1	**persecute**	to harm someone because of a difference of opinion

Chap/Part	Word	Meaning
15 4	**petition**	(verb) to ask for something in a legal way
2 3	**petroleum**	a very useful liquid mineral made up of carbon and hydrogen — the term includes both oil and gas
16	**photosynthesis**	the process used by green plants to change carbon dioxide of the air into oxygen
4 1	**pictograph**	a line drawing of an object, usually on the surface of a rock
14 2	**plastic**	a material made from chemicals that softens when it is heated
5 2	**plat**	(land) a plan for dividing a larger area of land into smaller areas for building houses or other structures
9 1	**politics**	the art of people living together in groups
3 3	**portage**	a path along which boats are carried from one body of water to another
6 3	**portrait**	a formal picture of a person
3 1	**prehistoric**	events that took place before humans were able to put their thoughts into written form
8 3	**preserve**	to save for future use
12 3	**prosperity**	time of high employment and general well-being
6 3	**psychic**	mental power that is not learned through regular schools
12 4	**quality**	the degree of "goodness"
2 3	**quarry**	a place where stone, or sand and gravel, are removed from the earth for use by humans
12 3	**recession**	(economic) a slow-down of economic activity
11 1	**record**	(verb) to write information about an event or object into a permanent note book
15 4	**referendum**	a public vote on an issue
10 1	**refine**	(petroleum) to separate useful chemicals from unwanted chemicals in petroleum

Chap/Part	Word	Meaning
5 2.....	**refugee**	a person looking for a safe place to live
15 3....	**register**	(vote) the process by which a citizen proves that she/he has a right to vote in a particular place
11 1....	**repeal**	to cancel a law
5 1.....	**representative**	a person selected to work for the interests of a group of people
14 2....	**research**	the search for a better understanding of something
6 3.....	**reservation**	(land) a place set aside for a particular use
5 1.....	**responsible**	being willing to take the blame or credit for a personal action
15 2....	**revenue**	money received by an organization
7 1.....	**right-of-way**	the right to move over land owned by someone else
8 3.....	**rural**	relating to an area where few people live
2 3.....	**salt lick**	a place where salt (sodium chloride) can be found on the surface of the earth
2 1.....	**sandstone**	the type of rock created from sand under a large body of water
2 1.....	**scholar**	a person who has great knowledge about a certain subject
5 1.....	**section**	(land) an area of land one-mile by one-mile in size
2 1.....	**sedimentary**	(rocks) rocks created under water from very small pieces of material
4 2.....	**sept**	a special, small group of natives
4 1.....	**settlement**	a place where a small group of migrants decide to locate their new homes
9 2.....	**sewage**	human wastes in liquid form
9 2.....	**sewer**	system of pipes to carry sewage from where it is created to a place where it can be treated
2 1.....	**shale**	sedimentary rock created from silt and clay

Chap/Part	Word	Meaning
11 4....	**slogan**	group of words that encourage people to act
9 2.....	**slum**	an area where people live who do not take care of their homes
2 3.....	**smelt**	to remove valuable minerals from their ores by heating
16	**smog**	a word created from fog and smoke
2 3.....	**soil**	the fine material on the surface of the earth in which plants grow
9 2.....	**soot**	small black bits of the chemical carbon
15 5....	**special district**	political body created to solve a problem that crosses the boundaries of other units of government
8 3.....	**spring**	(water) natural water that flows out of the surface of the earth
7 1.....	**station**	(railroad/bus) stopping place for trains and/or buses
11 1....	**statutory law**	a law created by a legislative body to deal with a particular problem
9 2.....	**street railway**	public transportation system that operates on rails in city streets
12 2....	**strike**	(labor) action taken by workers in the hope of forcing employers to deal more fairly with them
14 2....	**structure**	any type of object built on land for the benefit of people
2 3.....	**stump**	the base of a tree that is held to the ground by roots
5 2.....	**subdivision**	(land) plan for dividing a large piece of land into smaller pieces for construction of buildings
13 2....	**suburban**	an area that has a mix of urban and rural land uses
11 3....	**suffrage**	the right to vote
2 3.....	**sulphur**	a valuable yellow chemical that can cause "acid rain"
5 1.....	**survey**	(land) the process of establishing legal boundaries of pieces of land on the earth
6 3.....	**survive**	to continue to live

Chap/Part	Word	Meaning
5 1.....	**taxes**	money collected by the government to pay for services
8 1.....	**tolerant**	the willingness to let other people have ideas that are different
7 2.....	**toll**	the fee charged for use of a bridge, tunnel, or highway
9 1.....	**town**	a group of buildings in a planned subdivision that may, or may not, be part of a village or city
5 1.....	**township**	a unit of government that is part of a county, and may, or may not be related to the public land survey
4 3.....	**translator**	a person who changes ideas from the words of one language into the words of another language
4 2.....	**treaty**	an agreement, usually in writing, to settle an argument over control of land
2 1.....	**trilobite**	a small animal that lived in oceans millions of years ago, whose fossil is now a state symbol
12 4....	**tuberculosis**	a crippling disease of the lungs or bones
5 1.....	**turmoil**	troubles that interrupt peace and quiet
7 2.....	**turnpike**	a highway that requires users to pay a fee
9 1.....	**urban**	an area in which many people live freely
15 1....	**veto**	the ability of the chief executive to reject a law passed by the legislative body
9 1.....	**village**	an incorporated place having fewer than 5,000 people
6 3.....	**vision**	the ability to see, dream, and/or plan for the future
3 2.....	**volunteer**	a person who does valuable work for someone else without pay
3 3.....	**wampum**	patterns of beads sewn by leather by Native Americans to remember important events

Chap/Part	Word	Meaning
2 1.....	**weathering**	the natural process by which solid materials of earth are broken into small pieces
8 3.....	**well**	(water) a hole dig into the earth to find underground water
3 3.....	**wigwam - wigewa**	a simple building made by putting poles into the ground, bending them together at the top, and covering with material to make a shelter

Illustration Credits

Illustrations not listed were created by the author.

Page   2 Slaughter & Slaughter, Inc. (S&S) & Taylor Studio

Page   3 S&S

Page   4 Ohio Secretary of State

Page   7 Ohio Secretary of State

Page 14 Ohio Department of Natural Resources (ODNR)

Page 15 Ohio Caverns, Max Evans, President

Page 16 (left) ODNR

Page 17 ODNR

Pages 18-19 S&S

Page 23 ODNR

Page 24 S&S

Page 25 The Bettmann Archives (Bettmann) Color added (CA)

Page 27 ODNR

Page 29 ODNR

Page 34   S&S on Waldman: *Atlas of North American Indians*

Page 35 S&S based on Dunbar: *Historical Geology*

Page 36 ODNR, painting by James Glover

Page 37 Ohio Historical Society (OHS)

Page 40 (left) Woodward & McDonald: *Indian Mounds of Ohio Valley*

Page 40 (right) OHS

Page 41 (left) Squier & Davis: *Ancient Monuments* (CA)

Page 41 (right) Mound City Group National Monument Painting by
            Louis Glanzman

Page 42 (left and right) Squier & Davis

Page 45 (lower) S&S

Page 46-47 Mound City Group National Monument

Page 48 John Kahionhes Fadden

Page 54 S&S

Page 55 S&S based on Waldman

Page 57 (lower) Henry Howe: Historical Collections of Ohio (upper) OHS

Page 60 S&S based on Waldman

Page 64 S&S based on Waldman

Page 67 Bettmann (CA)

Page 77 ODNR Sherman: Ohio Land Subdivisions, Vol. 3

Page 79 S&S based on Sherman

Page 81 ODNR Sherman

Page 83 Hamilton County Recorder

Page 84 Henry Howe (CA)

Page 85 OHS (CA)

Page 87 Henry Howe (CA)

Page 91 S&S based on Waldman

Page 92 Darke County Historical Society, Inc., Garst Museum

Page 93 S&S

Page 94 ODNR Sherman

Page 102 Ohio Auditor of State (CA)

Page 104 OHS (CA)

Page 105 OHS (CA)

Page 113 Photo by Dennis Trimble for Author

Page 114 ODNR Sherman

Page 122 S & S based on Rose: *Historic American Roads*

Page 124 S&S based on Schneider: *The National Road*

Page 125 Hornung: *Wheels Across America* (CA)

Page 129 Hornung: *Wheels Across America* (CA)

Page 132 Henry Howe

Page 134 S&S based on Hahn: *The Best of American Canals*

Page 135 Jackson & Jackson: *The Colorful Era of the Ohio Canals*

Page 137 OHS

Page 140 Henry Howe

Page 141 S&S based on Scheiber: *Ohio Canal Era*

Page 148 S&S

Page 150 Bettmann (CA)

Page 151 Bettmann (CA)

Page 152 Bettmann

Pages 153-155 Schelbert, Leo: *New Glarus 1845-1970*

Page 154 Bettmann (CA)

Page 157 S&S based on map in display *Always a River*

Page 159 Cincinnati Art Museum

Page 162 Bettmann (CA)

Page 165 Bettmann

Page 168 Doyle Yoder, photographer

Page 174 Author and S&S

Page 177 ODNR

Page 179 Henry Howe

Bibliography of Books to Read

Note: (Chapter —) shows where book will be useful.

Altman, Susan. *Extraordinary Black Americans*.
Chicago: Childrens Press, 1989. 236 pages. (Chapter 12)

Ammon, Richard. *Growing Up Amish*.
New York: Atheneum, 1989. 102 pages. (Chapter 8)

Andrist, Ralph K. *The Erie Canal*.
New York: American Heritage Publishing Co. Inc., 1964. 153 pages. (Chapter 7)

Ash, Maureen. *The Story of Harriet Beecher Stowe*.
Chicago: Childrens Press, 1990. 32 pages. (Chapter 8)

Ashabranner, Brent. *An Ancient Heritage: The Arab-American*.
New York: Harper Collins, 1991. 147 pages. (Chapter 12)

Ashabranner, Brent and Conklin, Paul. *The New Americans*.
New York: Dodd, Mead & Company, 1983. 212 pages. (Chapter 12)

Beard, Charles A. *The Presidents in American History*.
New York: Julian Messner, 1973. 199 pages. (Chapter 11)

Bender, Lionel. *The Story of The Earth Cave*.
New York: Franklin Watts, 1989. 32 pages. (Chapter 2)

Berger, Gilda. *Alcoholism and The Family*.
New York: Franklin Watts, 1993. 123 pages. (Chapter 16)

Bial, Raymond. *Frontier Home*.
Boston: Houghton Mifflin Company, 1993. 37 pages. (Chapter 5 and 6)

Blumberg, Rhoda. *First Ladies*.
New York: Franklin Watts, 1981. 65 pages. (Chapter 11)

Branigan, Keith. *Prehistory*.
Warwick Press, 1984. 37 pages. (Chapter 3)

Brown, Trina. *Lee Ann, The Story of A Vietnamese-Amercian Girl*.
New York: G.P. Putnam's Sons, 1991. 47 pages. (Chapter 12)

Burger, Carl. *Beaver Skins and Mountain Men*.
New York: E.P. Dutton and Co. Inc., 1968. 191 pages. (Chapter 4)

Burt, Olive W. *Old America Comes Alive*.
New York: The John Day Company, 1966. 160 pages. (Chapter 4)

Carpenter, Allan. *The New Enchantment of America Ohio*.
Chicago, IL: Childrens Press, Inc, 1978. 96 pages. (Chapter 1)

Cavan, Seamus. *Daniel Boone and The Opening of The Ohio Country*.
New York: Chelsea House Publishers, 1991. 111 pages. (Chapter 5)

Charman, Andrew. *Energy: Science through Art.*
New York: Franklin Watts, 1992. 32 pages. (Chapter 13)

Charman, Andrew. *Materials: Science through Art.*
New York: Franklin Watts, 1992. 32 pages. (Chapter 13)

Coiley, John. *Train.*
New York: Alfred A. Knopf, Inc., 1992. 63 pages. (Chapter 7)

Cole, Michael D. *John Glenn — Astronaut and Senator.*
Hillsdale, NJ: Enslow Publishers, Inc., 1993. 104 pages. (Chapter 14)

Cook, Roy. *Leaders of Labor.*
Philadelphia: J.B. Lippincott Company, 1966. 152 pages. (Chapter 11 & 14)

Cooper, Kay. *Who Put The Cannon in The Courthouse Square?.*
New York: Walker and Company, 1985. 70 pages. (Chapter 1)

Cwiklik, Robert. *Tecumseh, Shawnee Rebel.*
New York: Chelsea House, 1993. 110 pages. (Chapter 6)

Davies, Eryl. *Transport on Land, Road and Rail.*
New York: Franklin Watts, 1992. 47 pages. (Chapter 7)

Dixon, Dougal and Matthews, Rupert. *The Illustrated Encyclpedia of Prehistoric Life.*
New York: SMITHMARK Publishers, Inc., 1992. 127 pages. (Chapter 2)

Eckert, Allan W. *Blue Jacket: War Chief of the Shawnees.*
Boston: Little, Brown & Co., 1969. 177 pages. (Chapter 5)

Everds, John. *The Spectacular Trains: A History of Rail Transportation.*
Northbrook, IL: Hubbard Press, 1973. 64 pages. (Chapter 7)

Farndon, John. *How The Earth Works.*
New York: Reader's Digest Books, 1992. 192 pages. (Chapter 2)

Feldman, Anne. *The Railroad Book.*
New York: David McKay Company, Inc., 1978. 58 pages. (Chapter 7)

Few, Roger. *Children's Guide to Endangered Species.*
New York: Macmillan Publishing Company, 1993. 96 pages. (Chapter 16)

Fitz-Gerald, Christine. *William Henry Harrison.*
Chicago: Childrens Press, 1987. 100 pages. (Chapter 5 and 11)

Fox, Mary Virginia. *Ohio.*
New York: Franklin Watts, 1987. 71 pages. (Chapter 1)

Freedman, Russell. *The Wright Brothers: How They Invented The Airplane.*
New York: Holiday House, 1991. 129 pages. (Chapter 14)

Fritz, Jean. *Shh! We're Writing The Constitution.*
New York: G.P. Putnam's Sons, 1987. 64 pages. (Chapter 6)

Gardom, Tim. *The Book of Dinosaurs.*
Rocklin, CA: Prima Publishing, 1993. 128 pages. (Chapter 2)

Graff, Nancy. *Where The River Runs.*
   Boston: Little, Brown & Company, 1993. 71 pages. (Chapter 12)

Graves, Charles. *The Wright Brothers.*
   New York: G.P. Putnam's Sons, 1973. 64 pages. (Chapter 14)

Greene, Carol. *John Chapman: The Man Who Was Johnny Appleseed.*
   Chicago: Childrens Press, 1991. 47 pages. (Chapter 8)

Grumet, Robert S. *The Lenapes: Indians of North America.*
   New York: Chelsea House Publishers, 1989. 111 pages. (Chapter 4)

Gutnik, Martin J. *Recycling, Learning The Four R's.*
   Hillside, NY: Enlow Publishers, 1993. 104 pages. (Chapter 16)

Handelsman, Judith F. *Gardens from Garbage.*
   Brookfield, CN: Millbrook Press, 1993. 48 pages. (Chapter 16)

Hartford, John. *Steamboat in A Cornfield.*
   New York: Crown Publishers, Inc., 1986. 35 pages. (Chapter 7)

Haskins, James. *Get on Board, The Story of The Underground Railroad.*
   New York: Scholastic Inc., 1993. 152 pages. (Chapter 8)

Henry, Joanne Landers. *Log Cabin in The Woods.*
   New York: Four Winds Press, 1988. 60 pages. (Chapter 6)

Herda, D.J. *Historical America, The North Central States.*
   Brookfield CN.: The Millbrook Press, 1993. 64 pages. (Chapter 4 thru 8)

Hoff, Mary King. *Our Endangered Planet: Rivers and Lakes.*
   Minneapolis: Lerner Publications Company, 1991. 64 pages. (Chapter 16)

Hyde, Margaret O. *The Homeless, Profiling The Problem.*
   Hillside, NJ: Enslow Publishers, Inc., 1989. 96 pages. (Chapter 12)

Jungreis, Abigail. *Know Your Hometown History.*
   New York: Franklin Watts, 1992. 61 pages. (Chapter 13)

Kent, Deborah. *America The Beautiful Ohio.*
   Chicago, IL: Childrens Press, Inc., 1989. 144 pages. (Chapter 1)

Knopf, Richard C. *Indians of the Ohio Country. : Modern Methods, 1959.*
   54 pages. (Chapter 3)

Koral, April. *Our Global Greenhouse.*
   New York: Franklin Watts, Inc., 1989. 64 pages. (Chapter 16)

LaFarge, Oliver. *The American Indian.*
   New York: Golden Press, 1960. 215 pages. (Chapter 4)

Lambert, David and Currant, Andrew. *The World Before Man.*
   New York: Facts on File, Inc., 1986. 64 pages. (Chapter 2)

Laycock, George and Ellen. *How The Settlers Lived.*
   New York: David McKay Company, Inc., 1980. 113 pages. (Chapter 6)

Lee, Susan. *George Rogers Clark: War in The West*.
New York: Childrens Press, 1975. 48 pages. (Chapter 4)

Levine, Ellen. *Freedom's Children*.
New York: G.P. Putnam's Sons , 1993. 167 pages. (Chapter 12)

Lomask, Milton. *Great Lives*.
New York: Charles Scribner's Sons, 1991. 258 pages. (Chapter 14)

Lopez, Gary. *Air Pollution*.
Mankato, MN: Creative Education, Inc., 1992. 50 pages. (Chapter 16)

Magocsi, Paul R. *The Russian Americans*.
New York: Chelsea House, 1989. 111 pages. (Chapter 8)

Mathieu, Joe. *The Olden Days*.
New York: Random House, 1979. 31 pages. (Chapter 8)

McKissack, Patricia and Long, Frederick A. *A Long, Hard Journey, The Story of The Pullman Porter*.
New York: Walker and Company, 1989. 144 pages. (Chapter 12)

McKissack, Patricia C. and Long, Frederick A. *Sojourner Truth, Ain't I a Woman*.
New York: Scholastic Inc., 1992. 186 pages. (Chapter 8)

McNeese, Tim. *West by Steamboat*.
New York: Crestwood House, 1993. 48 pages. (Chapter 7)

Meltzer, Milton. *Poverty in America*.
New York: William Morrow & Co., Inc., 1986. 122 pages. (Chapter 12)

Morrison, Velma Ford. *Going on A Dig*.
New York: Dodd, Mead & Company, 1981. 128 pages. (Chapter 3)

O'Toole, Thomas. *The Economic History of The United States*.
Minneapolis, MN: Lerner Publications Company, 1990. 112 pages. (Chapter 10 and 14)

Ogburn, Charlton. *Railroads: The Great American Adventure*.
Washington, DC: National Geographic Society, 1977. 204 pages. (Chapter 7)

Pack, Janet. *Fueling The Future*.
Chicago: Childrens Press, 1992. 127 pages. (Chapter 16)

Patterson, Wayne and Kim, Hyung-Chau. *The Koreans in America*.
Minneapolis, MN: Learner Publishing Co., 1977. 62 pages. (Chapter 12)

Pringle, Laurence. *Global Warning: Assessing The Greenhouse Threat*.
New York: Arcade Publishers of Little, Brown & Compnay, 1990. 46 pages. (Chapter 16)

Ray, Delia. *A Nation Torn The Story of How The Civil War Began*.
New York: Lodestar Books Dutton, 1990. 101 pages. (Chapter 11)

Robbins, Albert. *Coming to America, Immigrants from Northern Europe*.
New York: Delacarte Press, 1981. 214 pages. (Chapter 8)

Rutland, Jonathan. *See Inside An Airport*.
New York: Warwick Press, 1988. 31 pages. (Chapter 14)

Salomon, Julian Harris. *The Book of Indian Crafts & Indian Lore*.
New York: Harper & Row, Publishers, 1928. 418 pages. (Chapter 4)

Sandak, Cass R. *The Tafts*.
New York: Crestwood House, 1993. 48 pages. (Chapter 11)

Sattler, Helen Roney. *The Earliest Americans*.
New York: Clarion Books, 1993. 125 pages. (Chapter 3)

Schulte, William E. *The Mound Builders*.
Cleveland: The World Publishing Comapny, 1960. 61 pages. (Chapter 3)

Schwartz, Alvin. *Central City / Spread City*.
New York: Macmillan, 1973. 132 pages. (Chapter 13)

Schwartz, Alvin. *When I Grew Up Long Ago*.
Philadelphia: J.B. Lippincott, 1978. 224 pages. (Chapter 12, 13, 14)

Seymour, Simon. *Icebergs and Glaciers*.
New York: William Morrow and Company, 1987. 47 pages. (Chapter 2)

Siegel, Beatrice. *Fur Trappers and Traders*.
New York: Walker and Company, 1981. 64 pages. (Chapter 4)

Siegel, Beatrice. *Indians of The Northeast Woodlands*.
New York: Walker and Company, 1972. 96 pages. (Chapter 4)

Silverstein, Alvin and Virginia B. *The Robots Are Here*.
Engelwood Cliffs, NJ: Prentice-Hall, Inc., 1983. 128 pages. (Chapter 14)

Smead, Howard. *The African Americans*.
New York: Chelsea House Publishers, 1989. 127 pages. (Chapter 8)

Snow, Dean R. *The Archaeology of North America*.
New York: Chelsea House Publishers, 1989. 144 pages. (Chapter 3)

Spangenburg, Ray and Moser, Diane K. *Story of America's Canals*.
New York: Facts on File, 1992. 82 pages. (Chapter 7).

Spangenburg, Ray and Moser, Diane K. *The Story of America's Railroads*.
New York: Facts on File, 1991. 90 pages. (Chapter 7)

Steele, William O. *The Old Wilderness Road: An American Journey*.
New York: Harcourt, Brace & World, Inc., 1968. 175 pages. (Chapter 5)

Stein, R. Conrad. *The Great Depression*.
Chicago: Childrens Press, 1993. 33 pages. (Chapter 12).

Taylor, Paul D. *Eyewitness Books Fossil*.
New York: Alfred A. Knopf, 1990. 64 pages. (Chapter 2)

Thompson, Kathleen. *Portrait of America Ohio*.
Milwaukee, WI: Raintree Publishers, Inc., 1988. 48 pages. (Chapter 1)

Toone, Betty L. *Appalachia: The Mountains, The Place, and The People*.
New York: Franklin Watts, 1972. 90 pages. (Chapter 8)

Trevorrow, Frank W. *Ohio's Canals*.
Oberlin, OH: Frank W. Trevorrow, 1973. 151 pages. (Chapter 7)

Tribbel, John. *The Battle of Fallen Timbers*.
New York: Franklin Watts, Inc., 1972. 87 pages. (Chapter 5)

Tunis, Edwin. *Indians*.
New York: Thomas Y. Crowell, 1959. 158 pages. (Chapter 4)

Unstead, R. J., Series Editor. *See Inside A Galleon*.
New York: Warwick Press, 1977. 31 pages. (Chapter 7)

Whitman, Sylvia. *V Is for Victory*.
Minneapolis, MN: Lerner Publications Company, 1993. 77 pages. (Chapter 12)

Wise, Winifred E. Harriet Beecher Stowe. *Woman with A Cause*.
New York: G.P. Putnam's Sons, 1965. 190 pages. (Chapter 8)

Wood, Marion. *Ancient America*.
New York: Facts on File, 1990. 95 pages. (Chapter 3)

Wu, Dana Ying Hui and Tung, Jeffrey Dao-Shang. *The Chiness American Experience*.
Brookfield, CN: Millbrook Press, 1993. 61 pages. (Chapter 12)

Bibliography of References

The following sources of information were used in this book.

Auditor of State. *Ohio Land Grants*.
Columbus, OH: na, 46 pages.

Know Your Ohio Government.
Columbus, OH: League of Women Voters of Ohio, 6th Edition, 1987. 125 pages.

Bailey, L. Scott, Publisher. *The American Car Since 1775*.
New York: Autombile Quarterly Inc., 1971. 504 pages.

Boyd, T. A. *Professional Amateur, The Biography of Charles F. Kettering*.
New York: E.P. Dutton & Co., Inc., 1957. 242 pages.

Brewer, Priscilla J. *Shaker Communities, Shaker Lives*.
Hanover, NH: University Press of New England, 1986. 273 pages.

Cheek, William. *John Mercer Langston and the Fight for Black Freedom*.
Urbana, IL: University of Illinois Press, 1989. 478 pages.

Condit, Carl W. *The Railroad and the City*.
Columbus, OH: Ohio State University Press, 1977. 335 pages.

Crouch, Tom D. *The Bishop's Boys A Life of Wilbur and Orville Wright*.
New York: W. W. Norton & Company, 1989, 606 pages.

Dunbar, Paul Laurence. *Lyrics by the Hearthside*. New York:
  Dodd, Mead and Company, 1899. 277 pages.

Eckert, Allan W. *The Frontiersmen, A Narrative*.
  Boston, MA: Little, Brown and Company, 1967, 626 pages, and Gateway to Empire. Boston: Little,
  Brown & Company, 1983, 688 pages.

Giffin, William Wayne. *The Negro in Ohio, 1914-1939*.
  Ann Arbor, MI: University Microfilms, Inc., 1969. 499 pages.

Hahn, Thomas F. Editor-in-Chief. *The Best from American Canals*.
  York, PA: The American Canal Society Incorporated, 1980. 88 pages.

Hochstetter, Nancy, Editor. *Travel Historic Ohio*.
  Madison, WI: Guide Press Co., 1986. 168 pages.

Hornung, Clarence P. *Wheels Across America*.
  San Diego, CA: A.S. Barnes & Company, Inc. 1959. 341 pages.

Howe, Henry. *Historical Collections of Ohio*, in Two Volumes.
  Norwalk, OH: The State of Ohio, 1898. Vol. 1 - 992 pages, Vol. 2 -911 pages + Addenda.

Humphlett, Patricia E. *Astronauts and Cosmonauts Biographical and Statistical Data*.
  Washington: Government Printing Office, 1985. 402 pages.

Jackson, James S. *The Colorful Era of The Ohio Canal*.
  Akron, OH: The Summit County Historical Society, 1981. 24 pages.

Kunjufu, Jawanza. *Lessons from History - A Celebration of Blackness*
  (Elem. Ed.). Chicago, IL: African-American Images.

Lafferty, Michael B. Editor-in-Chief. *Ohio's Natural Heritage*.
  Columbus, OH: The Ohio Academy of Science, 1979. 324 pages.

Leslie, Stuart W. *Boss Kettering*.
  New York: Columbia University Press, 1983. 382 pages.

Levin, Phyllis Lee. *Abigail Adams: A Biography*.
  New York: St. Martin's Press, 1987. 575 pages.

Magill, Frank N. Editor. *The American Presidents: The Office and the Men*.
  Pasadena, CA: Salem Press, 1986. 869 pages.

Rose, Albert C. *Historic American Roads*.
  New York: Crown Publishers, Inc., 1976. 118 pages.

Scheiber, Harry N. *Ohio Canal Era: A Case Study of Government and the Economy*.
  Athens, OH: The Ohio University Press, 1969. 430 pages.

Schelbert, Leo, Editor. *New Glarus 1845-1970*.
  Glarus, Switzerland: Komissionverslag Tschudi & Co., 1970. 239 pages.

Schneider, Norris F. *The National Road, Main Street of America*.
  Columbus, OH: The Ohio Historical Society, 1987. 37 pages.

Siebert, Wilbur Henry: *From Slavery to Freedom*.
New York: Macmillan, 1898. 478 pages.

Siebert, Wilbur Henry. *The Mysteries Of Ohio's Underground Railroad*.
Columbus, OH: Long's College Book Company, 1951. 330 pages.

Siedel, Frank. *Out of the Midwest*.
Cleveland, OH: The World Publishing Company, 1953, 240 pages, and The Ohio Story. 1950, 288 pages.

Simmons, David A. *The Forts of Anthony Wayne*.
Fort Wayne, IN: Historic Fort Wayne, Inc., 1977. 26 pages.

Stokes, Carl B. *Promises of Power*.
New York: Simon and Schuster, 1973. 288 pages.

Thom, James Alexander. *Panther in The Sky*.
New York: Ballantine Books Division of Random House, Inc., 1989. 655 pages, and
Long Knife. 1979. 528 pages.

Tunis, Edwin. *Indians*.
Cleveland, OH: The World Publishing Company, 1959. 137 pages.

Waggoner, Madeline S. *The Long Haul West: The Great Canal Era*.
New York: G.P. Putnam's Sons, 1958. 320 pages.

Waldman, Carl. *Atlas of the North American Indian*.
New York: Facts on File Publications, 1985. 276 pages.

Woodward, Susan L. *Indian Mounds of The Middle Ohio Valley*.
Newark, OH: The McDonald & Woodward Publishing Company, 1986. 130 pages.

WPA, Writers' Program of the Works Projects Adminsitration. *The Ohio Guide*.
New York: Oxford University Press, 1940. 634 pages.

Zimmermann, George. *Off The Beaten Path*.
Charlotte, NC: The East Woods Press, Fast & McMillan Publishers, Inc., 1985. 158 pages.

Index

Aberdeen 123
Adams County 39, 169
Adams, Abigail Smith 99
Adams, John 99

Adena house 39, 106, 186
Adena people 38
AFL-CIO 258
Africa 98, 152
African-American 100, 105, 159, 227, 230, 233, 240, 250, 270, 309, 348, 359, 369, 370,

Afro-American Museum 268
agriculture 46, 207, 307
air pollution 372
airplane 120, 306
airport 118

Akron 248, 250, 300+, 318, 331
Alabama 108, 248
Alaska 2, 21, 34, 244, 310
Albany, NY 133
alcohol 56, 190, 233, 344, 370

Allegheny River 57
Allen County 169, 176, 283
amendment 222
American Federation of Labor 232, 256
American Revolution 66, 90, 149, 166

Amish 166, 209
amusement park 285
annexation 292
Appalachia 248
Appalachian Mountains 58, 66, 76, 83, 107, 148

apportionment 350
archaeologist 34, 42, 48, 214
Archbold 217, 312, 322
Arctic ice cap 21
ARMCO 321

Armed Services 293
Armstrong, Neil A. 330
Articles of Confederation 74
artifacts 38
arts 269

Ash Cave 14
Ashland, OH 165
Ashland County 165, 257, 280
Ashtabula County 29, 204, 216, 229, 321
Asia 55, 248, 251

asphalt 28, 202
asphaltic concrete 203
Athens County 229
Atlantic Ocean 24, 43, 48, 87, 149, 152
atomic energy 374

Atomic Energy Commission (United States) 374
attorney general 337
auditor 337
Auglaize County 136, 320
Auglaize River 90

automobile 118, 148, 206, 223, 257, 261, 276, 282+, 291, 294+, 299, 306, 311+, 374+

ballot 349
Baltimore and Ohio Railroad 139
Baltimore, MD 139, 153
bank 310

barrels 207
Battelle Memorial Institute (The) 324
Bedford, OH 271
Belmont County 39, 123, 272
Berea, OH 216

Bethlehem, PA 64
bicycle 284, 326
Bill of Rights 224
birth certificate 225
Black Swamp 25, 197, 363

Blooming Grove 243
Blue Jacket 59, 91, 269
board of education 363
board of elections 348
Boeing, William 306

booster 182
Boston, MA 83
bridge 121+, 176, 309
Bridgeport, OH 123
British 63

British colonies 368
British Empire 74
British Petroleum Company (plc) - BP 317
Brown County 123, 236
Brush, Charles F. 279

buckeye 6
Buckeye Furnace 30, 214, 321
Buckeye Lake 136
Buffalo, NY 133, 241
Bureau of the Census 368

burial places 37
bus 118, 126, 285, 299, 314
business 296, 304+
Butler County 90, 228, 375
C. J. Krehbiel Company (The) 316

Cahokia, IL 66
calcium 15
Caldwell, OH 204
California 3, 98
Cambodia 254

Cambridge, OH 214
Campus Martius 85
Canada 21, 88, 110+, 158
canal 133+, 149, 175+, 190, 209, 283
canal boat 137, 140, 282

Canal Fulton, OH 138
candidate 346+
canoe 47, 120, 131

Canton, OH 301
carbon dioxide 371+

Cardinal Power Plant 278
Caribbean Sea 44
Carillon Historical Museum 140, 328
carnation 4, 241
Cartier, Jacques 55

Cass, WV 283
cave - cavern 14
Cayuga people 60
Cedar Bog 25
Cedar Point 268

Celeron, Pierre Joseph 57, 76
Census, United States Bureau of 299, 355
Centerior Energy Corporation 376
central place 118, 182, 283, 288, 294
ceramics 214

Champaign County 25, 156, 369, 25
Chapman, John 165
charcoal 34
Charter Committee of Greater Cincinnati 365
chemicals 202, 372

Chief Little Turtle 90+
Chillicothe, OH 103, 181, 186, 233, 316
Chillicothe Gazette 103
Chilo OH 136
China 33, 43, 98, 251+

Chippewa people 94
Christy, Howard Chandler 93
Cincinnati, OH 86+, 98, 105, 115, 123, 133+, 155, 175, 184+, 192+, 217, 229+, 269, 300, 316+, 323

Cincinnati Law School 242
Cincinnati Museum of Natural History 21
Cincinnati, Hamilton and Dayton Railroad 140
Cincinnati, Society of the 89
Circleville, OH 39

circuit rider 164
citizenship 28, 226
city manager 365
Civil War 159, 213+, 233, 239, 325, 378
Civilian Conservation Corps 263, 363

Clark County 68, 178, 209
Clark, George Rogers 66+, 106, 179
clay 14, 212
Clear Creek Township 361
Cleaveland, Moses 87, 184

Clermont County 136, 235
Cleveland, OH 87, 127, 134+, 175, 184, 204, 217, 239+, 248, 255, 286, 312+, 320, 365

Cleveland Electric Illuminating Company 280, 375
Cleveland Hopkins Airport 286, 329
coal 26+, 161, 187, 199, 212, 276+, 283, 299, 321, 373+

Coffin, Catherine White 158
Coffin, Levi 158
cogeneration 374
Columbiana County 82, 212
Columbus, OH 36, 51, 127, 136, 188, 228, 232+, 297+, 310, 324
329, 336, 365, 372+

Columbus Municipal Electric Plant 374
Columbus, Christopher 43, 51
commission plan 365
common law 223+, 340
common law 224, 340

Communism 151, 254
Confederate Army 154, 237
Confederate States of America 159
Congress 74, 86, 100, 123, 146, 174, 213, 220, 237, 243, 256+, 261+, 280, 285, 349, 354+,

Congress Land 88
Congress of Industrial Organization 257
Conneaut, OH 229
Connecticut 74+, 87, 269
Connecticut Land Company 87, 184

Connecticut Western Reserve 94
Constitution of Ohio 223, 233+, 351
Constitution of United States 80, 98, 259, 348, 370
Constitutional Convention 225
constitutional law 223

construction 291, 309
Continental Congress 66, 79, 98, 220
Cooper Tire and Rubber Company (The) 319
corporation 175, 304
Coshocton County 138

council-manager plan 365
county commissioners 359+
county council 359
county fair 163
county seat 7, 179

court of appeals 340
court of common pleas 340
Covington, KY 236
Cox, James M. 244
craftsmen 163, 255

Crawford Auto-Aviation Collection 315
Crawford County 70, 177, 243
Crawford, William 70
Crestline, OH 177
Croghan, George 61

Cuba 241
Cuyahoga County 29, 126, 138, 169, 184, 206, 216, 271, 320+
Cuyahoga National Recreation Area 138
Cuyahoga River 87+, 94, 134, 184
Darke County 90

Dayton 42, 87, 134, 140, 244, 255+, 269+, 280, 301, 313, 327+, 369
Dayton Wright Airplane Company (The) 328
Dayton, Jonathon 86
Dearborn, MI 217, 279, 283, 328
Declaration of Independence 66, 74, 98+, 224, 271, 368

Deeds, Edward 328
Delaware, OH 53, 181, 237
Delaware County 181
Delaware people 53, 64, 69, 94
Delphos, OH 176, 209

Democratic Party 235, 346
Denman, Mathias 86
diesel power 276, 283, 373

dinosaur 20
Domestic Engineering Company 280

drainage 131, 359+
Dresser Industries, Inc. 321
Dublin, OH 181
Dunbar, Paul Laurence 269, 272, 326 272
Dunham Tavern 127

earthquake 109
East Indies 43, 55
East Liverpool, OH 61, 213
economics 120, 183, 195, 261, 304, 311
Edison, Thomas A. 279

education 226, 324, 344
efficiency 196, 206, 225
effigy pipe 46
Eighteenth Amendment 259, 344
elections 348+

electricity 199, 276+, 299, 368, 374+
Electrolux 312
energy 120, 178, 197, 202, 279, 288, 373
England 76, 126, 133, 201, 207, 299, 317
entrepreneur 139, 178, 215, 276, 283+, 292+, 306, 368+

Environmental Protection Administration 364
Erie and Kalamazoo Railroad 139
Erie Canal 133
Erie County 56, 88, 139, 268, 279
Erie people 56

Erie, PA 112
erosion 13, 309
Europe 5, 55, 133, 175, 247, 287
executive branch 220, 336

factory 199, 208, 231, 258, 276, 283, 292, 307
Fadden, John Kahionhes 48
Fairfield County 88, 136, 186, 239
Fallen Timbers, Battle of 90, 105
farming 63, 136, 149, 152, 165, 176, 228, 289+, 307+, 370

Federal Aid Road Act of 1916 285
Federal Housing Administration 264, 291, 364
Federated Department Stores, Inc. 323
Findlay, OH 205, 318+
Fire Lands 88

fire protection 292, 361
Firestone, Harvey S. 318
fishing 73, 307
flatboat 120, 131
flint 4, 36

Flint Ridge State Memorial 37
food 46, 125, 149, 162, 175, 189, 196, 204, 209, 345
forest 121, 207, 307
Fort Ancient 41
Fort Ancient people 38, 42, 58

Fort Definance 90
Fort Detroit 63, 68, 90, 112
Fort Duquesne 64
Fort GreeneVille 90+
Fort Hamilton 90

Fort Jefferson 90
Fort Laurens 68, 94

Fort McIntosh 68
Fort Meigs 110+
Fort Miami 91, 105

Fort Pitt 63+, 84, 121
Fort Recovery 90+
Fort Washington 90, 102+, 184
Fort Wayne, IN 89, 177
fossil 16
4-H Program 304

France 133, 146+, 299
Franklin County 181, 283, 310, 330, 361
Franklinton 181
Fremont, OH 237
French Grant 63, 148

Fulton County 169, 217, 312
Fulton, Robert 133
furs 56, 73, 121, 131
Gallipolis, OH 148, 197
Galloway, James and Rachael 106

Gamble, James 210
Garfield, James A. and Lucretia 238+
Garst Museum 93
gasoline 297, 373+
Geauga County 169, 239

General Assembly 80, 102+, 126, 133, 175, 181, 222+, 234, 239+, 336+, 344, 351+, 363

General Electric Aircraft Engines 329
General Motors Corporation 175, 257, 313
General Tire and Rubber Company 318
general welfare 190, 223
geology 12, 16, 200, 214

Georgetown, OH 236
Georgia 248
Germany 61+, 133, 149, 201, 251, 311
Girty, Simon 65+, 88
glass 214, 312

Glendale, OH 193
Glenn, John H. Jr. 329
Gnadenhutten 65, 269
Golden Lamb Inn 127

Goodrich, Benjamin F. 318
Goodyear Tire & Rubber Company 318
Goodyear, Charles 318
governor 74, 84, 222, 237, 336+,
Grand Lake St.Mary 136

Grandview Heights, OH 330
Grant, Ulysses S. and Julia Dent 235+, 346
Great Britain 56, 66, 73, 98, 146+, 226, 251+
Great Depression 248, 260+, 272, 280, 371, 378
Great Lakes 25, 55, 63, 89, 112, 131, 215

Great Miami Conservancy District 363
Great Miami River 86, 90, 94, 103, 229, 281, 363
Great Seal of Ohio 4
Great Spirit 76, 94, 105
Greene County 59, 106, 217, 268+

Greenfield Village 217, 279, 328
Greenville, OH 90
Guernsey County 123, 214

Gulf of Mexico 24, 48
guns 56, 63, 68, 226

Hale Farm 228
Hamilton County 89, 126, 169, 184, 193, 235, 240, 329, 361, 372+
Hancock County 204+, 319
Hanging Rock Iron Region 30, 214, 320
Hanna, Marcus A. 241

Harding, Warren G. and Florence 243+
Harmar, Josiah 89
Harrison, Anna Symmes 235
Harrison, Benjamin and Caroline 240
Harrison, William Henry 7, 101+, 112+, 234, 240+

Hawaii 2
Hayes Presidential Center 238
Hayes, Rutherford B. and Lucy 237
Heckewelder, John 65
Henry Ford Museum 217, 283+

Highland County 233
highway 119+, 121, 126, 149, 282+, 287+, 309, 361
highway - I-70 88, 124
highway - interstate 292+
highway - S.R. 3 126

highway U.S. 40 78, 123
Hillsboro, OH 233
Historical Society - Greene County 106
Hocking County 14, 214
Hocking River 123

Holmes County 167+, 209
Hopewell people 38, 319
horse 47, 120, 126, 133, 192, 209, 223, 287
hospital 183, 296+
houses 45, 132, 185, 207, 290+

House of Representatives 340, 351, 370
Housing Act of 1968 293
Howe, Henry 227, 316
Howells, William Dean 272
Huron County 88

Huron people 56, 60
Ice Age 21, 35
Illinois 55, 64+, 77, 107, 123, 158, 209, 310
immigrant 226+
incinerators 372

India 43, 254
Indian Lake 136
Indiana 3, 21, 39, 77, 107, 123, 158, 209, 310, 320
Indiana Territory 103+
Indianapolis, IN 240

Industrial Revolution 207
industry 195, 248, 276, 304+
Inscription Rock 56
International Ladies Garment Workers Union 256
interurban lines 281

inventor 276, 314
Iowa 209
Iran 251
Ireland 56, 149
Iroquois people 98

iron 26+, 160, 212+
Iron Age 29, 55
Ironton, OH 30
Iroquois people 6, 53, 60+
Italy 149, 251

Jackson County 29
Japan 33, 251+, 311, 320
Jefferson County 136
Jefferson, Thomas 77, 103, 123
Jews 150

Johnny Appleseed 165
judicial branch 220, 340
Junior Achievement 304
Kaskaskia, IL 66
Kelleys Island 21, 56

Kenton, Simon 65, 86, 90, 179
Kentucky 3, 39, 53, 59, 66, 77, 108, 156+, 179, 214, 248
Kenyon College 237
kerosene 202, 206, 297
Kettering, OH 257

Kettering, Charles F. 255+, 279, 328
Kettering, Olive Williams 257
Kilbourne, James 181
Kings Island 268
Kitty Hawk, NC 327

Knox County 237
Korea 33, 251+
Kroger Company (The) 295, 323
Kroger, Bernard H. 295

labor movement 230, 248, 256, 371
LaChoy Food Products Company 312, 322
Lake County 29, 216, 239, 321
Lake Erie 5, 21+, 112, 131+, 175, 209, 216, 267, 278, 372+
Lake Hope State Park 263

Lake Huron 63
Lake Loramie 136
Lake Ontario 24
Lancaster, OH 186, 280
Langston, John Mercer 233

LaSalle, Robert Cavelier 55, 76
Lawrence County 30, 214
Lazarus stores 323
League of American Wheelmen 284
leather 210, 277, 306, 319

Lebanon, OH 86, 127
Lebanon - nation 252
Lee, Ann 169
Lee, Robert E. 237
legislative branch 220

Lenape people 53, 58, 98
Lewis Research Center 329
Licking County 29, 36, 88, 103, 297
Lima, OH 283
limestone 15, 27, 214

Lincoln, Abraham 233
Little Miami River 41, 59, 82, 86
lobbying 356
Lockington 136
locomotive - steam 139, 158, 282+

Logan, OH 30
Logan County 136
logging industry 283
Logstown 61, 68
Lorain, OH 315

Lorain County 16, 271
Loramie, Peter 63, 94
Lordstown, OH 315
Losantiville 86+
Loudonville 257

Louisiana 248, 278
Lucas County 7, 91, 214
Ludlow, Israel 83+
lumber 28, 73, 132, 207

machinery 231, 276+, 312
Madison County 169
Mahoning County 215, 320
Maimi and Erie Canal 184
manufacturing 207, 310+, 322, 371

Marathon Oil Company 318
Marietta, OH 84+, 89, 123, 175
Marion, OH 243
Marion County 243, 321
Maryland 53, 123

Massachusetts 3, 74+, 99, 126
Massie, Nathaniel 181
mastodon 35
Maumee, OH 91, 167
Maumee Bay 132

Maumee River 64, 90, 112, 134
mayor 365
mayor's court 365
McGuffey Readers 229
McGuffey, William Holmes 228

McIntosh, Lachlan 68
McKinley, William Ida Saxton 240+
Mead paper 316
Mead, Daniel 316
meat 203

Mechanicsburg, OH 156
Medina County 29
Meigs, Return J. 112
Mennonites 166
Mentor, OH 239

Mercer County 90, 136
merchants 163, 255
metropolitan area 299, 359
Metropolitan Housing Authority 264
Miami and Erie Canal 136, 177, 281, 316

Miami County 61, 138
Miami people 60, 90
Miami Purchase 86
Miami University 228+, 240
Miamisburg mound 39

mica 48, 319
Michigan 3, 21, 48, 63, 77, 107, 279, 308+, 368
Middle East 248+, 272, 373
Middletown, OH 321
migrant worker 308

migration 146+, 248
Milan, OH 279
militia 66, 224
mill 136, 161+, 178, 198, 216

Millenium Church of United Believers 169
Miner's National Association 232
Mingo people 60
mining 152, 201, 212, 321
Minnesota 3, 77, 215

Mississippi 108, 248
Mississippi River 39, 55, 61, 66, 87, 109, 122+, 131, 326
Missouri 3, 236
Mohawk people 61
Moneto 108+

money 223, 378
Montgomery County 22, 39+, 169, 328, 359
Moraine, OH 22, 315, 328
Moravians 64
Morrill Act 229

motor vehicle 286, 289, 314, 368, 376
Mound builders 38
Mound City Group 39
Moundsville, WV 39
municipal courts 365

Museum of Natural History—Cleveland 36
Muskingum Conservancy District 263
Muskingum County 123, 214+, 330
Muskingum River 84, 94, 123, 263
Muskingum River Conservancy District 363

Nashville, TN 123
Natchez Trace 123
Natchez, MS 123
National Aeronautics and Space Administration 329
National Cash Register Company (NCR) 255+, 311, 328, 363

National Industrial Congress 232
National Labor Relations Act 256, 378
National Park Service 193
National Rifle Association 226
National Road 123, 285

National System of Interstate and Defense Highways 285
Native Americans 5, 38, 74+, 99, 104, 120, 196, 368+
natural gas 202, 299, 373
natural resources 26, 361, 368+

Navistar International Transportation Company 315
Neil Armstrong Air and Space Museum 330
Neutral people 56
New Concord, OH 330
New Jersey 53, 86, 279

New Madrid, MO 109, 133
New Orleans boat 133
New Orleans, LA 122, 132
New Vienna, OH 233
New York 184, 205

New York City 98, 237, 314
New York State 6, 53, 57, 63, 133, 229, 368
Newark, OH 41
Niles, OH 240
NIMBY 373

Nineteenth Admendment 259
Noble County 204
North Bend, OH 86, 234, 240
North Carolina 48, 248
Northwest Ordinance 79, 95, 99, 157, 220

Northwest Territory 6, 89, 95, 311
Norwich, OH 124
nuclear energy 279, 374+
Oakwood, OH 328
Oberlin College 230+, 326

Ohio and Erie Canal 138, 184
Ohio and Indiana Railroad 177
Ohio Cavern 15
Ohio Company of Associates 83, 148, 229
Ohio Historical Society 30, 36, 41, 170

Ohio Oil Company 318
Ohio pipe stone 47
Ohio Railroad Museum 283+
Ohio Revised Code 355, 364
Ohio River 6, 24, 57+, 94, 131, 136, 148+, 175, 184, 209, 235,
267, 278, 320, 372, 375

Ohio State Capitol 113
Ohio State Fair 267
Ohio State University (The) 230, 257
Ohio University 229
Ohio Village 228

Old Man's Cave 14
omnibus 187, 285
Ottawa County 112, 375
Ottawa people 94
Otterbein Retirement Community 169

Owens Bottle Machine Company 312
Owens, Michael J. 312
Pakistan 254
paper making 136, 316
Parker, John Percial and Miranda Boulden 158

parking 295+, 336
Pataskala, OH 297
Patterson, John Henry 255, 363
Patterson, Robert 86, 255
Pearl Harbor, HI 251

Penn, William 166
Pennsylvania 3, 53, 58+, 82, 112, 122, 158, 166, 214
Perry, Oliver Hazzard 112
Perrysburg, OH 112, 267
petroleum 26+, 184, 202, 212, 276, 317, 368, 371+

Philadelphia, PA 66, 74, 121, 271
photosynthesis 371
Pickaway County 39
Pickawillany 61
pictograph 56

pipeline 276
Piqua, OH 138
Pittsburgh, PA 121, 133, 153
plastic 319, 376
Point Pleasant, OH 235

political parties 336, 345
politics 179, 345
Pontiac 63

Pope, Hawk 369
population 288, 304

Portage County 268, 359
Portage Lakes 136
Portland cement 28, 217
Portsmouth, OH 133+, 211
Potawatomi people 60

pottery 46, 213
Pottery Museum 213
Powell, William H. 112
President of the United States 220, 349
Presque Isle 112

Proctor & Gamble Company 210
Proctor, William 210
Prophet, The 108
Prophets Town 109
Public Land Act 77, 86, 226+

Public Land Survey 79, 85, 95
public transportation 285, 292, 344
Public Works Administration 262
Put-in-Bay 112
Putnam, Rufus 83+

Quakers 58, 64, 158
quarrying 27, 321
Quebec 63
raft 131
railroad 119, 127, 139, 149, 165, 175+, 193, 199, 209, 276, 283,
288+, 332

Rankin, John and Jane Lowery 158, 236
raw materials 196, 283, 373
Ray, Joseph 229
recreation 183, 267
recycling 320, 373+

referendum 356
Refugeee Tract 88
registering to vote 348
religion 166, 266
Religious Society of Friends 158

Republic of China 254
Republican Party 237+, 241+, 346
reservation -native 115
Resnick, Judith 331
Revco D. S. Inc. 323

revenue 341
Revolutionary War 224
Rhode Island 74
Richland County 239, 243
right-of-way 118, 125

Ripley, OH 158, 236
Rittman, OH 216
Rockefeller, John D. 205, 255, 317
rocks 12+, 212+
Rocky Mountains 48

Roman Catholic Church 228
Roosevelt, Franklin D. 261
Roosevelt, Theodore 241+
Roscoe Village, OH 138
Ross County 39, 46, 103, 181, 269, 316

rubber 250, 318, 376
Rubbermaid, Inc. 319
rule of law 220, 225, 230
Rural Electrification Administration 280
Russia 150, 251, 299

Salem, OH 69
sales tax 344+
salt 26, 29, 203, 212, 216, 321
San Francisco 244, 314
San Salvador 53

Sandusky Bay 60, 132
Sandusky County 237
Sandusky River 69+
sanitary land fill 372
Santa Maria 51

Sauder Farm and Craft Museum 217
Schoenbrunn 65, 69
schools 165, 183, 226, 286, 296, 349, 363
Scioto County 30, 133, 211, 214, 263
Scioto River 47, 82, 89, 123, 133, 148, 181

Scotland 56, 149, 250
Sea World 268
secretary of state 337
Seiberling, F. A. 318
Senate 340, 351

Senate of the United States 330
Seneca people 60
Seven Ranges 82
sewage 187, 292
sewers 187, 292, 363+, 371

Shaker Heights 169, 286
Shakers 169
Shawnee Nation United Remnant Band 369
Shawnee people 53, 58+, 113, 269, 368+
Shawnee State Park 263

Shelby County 63, 136
Sherman, John 239
Shippingport, PA 376
shopping 292+
slavery 100, 149, 156, 233, 269

Smithsonian Insitution 112, 328
smog 374
Social Security 225, 378
Society of Friends 58
Society of Separates 169

SOHIO 317
solid wastes 372+
South Bass Island 112
South Carolina 48, 248
space exploration 329

Spanish-American War 241+
special districts 361
special interest groups 358
Spencer, Platt Roger 229
Spirit of '76 (The) 269

Springboro, OH 361
Springfield, OH 68, 179, 209, 304, 315
St.Clair, Arthur 84, 89, 101
St.Lawrence River 24, 55, 63, 89, 131

St.Marys River 94

Standard Oil Company 206, 297, 317
Stark County 138, 241
State Board of Education 340, 344   340
state flag 4
state flower 4, 241

state motto 4
state symbols 4
statutory law 223, 340
steam 178, 199, 207, 211, 276, 282, 374
steamboat 131+, 154

steel 184, 311, 320
Stites, Benjamin 86
Stokes, Carl 264
Stokes, Louis 264
Stone Age 27, 48, 55

Stone, Lucy 232
Stowe, Calvin and Harriet Beecher 269
Stratton, OH 136
streetcar 188, 280, 285, 290, 298+
Strongsville, OH 206

subdivisions 285, 293
suburban areas 290+, 299
suffrage 232
Summit County 136+, 228, 323, 359
Sun Watch 42

Superintendent of Public Instruction 340
Supreme Court 220+, 243, 336+
Sweden 201, 312+
Switzerland 152, 166
Symmes Purchase 86

Symmes, John Cleves 86, 229, 235
Taft, William Howard and Helen Herron 192, 242+
Taiwan 254
taxes 76, 224, 341+, 349
Tecumseh 59, 91+, 105, 112, 269, 369

Tennessee 108+, 248
Texas 278, 308
Thames, Battle of the 112
Tipp City, OH 178
Tippecanoe, Battle of 108+

tires 295, 311, 377
Tobacco people 56
Toledo 216, 300, 312, 315
Toledo Edison Company 375
Toledo Museum of Art 214

tools 196+, 208, 214
township government 359+
township — Public Land Survey 79
trade 48, 322
transportation 47, 118, 281, 288+, 376

treasurer 340
Treaty of GreeneVille 92, 103, 121, 179
trilobite 4, 18
trucks 283, 287+, 299, 314, 376
Trumbull County 228, 240

Trumpet in the Land 268
turmoil 224, 377

turnpike 126, 174+, 184, 216
Tuscarawas County 68, 169, 268
Tuscarawas River 68+, 169

Tuscarora people 53, 60
Twenty-first Amendment 344
Twenty-sixth Amendment 348
Twinsburg, OH 323
Tyler, James 235

U.S. Military District 88
Uncle Tom's Cabin 269
Underground Railroad 158, 230, 269
Union of Soviet Socialist Republics 151, 329
United Airlines 306

United Automobile Workers 257
United Brethren in Christ, The Church of 326
United Mine Workers 232, 257+
United Nations 251+
United Rubber Workers 257

United States Army 39, 123, 237
United States Military Academy 236
United States Shoe Company (The) 323
United States Steel Corporation 318
United Steel Workers 257

University of Cincinnati 331
Upper Sandusky, OH 69
uranium 374+
Urbana, OH 179
USX Corp. 318

Van Buren, Martin 235
Van Wert County 176
Vicksburg, MS 154
Vietnam 43, 254, 348
Vincennes, IN 66, 107

Vinton County 214, 263
Virginia 53, 65+, 77, 233, 244, 248, 314
Virginia Military District 82
voting 348
Washington County 320

Wabash River 68, 90, 107+
Walcott House 167
Wales 56, 149, 201
wampum 48, 56, 98
Wapakoneta, OH 330

War of 1812 98, 110, 133, 145
Warren County 22, 41, 86, 127, 169, 268, 331, 361
Washington County 89
Washington, DC 112, 235, 328
Washington, George 68, 80, 90

water 160, 187, 265, 292
Watiker & Sons, Inc. 309
Watiker, Albert D. Jr. 309
Wayne County 126, 216, 319+
Wayne National Forest 28

Wayne, Anthony 90, 102+
Weather Service, The United States 327
weathering 13, 309
Webber, Charles T. 158
Weiser, Conrad 61

Wellington 271
Wellston 29
West Virginia 39, 66, 77, 214, 248, 318
Western Reserve Historical Society 315
Western Reserve of Connecticut 87

Wheeling, WV 123
Whig Party 235
White Company (The) 314
White Consolidated Industries 312
White Sewing Machine Company (The) 312

White, Thomas 312
Whittlesey people 42, 58
wigwam—wigewa 45
Willard, Archibald M. 269+
Williams County 169

Williamson, David 69+
Winton, Alexander 314
Wisconsin 77, 107, 310
women 98, 190, 232, 258, 348, 359, 370
Women's Temperance Crusade 233

wood 187, 199, 276
Wood County 112
Woodland people 38
Wooster 126, 319
working 255, 290, 304, 379

Workmen's Compensation Program 378
Works Progress Administration 261
World War I 39, 248, 259, 318, 328
World War II 251+, 258+, 264, 276, 288, 293+, 329, 359, 371+
Worthington, OH 181

Worthington, Thomas and Eleanor 39, 106, 186
Wright, Katharine 326
Wright, Milton and Susan 325
Wright, Orville 270, 306, 326+
Wright, Wilbur 270, 326

Wyandot people 60, 69, 94
Xenia, OH 106
Youngstown, OH 205, 215, 301
Zane's Trace 121
Zane, Ebenezer 123

Zanesville, OH 123, 181, 309
Zeisberger, David 64, 69
Zoar 169